T0178908

Real-time Systems Scheduling 2

Series Editor
Abdelhamid Mellouk

Real-time Systems Scheduling 2

Focuses

Edited by

Maryline Chetto

WILEY

First published 2014 in Great Britain and the United States by ISTE Ltd and John Wiley & Sons, Inc.

Apart from any fair dealing for the purposes of research or private study, or criticism or review, as permitted under the Copyright, Designs and Patents Act 1988, this publication may only be reproduced, stored or transmitted, in any form or by any means, with the prior permission in writing of the publishers, or in the case of reprographic reproduction in accordance with the terms and licenses issued by the CLA. Enquiries concerning reproduction outside these terms should be sent to the publishers at the undermentioned address:

ISTE Ltd
27-37 St George's Road
London SW19 4EU
UK

www.iste.co.uk

John Wiley & Sons, Inc.
111 River Street
Hoboken, NJ 07030
USA

www.wiley.com

© ISTE Ltd 2014
The rights of Maryline Chetto to be identified as the author of this work have been asserted by her in accordance with the Copyright, Designs and Patents Act 1988.

Library of Congress Control Number: 2014946162

British Library Cataloguing-in-Publication Data
A CIP record for this book is available from the British Library
ISBN 978-1-84821-789-8

Contents

Preface

We refer to a system as real-time when it has to meet deadlines when reacting to stimuli produced by an external environment. Punctuality therefore constitutes the most important quality of a real-time computer system, which, moreover, distinguishes it from conventional computer systems. We refer to a system as embedded when it is physically integrated into a physical device whose control and command it ensures, which have a particular impact on its sizing and the selection of its components.

The rapid evolution of microelectronic techniques and communication infrastructures in recent years has led to the emergence of often-miniaturized interconnected embedded systems (wireless nodes processing data coming from sensors), leading to the birth of the concept of the "Internet of things". The real-time qualifier therefore remains relevant for all these autonomous and intelligent objects as it was in the 1970s with the advent of microcomputers, when this qualifier was restricted to industrial process controlling systems.

The large variety of appliances in which real-time systems are now integrated requires increasingly strict constraints to be taken into account in terms of physical size, computational power, memory capacity, energy storage capacity and so on, in their design. It is therefore in this direction that research efforts have turned for several years.

Every piece of software with real-time application is composed of tasks, programs whose execution requires a concurrent access to shared resources limited in number (processor, memory, communication medium). This raises the central issue of scheduling whose solution leads to a planning of tasks that respects the time constraints.

Since the early 1970s, in particular following the publication of the crucial article by Liu and Layland, research activity in the field of real-time scheduling, both through its theoretical results and integration in operating systems, has allowed us to overcome numerous technological barriers.

Real-Time Systems Scheduling constitutes a learning support regarding real-time scheduling intended for instructors, master's degree students and engineering students. It also aims to describe the latest major progress in research and development for scientists and engineers. The book groups together around 30 years of expertise from French and Belgian universities specialized in real-time scheduling. It was originally published in French and has now been translated into English.

This book is composed of two volumes with a total of 13 chapters.

Volume 1 entitled *Fundamentals* is composed of six chapters and should be of interest as a general course on scheduling in real-time systems. Reading the chapters in order, from 1 through to 6, is recommended but not necessary. Volume 1 is structured as follows: Chapter 1 constitutes a conceptual introduction to real-time scheduling. Chapters 2 and 3, respectively, deal with uniprocessor and multiprocessor real-time scheduling. Chapter 4 discusses results on scheduling tasks with resource requirements.

Chapter 5 relates to the scheduling issue in energy-constrained systems. Chapter 6 presents the techniques of computing the worst-case execution time (WCET) for tasks.

Volume 2 entitled *Focuses* is composed of seven chapters. This volume aims at collecting knowledge on specific topics and discussing the recent advances for some of them. After reading Chapter 1 of Volume 1, a reader can move to any chapters of Volume 2 in any order. Volume 2 is structured as follows: Chapter 1 highlights the newer scheduling issues raised by the so-called energy-autonomous real-time systems. In Chapter 2, the authors consider a probabilistic modelization of the WCET in order to tackle the scheduling problem. In Chapter 3, the authors show how automatic control can benefit real-time scheduling. Chapter 4 deals with the synchronous approach for scheduling. In Chapter 5, the authors focus on the optimization of the Quality-of-Service in routed networks. Chapter 6 is devoted to the scheduling of messages in industrial networks. Finally, Chapter 7 pertains specifically to resolution techniques used in avionic networks such as AFDX.

Maryline CHETTO
July 2014

List of Figures

Chapter 3

Chapter 4

Chapter 5

Chapter 6

Chapter 7

List of Tables

Chapter 4

Chapter 5

Chapter 6

Chapter 7

Scheduling in Energy Autonomous Objects

In an autonomous system, in other words a system supplied during its entire lifetime by ambient energy, the issue of scheduling must be addressed in jointly taking into account the two physical constraints: time and energy. The fundamental scheduling questions can be raised as follows: is a scheduler as efficient, simple and high-performance as earliest deadline first (EDF) is appropriate? Is there, in this new context of perpetual energy autonomy, a scheduler which is optimal with acceptable implementation costs? How do we dimension the energy storage unit in such a way that no energy starvation, and therefore no deadline violation can occur at any time?

This chapter proposes to answer these questions according to the following plan:

– description of the real-time energy harvesting (RTEH) system model;

– study of the behavior of EDF for the RTEH model;

Chapter written by Maryline CHETTO.

– specification of the earliest deadline-harvesting (ED-H) scheduler, optimal for the RTEH model;

– description of a necessary and sufficient schedulability test.

1.1. Introduction

Electrical energy supply is a crucial issue, in particular in the design of portable systems that by nature have to be autonomous from an energy point of view. Today, this issue is mainly handled by dynamic voltage scaling (DVS) or dynamic power management (DPM) methods that aim to reduce the energy consumption of electronic circuits. Thus, the proposed solutions allow us to extend the durations separating two successive recharges of a battery without overcoming them.

However, the new generations of embedded systems, in particular those functioning in hostile or inaccessible environments, limit human intervention. They function with the help of batteries (or any other kind of energy storage unit), which are continuously recharged over time from a renewable energy source. There is no doubt that the DVS and DPM techniques prove to be very useful in autonomous systems: they lead to using lower capacity batteries, smaller solar panels, etc. But these techniques do not allow, by themselves, to ensure infinite operation, called *energy-neutral*. Energy-neutrality is defined here by the property of the embedded system to operate in such a way as to respect all of its timing constraints and this, by only using the energy available in the storage unit without ever lacking any.

An autonomous system is built around three components (see Figure 1.1):

– The *energy harvester* whose choice depends on the nature of the environmental energy, the amount of energy required, etc.

– The *energy storage unit,* such as a battery or a super-capacitor, whose choice depends on the dynamics of the system, the design constraints and/or cost constraints, etc.

– The *energy consumer* that here represents the execution support of the real-time tasks. In this chapter, we assume that the energy consumed by the operational part of the embedded system (actuator, LED, etc.) is separately powered, as is the transmitter/receiver module. Therefore, the energy consumer denotes the electronic card built around a microcontroller or a microprocessor.

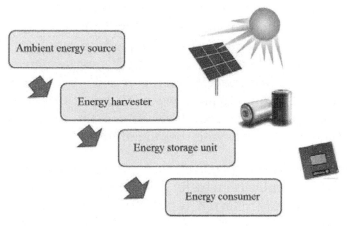

Figure 1.1. *Diagram of an ambient energy harvesting system*

Designing such a system requires the resolution of a certain number of issues related to the harvesting, storage and the use of ambient energy [PRI 09]. It has to be provided with a durable autonomy (from one to tens of years) while maintaining an acceptable real-time performance level. In this chapter, we focus on the consumer of energy, a machine whose energy needs are variable in time. These needs are required by the real-time tasks whose processing has to be done in predefined time intervals. Therefore, the energy needs are not identical and continuous over time. They depend on the timing profile of the tasks, very generally characterized by a period and/or a deadline. An embedded system and mainly an autonomous intelligent sensor has to function during several years or even several tens of years without any possibility of intervention. This is why guaranteeing offline that it will respect its constraints is of importance. The implementation will be made difficult or even impossible by the uncertainty attached to the quantity of harvested energy. We can, therefore, see that the design of an autonomous system leads to several fundamental questions. Assuming that the energy supply is perfectly characterized (energy source profile, size of the storage battery, etc.), how do we verify and guarantee before the system becomes operational that it will have a continuous autonomy with an always acceptable performance level? This, therefore, means, first of all, to define this performance, often called Quality-of-Service, characterized by application constraints. In this chapter, we consider a firm real-time system whose performance level is mostly related to the percentage of jobs satisfying their deadlines.

From a software point of view, a real-time system is composed of application tasks and the real-time operating system (commonly referred to as RTOS) that ensures their scheduling. In Chapter 1, Volume 1 [CHE 14d], we have recalled the real-time schedulers typically implemented in current RTOSs. These schedulers have, for the most part, the particularity of being online, non-idling, priority-driven and preemptive. Their implementation does not lead to any major difficulty: one or more data structures organized in lists have to be managed. The role of the scheduler is to order these lists and update them, either using a fixed-priority policy such as rate monotonic or a dynamic-priority policy such as EDF [LIU 73]. However, these optimal schedulers offer their performance under the assumption that there is no energy limitation. Indeed, their optimality assumes that the processor has, at any time, the energy required for the execution of any job. Thus, we can see that the only constraint to be handled by the scheduler is a timing one.

Schedulability conditions associated with these schedulers are, therefore, centered around the utilization factor of the processor or the processor demand by time interval.

In an energy-autonomous system, the issue of scheduling is related to jointly taking into account the two physical constraints: time, which is measured in seconds and energy, which is measured in joules. The following fundamental questions are, therefore, raised: can an efficient and capable scheduler, such as EDF, be suitable for systems subject to, besides timing constraints, energy constraints? Are there, in this new context proper to renewable energy harvesting, schedulers which are at the same time optimal and easily implementable? The initial studies related to these questions date back to the 2000s [ALL 01].

1.2. Modeling and terminology

1.2.1. *System model*

Hereafter, we describe the RTEH model that comprises a computing element, a set of jobs, an energy storage unit, an energy harvesting unit and the environmental energy source (see Figure 1.2).

1.2.1.1. *Job model*

We consider a set of real-time jobs that is executed on a single processing unit. A single operating frequency is supported. We assume the energy consumed in the idle state to be negligible. The energy consumption comes integrally from dynamic switching. The jobs are executed by exclusively using the energy generated by the environmental source. We denote by $\tau = \{\tau_i, i = 1, \ldots, n\}$ the set of n preemptible jobs. The jobs are independent from one another. We associate the four-tuple (r_i, C_i, E_i, d_i) with the job τ_i. This job arrives at time r_i called release time, and requires a worst-case execution time of C_i time units and consumes E_i energy units in the worst case. The quantity E_i is not necessarily proportional to C_i [JAY 06]. In other words, the effective energy consumption of a job does not vary linearly with its effective execution time. During each time unit, we know an upper bound on the energy consumption of every job equal to e_{Max} energy units. The exact amount of energy effectively drained in every time unit is, however, not known beforehand. The deadline of τ_i denoted by d_i represents the date at which τ_i has to have terminated its execution. We assume that $\min_{0 \leq i \leq n} r_i = 0$. Let $d_{Max} = \max_{0 \leq i \leq n} d_i$ and $D = \max_{0 \leq i \leq n} (d_i - r_i)$ be, respectively, the latest absolute deadline and the greatest relative deadline among those of the jobs of τ. $E_c(t_1, t_2)$ denotes the energy consumed by the jobs on the time interval $[t_1, t_2)$. If the energy consumed by a job in each time unit is no less than the energy harvested on this same time unit, we say that the job is discharging [ALL 01]. Every job of τ is discharging. Consequently, the residual capacity of the energy storage unit never increases every time a job executes.

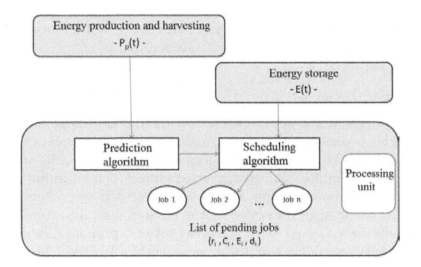

Figure 1.2. *The RTEH model*

1.2.1.2. *Energy production model*

The energy produced by the environmental source is assumed to be uncontrollable. We characterize it by a so-called *instantaneous charging rate* denoted by $P_p(t)$. This includes all the losses induced by the energy conversion and storage processes. The energy produced by the source on the time interval $[t_1, t_2)$ is denoted by $E_p(t_1, t_2)$ and is obtained by the following formula: $E_p(t_1, t_2) = \int_{t_1}^{t_2} P_p(t)dt$. We assume that the production and consumption of energy can occur simultaneously. Even though the power output at any time by the environmental source fluctuates with time, we assume to be able to predict it with precision in an immediate future and with negligible processing and energy costs.

1.2.1.3. *Energy storage model*

Our system uses an ideal energy storage unit with a nominal capacity denoted by C that is expressed in units of energy such as joule or watt per hour. The capacity may be less than the total energy consumption of a job. Let us denote by $E(t)$ the residual capacity of the storage unit at time t, which gives the current level of energy available.

We consider the energy to be wasted when the storage unit is fully charged while we continue to charge it. In contrast, the storage unit is considered fully discharged at time t if $0 \leq E(t) < e_{Max}$ denoted by $E(t) \approx 0$. The application starts with a fully charged storage unit (i.e. $E(0) = C$). The stored energy may be used at any later time and does not leak energy over time.

1.2.2. *Types of starvation*

According to the RTEH model described in the previous section, a job τ_i can miss its deadline if one of the two following situations occurs:

– *Time starvation*: when τ_i reaches its deadline at time t, its execution is incomplete because the time required to process τ_i by its deadline is not sufficient. However, there is enough energy in the storage unit when the deadline violation occurs, i.e. $E(t) > 0$.

– *Energy starvation*: when τ_i reaches its deadline at time t, its execution is incomplete because the energy required to process it by its deadline is not sufficient. The energy in the storage unit is exhausted when the deadline violation occurs, i.e. $E(t) \approx 0$.

1.2.3. *Terminology*

We now give definitions that we will be requiring throughout the remainder of the chapter.

DEFINITION 1.1.– *A schedule Γ for τ is said to be valid if the deadlines of all jobs of τ are respected in Γ starting with a full energy storage unit.*

DEFINITION 1.2.– *A system is said to be feasible if there exists at least one valid schedule for τ with a given energy storage unit and environmental energy source. Otherwise, the system is said to be infeasible.*

In infeasible systems, the limiting factors are either time, energy or both time and energy. In this chapter, we focus on feasible systems only. As in classical scheduling theory, we say that a scheduling algorithm is:

– *optimal* if it finds a valid schedule whenever one exists;

– *online* if it makes its decisions at run-time;

– *semi-online* if it is online with necessary lookahead on a certain time interval;

– *lookahead-ld* if it is semi-online with lookahead on ld time units;

– *idling* if it is allowed to keep the processor idle even when there are pending jobs. Otherwise, it is called *non-idling*;

– *clairvoyant* if it has knowledge of the future (characteristics of released jobs and energy production profile) at any time including the initial instant.

We introduce a terminology proper to the RTEH model.

DEFINITION 1.3.– *A schedule* Γ *for* τ *is said to be time-valid if the deadlines of all jobs in* τ *are met in* Γ, *considering that* $E_i = 0 \ \forall i \in \{1, \ldots, n\}$.

DEFINITION 1.4.– *A set of jobs* τ *is said to be time-feasible if there exists a time-valid schedule for* τ.

DEFINITION 1.5.– *A schedule* Γ *for* τ *is said to be energy-valid if the deadlines of all jobs in* τ *are met in* Γ, *considering that* $C_i = 0 \ \forall i \in \{1, \ldots, n\}$.

DEFINITION 1.6.– *A set of jobs* τ *is said to be energy-feasible if there exists an energy-valid schedule for* τ.

DEFINITION 1.7.– *A scheduling algorithm* A *is said to be energy-clairvoyant if it needs knowledge of the future energy production to take its run-time decisions.*

1.3. Weaknesses of classical schedulers

1.3.1. *Scheduling by EDF*

We show by a simple example that a conventional priority-driven real-time scheduler cannot build an optimal schedule for the RETH model. We consider the EDF algorithm, the most popular approach to schedule independent jobs in the absence of energy limitation and processing overload [LIU 73, DER 74]. EDF is an online scheduler that selects the ready job with the closest relative deadline. An online scheduling represents the only option in a system whose processing overload is unpredictable, since it accommodates itself in an adaptive way to processor demand variations.

Let us give several useful definitions for the evaluation of the performance of online schedulers. The *value of a job* defines its contribution to the global performance of the system. The system obtains the value of the job if it terminates its execution before its deadline. Otherwise, the system obtains no value [BAR 91, BUT 05]. We say that an online scheduler has a *competitive factor* r ($0 < r < 1$) if it guarantees a total cumulated value of at least r times the value that the best clairvoyant scheduler may provide [BAR 92]. We say that an online scheduler is *competitive* if its competitive factor is strictly higher than 0. Otherwise, it is *non-competitive*.

The optimality of EDF remains true as long as we allow preemption between the jobs, and the jobs do not enter into competition for the access to shared resources. However, if a processing overload occurs, the optimality of EDF disappears. Let us consider the value of a job as being proportional to its execution time. Baruah *et al.* proved that no online scheduler, including EDF, can guarantee, in an overload situation, a competitive factor higher than 0.25 when jobs have uniform value densities [BAR 92]. A recent analysis shows that for the RTEH model, the competitive factor of EDF becomes zero.

THEOREM 1.1.– [CHE 14a] EDF is non-competitive for the RTEH model.

The EDF scheduler can be implemented under two distinct variants, called, respectively, as soon as possible (ASAP) and as late as possible (ALAP). It also possesses very important qualities: easy implementation, fast execution (low overhead) and reduced preemption rate. It is, therefore, natural to ask ourselves whether the EDF algorithm, even though non-competitive, remains optimal or not when the jobs present energy needs in the context of RTEH.

1.3.2. *ASAP strategy*

The EDF variant that applies the ASAP policy is also called Earliest Deadline as Soon as possible (EDS). It consists of immediately rendering the highest priority ready job executable. We illustrate below this non-idling scheduling policy.

Example: let us consider a time-feasible set of two jobs τ_1 and τ_2 with $\tau_1 = (0, 4, 32, 9)$ and $\tau_2 = (2, 3, 24, 5)$. We harvest energy from the environment with the same power over time, $P_p = 6$. The energy storage unit has a capacity of $C = 8$ and is initially full ($E_c(0) = 8$). We notice that τ_2 misses its deadline at time 5 (see Figure 1.3). The weak point of EDS resides in its greedy way of consuming energy, which leads to emptying the energy storage unit and preventing the job τ_2 to be completely executed. This example shows that, despite a sufficient amount of energy and processing capacity, the non-idling schedulers commonly integrated into existing operating systems turn out to be incapable of efficiently dealing with energy limitations. Theorem 1.2 establishes that the EDF scheduler remains, however, the best non-idling scheduler for the RTEH model.

THEOREM 1.2.– [CHE 14a] EDF is optimal in the class of non-idling schedulers for the RTEH model.

1.3.3. *ALAP strategy*

In symmetry with the ASAP variant of EDF, let us examine the behavior of the ALAP variant, also called earliest deadline as late as possible (EDL). This consists of postponing the execution of the jobs as much as possible while respecting their deadlines. EDL is particularly adapted to situations in which the processor must be put in an idle state for as long as possible [CHE 89]. The idea of delaying the execution of the jobs of critical periodic tasks permits us to recover the availability of the processor and to serve non-critical aperiodic tasks as soon as possible for minimizing their response time [CHE 99].

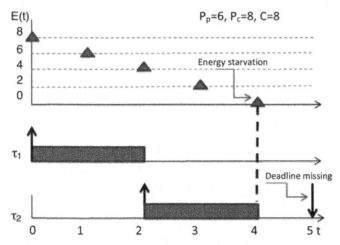

Figure 1.3. *Schedule produced by EDF with ASAP*

Example: We go back to the previous example and apply the ALAP variant of EDF (see Figure 1.4).

At the release of τ_1, its latest starting time for ALAP is computed, equal here to 5 and given by its deadline minus its execution time. The processor, in the idle state from instant 0, therefore, does not consume any energy, which allows the storage unit to fill up until time 1. The storage unit has then reached its full capacity. Thus, the energy harvested after time 1 is wasted. At time 2, the job τ_2 is released. Its latest starting time corresponds to its release time. τ_2 is executed from time 2 to time 5. Hence, this is causing a discharge of the storage unit which, at time 5, contains 2 units of energy. τ_2 starts its execution, which leads to completely emptying the storage unit at time 6, when the application is prematurely stopped.

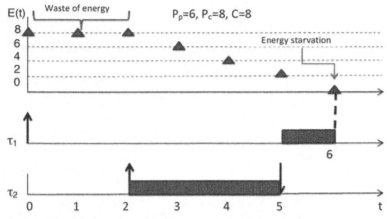

Figure 1.4. *Schedule produced by EDF with ALAP*

Contrarily to EDS, EDL does not turn out to be greedy enough, since it delays the energy consumption of the jobs. This first of all leads to a waste given the limited capacity of the storage unit that cannot store all the harvested energy. This is followed by an energy starvation depriving the job from terminating its execution before its deadline even though it has enough time to do so.

From a practical point of view and with regard to simplicity, EDF remains a first-choice scheduler for systems powered by renewable energy. Its integration does not require any particular technological device: it does not need to know the current level of energy in the storage unit, and to complete a predictive estimation of the harvested energy.

1.4. Fundamental properties

From the above, we conclude that every energy starvation (i.e. the situation in which the available energy proves to be insufficient to execute a job with respect to its deadline) has to be anticipated sufficiently in advance in order to prevent it from exceeding a deadline. In other words, the optimality of a scheduler assumes a clairvoyance capacity.

THEOREM   1.3.– [CHE 14a]   A   non-clairvoyant   online scheduling algorithm cannot be optimal for the RTEH model.

Thus, theorem 1.3 indicates that having a prediction on a part of the future may help in building a better schedule than that produced by a totally non-clairvoyant scheduler such as EDF. Moreover, theorem 1.4 establishes a lower bound on the omniscience of the scheduler in order for it to build an energy-valid schedule.

THEOREM 1.4.– [CHE 14a] Let D be the largest relative deadline of the application. No lookahead-ld online scheduling algorithm is optimal for the RTEH model if $ld < D$.

Thus, theorem 1.4 gives us the clairvoyance horizon required by any optimal scheduler. The value of the largest relative deadline appears as a key parameter in the application. If, for a given application we cannot predict the harvested energy profile on a time interval of length equal to at least this relative deadline, then it is illusory to benefit from an optimal online scheduler.

Estimating the amount of energy drained from the environment on a given time interval constitutes a central issue on the design of an RTEH system. The source of environmental energy can be formally modeled or even precisely determined offline in certain applications. However, when it is uncontrollable and highly unstable, only the prediction techniques applied online and cyclically on timing sliding windows allow us to determine lower bounds on the future harvested energy.

1.5. Concepts related to energy

1.5.1. *Processor demand*

The processor demand on $[t_1, t_2)$ is defined by the amount of execution time required by all jobs with release time at or after t_1 and deadline before or at t_2 (see definition 1.8). When the set of jobs τ under-utilizes the processor, the result is a residual processing availability and a timing flexibility in the execution of the jobs, hence the notion of slack time.

DEFINITION 1.8.– *The processor demand of a set of jobs τ on the time interval $[t_1, t_2)$ is given by*

$$h(t_1, t_2) = \sum_{t_1 \leq r_k, d_k \leq t_2} C_k \qquad [1.1]$$

The schedulability analysis of EDF based on the so-called processor demand approach needs to compute the processor demand for every time interval starting with a release time and finishing with a deadline. We then verify whether there is a processing overload on each tested interval. This approach comes down to compute the *static slack time* denoted by $SST_\tau(t_1, t_2)$ (see definition 1.9). For applications in which the jobs arrive in an unpredictable manner, the schedulability analysis takes the form of an online test (we then refer to an admission test) in such a way as to decide whether to accept or reject a new job [BUT 05].

DEFINITION 1.9.– *The static slack time of a set of jobs τ on the time interval $[t_1, t_2)$ is given by*

$$SST_\tau(t_1, t_2) = t_2 - t_1 - h(t_1, t_2) \qquad [1.2]$$

$SST_\tau(t_1, t_2)$ represents the longest duration of the interval included within $[t_1, t_2)$ during which the processor can remain inactive while guaranteeing the execution of the jobs of τ released at or after t_1 and with deadline at most equal to t_2. From this, we deduce the static slack time of the set τ.

DEFINITION 1.10.– *The static slack time of a set of jobs τ, SST_τ, is given by*

$$SST_\tau = \min_{0 \le t_1 < t_2 \le d_{Max}} SST_\tau(t_1, t_2) \tag{1.3}$$

Let t_c be the current time in the schedule produced for the set of jobs τ by a certain scheduling algorithm. Let AT_i be the remaining execution time of the uncompleted jobs at time t_c with deadlines smaller than or equal to d_i.

DEFINITION 1.11.– *The slack time of the job τ_i at the current time t_c is given by*

$$ST_{\tau_i}(t_c) = d_i - t_c - h(t_c, d_i) - AT_i \tag{1.4}$$

$ST_{\tau_i}(t_c)$ represents the total amount of processor time available in $[t_c, d_i)$ after having executed all the jobs with deadlines smaller than or equal to d_i. We can define the slack time of τ at the current time t_c as follows:

DEFINITION 1.12.– *The slack time of the set of jobs τ at the current time t_c is given by*

$$ST_\tau(t_c) = \min_{d_i > t_c} ST_{\tau_i}(t_c) \tag{1.5}$$

The slack time as computed with [1.5] represents the maximum continuous processor time that could be available from t_c during which the processor could remain inactive or execute other jobs than those of the set τ. The computation of $ST_\tau(t_c)$ uses the construction of the EDL schedule from time t_c initially described in [CHE 89].

1.5.2. *Energy demand*

We introduce here new concepts for the feasibility analysis of a set of jobs characterized by their energy needs. Let $E_p(t_1, t_2)$ be the amount of energy harvested between t_1 and t_2.

DEFINITION 1.13.– *The energy demand of a set of jobs τ on the time interval $[t_1, t_2)$ is given by*

$$g(t_1, t_2) = \sum_{t_1 \leq r_k, d_k \leq t_2} E_k \qquad [1.6]$$

DEFINITION 1.14.– *The static slack energy of a set of jobs τ on the time interval $[t_1, t_2)$ is given by*

$$SSE_\tau(t_1, t_2) = C + E_p(t_1, t_2) - g(t_1, t_2) \qquad [1.7]$$

$SSE_\tau(t_1, t_2)$ represents the maximum amount of energy available during the time interval $[t_1, t_2)$ and this, while guaranteeing the execution of the jobs of τ released at or after t_1 and with deadlines smaller than or equal to t_2. We can then define the static slack energy of τ as follows:

DEFINITION 1.15.– *The static slack energy of a set of jobs τ is given by*

$$SSE_\tau = \min_{0 \leq t_1 < t_2 \leq d_{Max}} SSE_\tau(t_1, t_2) \qquad [1.8]$$

The static slack energy of τ represents the energy surplus that could be consumed at any time while guaranteeing the energy needs of the jobs of τ.

DEFINITION 1.16.– *The slack energy of a job τ_i at the current time t_c is given by*

$$SE_{\tau_i}(t_c) = E(t_c) + E_p(t_c, d_i) - g(t_c, d_i) \qquad [1.9]$$

$SE_{\tau_i}(t_c)$ represents the maximum amount of energy consumed in $[t_c, d_i)$ while guaranteeing the energy needs of the jobs released from time t_c with deadlines smaller than or equal to d_i. If there is a job τ_i such that $SE_{\tau_i}(t_c) = 0$, then the execution between t_c and d_i of any job with a deadline higher than d_i will provoke an energy starvation for τ_i. We can now describe ED-H, the optimal scheduler for the RTEH model.

1.6. ED-H scheduling

1.6.1. *Informal description*

The intuition behind the ED-H scheduler is to run jobs according to the EDF rule in time intervals determined following energy constraints. A job is only allowed to be executed after having verified that its execution during a time unit will not lead to energy starvation neither for the job nor for a job that will arrive in the future. ED-H does not correspond either to EDS, nor to EDL. This scheduler is, therefore, based on the timing and energy characteristics of the jobs as well as on the replenishment rate of the storage unit to make decisions concerning the state of the processor. Schematically, ED-H constitutes a variant of EDF that could be qualified as energy aware, since it is capable of preventing energy starvation.

The conventional EDF scheduler is said to be greedy since it executes systematically jobs as soon as possible, and thus spends the energy stored in the storage unit disregarding needs of future occurring jobs. Let us consider a set of jobs that is time-feasible by EDF. The energy starvation for a job τ_i can only come from the execution of a job τ_j that is executed before the arrival of τ_i with $d_j > d_i$. Indeed, the energy starvation of τ_i caused by τ_j with $d_j \leq d_i$ cannot be avoided by any other scheduler. Intuitively, a minimum of clairvoyance relative to the arrival of jobs and to the production of energy will help EDF to anticipate an energy starvation, and consequently a deadline miss. The key principle of ED-H consists of allowing the execution of jobs while no energy starvation can occur. We are, therefore, led to introducing the concept of *preemption slack energy* at the current time t_c as the largest quantity of energy consumable by the active job that does not put into question the feasibility of the jobs susceptible to preempt it.

DEFINITION 1.17.– *Let d be the deadline of the active job at time t_c. The preemption slack energy of the set τ at time t_c is given by*

$$PSE_\tau(t_c) = \min_{t_c < r_i < d_i < d} SE_{\tau_i}(t_c) \qquad\qquad [1.10]$$

1.6.2. *Rules of ED-H*

Let $L_r(t_c)$ be the list of jobs ready for execution at time t_c. The ED-H scheduling algorithm respects the following rules:

– *Rule 1:* the EDF priority order is used to select the future running job in $L_r(t_c)$.

– *Rule 2:* the processor is imperatively idle in $[t_c, t_c + 1)$ if $L_r(t_c) = \emptyset$.

– *Rule 3:* the processor is imperatively idle in $[t_c, t_c + 1)$ if $L_r(t_c) \neq \emptyset$ and one of the following conditions is satisfied:

   1) $E(t_c) \approx 0$;

   2) $PSE_\tau(t_c) \approx 0$.

– *Rule 4:* the processor is imperatively busy in $[t_c, t_c + 1)$ if $L_r(t_c) \neq \emptyset$ and one of the following conditions is satisfied:

   1) $E(t_c) \approx C$;

   2) $ST_\tau(t_c) = 0$.

– *Rule 5:* the processor can equally be idle or busy if $L_r(t_c) \neq \emptyset$, $0 < E(t_c) < C$, $ST_\tau(t_c) > 0$ and $PSE_\tau(t_c) > 0$.

Rule 3 states that no job can be executed if the energy storage unit is empty or if this execution unavoidably leads to energy starvation, the preemption slack energy being insufficient. Rule 4 states that the processor cannot be inactive if either the energy storage unit is fully replenished or making the processor idle would lead to missing a deadline due to a zero slack time. If the storage unit is neither empty nor full and if the system has a non-zero slack time and a non-zero preemption slack energy, rule 5 states that the processor can equally take the idle or busy state without compromising the validity of the resulting schedule. Note that according to ED-H, a waste of energy is only produced when the storage unit is full and no job is waiting to be executed.

This description of ED-H does not mention the particular situation in which the storage unit is full $(C \leq E(t_c) < C + e_{Max})$ with a zero preemption slack energy $(0 \leq PSE_\tau(t_c) < e_{Max})$. In order to avoid a waste of energy by putting the processor into an idle state, the execution of the highest priority job in $[t_c, t_c + 1)$ may be allowed, leading then to an energy consumption equal to at most e_{Max} units of energy. The processor then remains passive during a sufficient amount of time for the storage unit to be fully replenished. Thus, ED-H provokes a continuous switching from a busy state to an idle state in such a way that over this period the consumption of energy remains the same as the production of energy. The result is an energy waste of at most e_{Max} units.

Various implementations can be taken from ED-H depending on the choice of rule 5. ASAP and ALAP are the only special cases that can be reduced to executing jobs either systematically at the earliest as soon as the energy proves to be sufficient or at the latest without, however, provoking an overflow of the energy storage unit. The rule selected for deciding when to start and when to stop the recharging phase of the storage unit determines the variant of ED-H. Thus, we will be able to choose to execute jobs while the energy level is above a certain threshold and leaving the processor inactive in order to replenish the storage unit while its level has not reached a predefined upper value. The ED-H scheduler, therefore, presents a great flexibility in its implementation with the only conditions that we forbid at all times the waste of energy and we prevent the system from a negative slack time and a negative preemption slack energy.

Example: let us go back to the previous example. Equation [1.9] gives us

$$SE_{\tau_2}(0) = E(0) + E_p(0, d_2) - g(0, d_2) = 8 + 30 - 24 = 12.$$

$SE_{\tau_2}(0)$ represents the maximum quantity of energy that any active job may consume from instant zero in order to preserve to feasibility of τ_2. τ_1 is allowed to consume at most 12 units of energy and is stopped at time 1, since $SE_{\tau_2}(1) \approx 0$. Rule 3 imposes that the processor be put into an idle state until the storage unit is again full or that the slack time becomes zero. Note the simultaneous fulfillment of these two conditions at time 2. $ST_{\tau_2}(1)$ is given by $d_2 - 1 - h(2, d_2) - AT_2$. Consequently, $ST_{\tau_2}(1) = 1$. $ST_{\tau_1}(1)$ is given by $d_1 - 1 - h(2, d_1) - AT_1 = 9 - 1 - (3 + 3) - 1$. $ST_{\tau_1}(1) = 3$. From formula [1.5], $ST_{\tau}(1) = 1$. The processor switches back to the active state at time 2 when $E(2) = 8$. τ_2 is executed until its completion at time 5 where $E(5) = 2$. τ_1 resumes its execution until the storage unit is empty at time 6. The processor becomes inactive in order to refill the storage unit until time 7, the time when the slack time of the system becomes zero, imposing the execution of τ_1 that is thus terminated at time 9, its deadline where $E(9) = 2$ (see Figure 1.5).

1.6.3. *Optimality analysis*

The optimality of ED-H means that if ED-H is unable to build a valid schedule for a set of jobs τ, then no other scheduler will be able to. The proof of optimality is based on lemmas 1.1 and 1.2 in which we assume that the deadline d_1 of the job τ_1 is the first missed deadline in the ED-H schedule produced for the set τ.

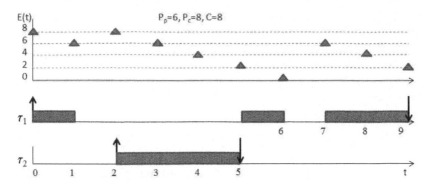

Figure 1.5. *Schedule produced by ED-H*

LEMMA 1.1.– [CHE 14c] If d_1 is missed in the ED-H schedule because of time starvation, then there exists a time instant t such that $h(t, d_1) > d_1 - t$ and no schedule exists where d_1 and all earlier deadlines are met.

LEMMA 1.2.– [CHE 14c] If d_1 is missed in the ED-H schedule because of energy starvation, then there exists a time instant t such that $g(t, d_1) > C + E_p(t, d_1)$ and no schedule exists where d_1 and all earlier deadlines are met.

The ED-H scheduler produces a valid schedule as long as there are no time intervals where the processor demand on this interval exceeds its duration and the energy demand exceeds the total available energy in this interval. Lemmas 1.1 and 1.2 then lead us to theorem 1.5.

THEOREM 1.5.– [CHE 14c] The ED-H scheduling algorithm is optimal for the RTEH model.

ED-H provides an optimal solution that is less restrictive than the lazy scheduling algorithm (LSA) algorithm described in [MOS 07]. In these works, the energy consumed by any job being executed varies linearly with its execution time.

1.6.4. *Clairvoyance analysis*

In accordance with the result outlined in theorem 1.4, we know that no online scheduling algorithm can be optimal without a clairvoyance of at least D time units. In order to make a decision at any time t_c, ED-H requires to know at the same time the arrival process of the jobs and the energy production process recovered over the following D time units, hence theorem 1.6.

THEOREM 1.6.– [CHE 14c] The ED-H scheduling algorithm is lookahead-D.

The main technological limitation associated with the implementation of ED-H is due to the estimated measure of the energy harvested over D time units. This problem is handled by targeted prediction methods that depend on the energy source.

1.6.5. *Schedulability test*

The essential question "is the set τ feasible?" refers to that of the schedulability of τ by ED-H. It has to be verified by a simple test whether there exists a valid ED-H schedule for τ, given an energy storage unit characterized by its capacity and an energy harvesting system characterized by an instantaneous production power $P_p(t)$. Theorem 1.7 shows that this feasibility test is reduced to two independent tests, one relative to the timing feasibility and the other to the energy feasibility. In other words, we show that τ is feasible if and only if τ is time-feasible and energy-feasible.

THEOREM 1.7.– [CHE 14c] A set of jobs τ compliant with the RTEH model is feasible if and only if

$$SST_\tau \geq 0 \text{ and } SSE_\tau \geq 0 \qquad [1.11]$$

This feasibility test is implemented in $O(n^2)$, since n^2 time intervals are the object of a static slack time calculation. Let us assume that we predict the ambient energy on each time interval by a finite number of values. We then show that the complexity of the energy feasibility test is in $O(n^2)$.

Example: we go back to the previous example and apply theorem 1.7 in order to test the feasibility of the two jobs τ_1 and τ_2. Since $SST_\tau(0,9) = 2$ and $SSE_\tau = 6$, we deduce that the set τ is feasible and consequently feasibly schedulable by ED-H.

1.7. Conclusion

The technology known as *energy harvesting* consists of generating electrical energy from the environment. This technology is becoming an undeniable asset for the development of autonomous communication devices, with as much regards to civil applications as military defense applications. Energy harvesting is turning out to be potentially attractive and promising. Nevertheless, its implementation assumes to resolve numerous theoretical and technological issues relative to the harvesting, conversion, storage and consumption of energy. We do not seek here to minimize the energy consumption in order to maximize the lifetime of the system (low-power technology) as in traditional portable devices. An *energy-neutral* mode of functioning has to be ensured in which the system never consumes more energy than it harvests. More precisely, the question that we have provided an answer for, is formulated as follows: how do we schedule the jobs in order to continuously respect their timing constraints by an adequate exploitation of the *processor* resource and the *ambient energy* resource?

This assumes providing the operating system with DPM functions capable of adapting the energy consumption of the processor to the energy production profile and respecting the deadline constraints attached to the jobs.

In this chapter, we have restricted our study to a monofrequency uniprocessor platform. We have presented an optimal scheduler, ED-H, a variant of the EDF scheduler. Energy autonomous real-time systems are also the subject of studies that relate to platforms equipped with DVFS functionalities [LIU 08, LIU 09, LIU 12], to fixed-priority driven systems [ABD 13] or to multiprocessor architectures [LU 11].

1.8. Bibliography

[ABD 13] ABDEDDAIM Y., CHANDARLI Y., MASSON D., "The optimality of PFPasap algorithm for fixed-priority energy-harvesting real-time systems", *25th Euromicro Conference on Real-Time Systems*, 2013.

[ALL 01] ALLAVENA A., MOSSE D., "Frame-based embedded systems with rechargeable batteries", *Workshop on Power Management for Real-Time and Embedded Systems*, 2001.

[BAR 91] BARUAH S., KOREN G., MISHRA B., *et al.*, "Online scheduling in the presence of overload", *Symposium on Foundations of Computer Science*, 1991.

[BAR 92] BARUAH S., KOREN G., MAO D., *et al.*, "On the competitiveness of on-line real-time job scheduling", *Real-Time Systems*, vol. 4, no. 2, pp. 125–144, 1992.

[BUT 05] BUTTAZZO G., *Hard Real-Time Computing Systems: Predictable Scheduling Algorithms and Applications*, Springer, 2nd. ed., 2005.

[CHE 89] CHETTO H., CHETTO M., "Some results of the earliest deadline scheduling algorithm", *IEEE Transactions on Software Engineering*, vol. 15, no. 10, pp. 1261–1270, 1989.

[CHE 99] CHETTO-SILLY M., "The EDL server for scheduling periodic and soft aperiodic tasks with resource constraints", *Real-Time Systems*, vol. 17, no. 1, pp. 87–111, 1999.

[CHE 14a] CHETTO M., QUEUDET A., "Clairvoyance and online scheduling in real-time energy harvesting systems", *Real-Time Systems*, vol. 50, no. 2, pp. 179–184, 2014.

[CHE 14b] CHETTO M., QUEUDET A., "A note on EDF scheduling for real-time energy harvesting systems", *IEEE Transactions on Computers*, vol. 63, no. 4, pp. 1037–1040, 2014.

[CHE 14c] CHETTO M., "Optimal scheduling for real-time jobs in energy harvesting computing systems", *IEEE Transactions on Emerging Topics in Computing*, 2014.

[CHE 14d] CHETTO M., (ed.), *Real-time Systems scheduling 1: Fundamentals, ISTE*, London and John Wiley & Sons, New York, 2014

[DER 74] DERTOUZOS M.-L., "Control robotics: the procedural control of physical processes", *International Federation for Information Processing Congress*, 1974.

[JAY 06] JAYASEELAN R., MITRA T., LI X., "Estimating the worst-case energy consumption of embedded software", *12th IEEE Real-Time and Embedded Technology and Applications Symposium*, 2006.

[LIU 73] LIU C.-L., LAYLAND J.-W., "Scheduling algorithms for multiprogramming in a hard real-time environment", *Journal of the Association for Computing Machinery*, vol. 20, no. 1, pp. 46–61, 1973.

[LIU 08] LIU S., QIU Q., WU Q., "Energy aware dynamic voltage and frequency selection for real-time systems with energy harvesting", *Design, Automation and Test in Europe*, 2008.

[LIU 09] LIU S., WU Q., QIU Q., "An adaptive scheduling and voltage/frequency selection algorithm for real-time energy harvesting systems", *ACM / IEEE Design Automation Conference*, 2009.

[LU 11] LU J., QIU Q., "Scheduling and mapping of periodic tasks on multi-core embedded systems with energy harvesting", *Conference on Green Computing*, 2011.

[LIU 12] LIU S., LU J., WU Q., *et al.*, "Harvesting-aware power management for real-time systems with renewable energy", *IEEE Transactions on Very Large Scale Integration (VLSI) Systems*, vol. 20, no. 8, pp. 1473–1486, 2012.

[MOS 07] MOSER C., BRUNELLI D., THIELE L., *et al.*, "Real-time scheduling for energy harvesting sensor nodes", *Real-Time Systems*, vol. 37, no. 3, pp. 233–260, 2007.

[PRI 09] PRIYA S., INMAN D.-J., *Energy Harvesting Technologies*, Springer-Verlag, 2009.

2

Probabilistic Scheduling

In this chapter, we present the probabilistic real-time approaches. First, we present the context of these approaches as well as the notations and definitions commonly accepted by the real-time community. By introducing several possible values for the task parameters, the probabilistic constraints also have to be defined and we then refer to properties imposed by the designer. Two main classes of probabilistic models exist, worst-case and average, and we show their differences with respect to a task response time analysis. We continue by presenting the non-optimality of Rate Monotonic and by underlining the applicability of Audsley's principle. This allows us to give an optimal algorithm of assigning task priorities with worst-case execution times described by random variables in the context of a single processor and using a preemptive scheduler. In the same scheduling context, a response time analysis is possible and we present an example of this. A classification of the main results and open problems for probabilistic real-time systems closes this chapter.

Chapter written by Liliana CUCU-GROSJEAN, Adriana GOGONEL and Dorin MAXIM.

2.1. Introduction

Since the seminal article of Liu and Layland, the temporal analysis of critical systems has for a long time been studied through worst-case approaches. These approaches can become too pessimistic in the presence of an increasing need for performance; proposing solutions in these conditions is a real challenge for the real-time community.

The important variation in the execution times of a program in the presence of complex architectures implies that the worst-case approaches can be concluded with the non-feasibility of a system when the probability of such a failure during the lifetime of the system is extremely small. This way, the worst-case approaches can in some cases impose an important over-sizing of the architectures by limiting the introduction of new functionalities.

Another example concerning the limits of worst-case analysis are event management systems for which it is not always useful to propose a bound for the arrival of jobs generated by the interruptions coming from the sensors [BRO 04]. The most widely known example of such systems are controller area networks (CAN) with magnetic interference faults [BRO 04, NAV 00].

Some industries propose probabilistic solutions by defining parameters described by random variables. For instance, in the automotive industry, we find parking aid sensors that have randomly chosen frequencies in order to avoid collision situations between two vehicles facing back-to-back (see Figure 2.1) [BUT 12]. In case of identical frequencies, the parking aids might be less efficient or even inefficient. In this case, the sensors generate jobs that have random arrival sequences. These jobs belong to tasks that can be seen as sporadic with a period equal to the minimum time between the arrival of two consecutive jobs.

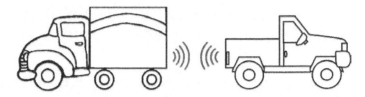

Figure 2.1. *Two vehicles reversing with radars emitting on the same frequency might not "see" each other*

The probabilistic approaches are alternatives to worst-case approaches. The feasibility of real-time systems is, in general, expressed in terms of probabilities associated with various possible values for the parameters of a system. In recent years, the probabilistic analysis of real-time systems has gained momentum, various works currently exist on this subject and in this chapter we present the main results and concepts that then allow a more in-depth reading of the existing literature.

The implicit task model, also known as the Liu and Layland model, is the first real-time task model. The tasks have two parameters, the execution time and the period, the deadline being equal to the period. The periodicity constraint relaxed in the framework of sporadic tasks as well as this model is, in the worst case of a single processor, equivalent to the periodic model. In the above mentioned models, there can be no variation in the execution time.

The following level of generalization is attained by the *multi-frame* (MF) task model, the *generalized multi-frame* (GMF) model and the *recurrent real-time* (RRT) model. These models allow the tasks to have different execution times as well as different inter-arrival times and deadlines, in a cyclical manner. In the MF and GMF models, if a task has n possible types of jobs, then the parameters of a job i are the same parameters as of a job $i + n, \forall i$.

The cyclicity hypothesis in the GMF model implies that the instructions inside the tasks are always executed in the same order, which is not necessarily true.

The cyclicity hypothesis has been removed from the non-cyclical GMF task model, the RRT non-cyclical task model and the real-time graph-oriented model.

A hierarchy of the models mentioned earlier is presented in Figure 2.2. A model is as general as it is expressive, it is therefore placed higher on the figure.

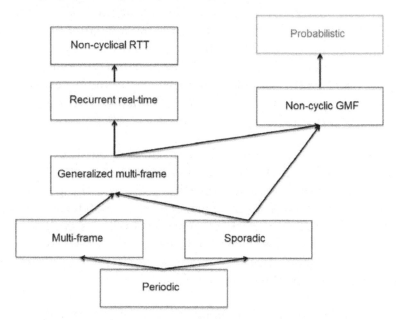

Figure 2.2. *Hierarchy of models used to describe real-time systems. The arrows indicate the relations between the models*

The probabilistic model has the potential to be the most expressive model of our time. This is driven by the possibility, in the probabilistic model, to associate a combination of values for every parameter of a task. A probabilistic model, which would allow us to describe the dependencies between the jobs of the same task, would be the closest model to the RRT model for tasks.

The organization of this chapter is as follows: section 2.2 presents the main notations and definitions. In section 2.3, we present the probabilistic real-time systems model employed in this chapter.

2.2. Notations and definitions

A probabilistic real-time system is a real-time system with at least one parameter defined by a random variable.

A random variable $\mathcal{X}$ has a distribution function (PF) $f_{\mathcal{X}}(\cdot)$ with $f_{\mathcal{X}}(x) = P(\mathcal{X} = x)$. The values possible for $\mathcal{X}$ belong to the interval $[x^{min}, x^{max}]$. In this work we associate probabilities to possible values of a random variable $\mathcal{X}$ using the following notation:

$$\mathcal{X} = \begin{pmatrix} X^0 = X^{min} & X^1 & \cdots & X^k = X^{max} \\ f_{\mathcal{X}}(X^{min}) & f_{\mathcal{X}}(X^1) & \cdots & f_{\mathcal{X}}(X^{max}) \end{pmatrix} \qquad [2.1]$$

where $\sum_{j=0}^{k_i} f_{\mathcal{X}}(X^j) = 1$. A random variable can also be defined by indicating its cumulative distribution function (CDF) $F_{\mathcal{X}}(x) = \sum_{z=x^{min}}^{x} f_{\mathcal{X}}(z)$.

For instance, the random variable $\mathcal{X} = \begin{pmatrix} 1 & 2 & 5 \\ 0.9 & 0.05 & 0.05 \end{pmatrix}$ has a cumulative distribution function

$$F_{\mathcal{X}}(x) = \begin{cases} 0.9, & \text{if } x = 1; \\ 0.95, & \text{if } x = 2; \\ 1, & \text{otherwise} \end{cases}.$$

Throughout this chapter we will be using cursive characters to denote random variables.

Two random variables $\mathcal{X}$ and $\mathcal{Y}$ are (probabilistically) independent if they describe events in such a way that the result of one of the events has no effect on the other.

The sum $\mathcal{Z}$ of two independent random variables $\mathcal{X}$ and $\mathcal{Y}$ is the convolution $\mathcal{X} \otimes \mathcal{Y}$ where $P\{\mathcal{Z} = z\} = \sum_{k=-\infty}^{k=+\infty} P\{\mathcal{X} = k\}P\{\mathcal{Y} = z - k\}$.

For instance, the sum of $\mathcal{X} = \begin{pmatrix} 3 & 7 \\ 0.1 & 0.9 \end{pmatrix}$ and $\mathcal{Y} = \begin{pmatrix} 0 & 4 \\ 0.9 & 0.1 \end{pmatrix}$ is equal to

$$\mathcal{Z} = \begin{pmatrix} 3 & 7 \\ 0.1 & 0.9 \end{pmatrix} \otimes \begin{pmatrix} 0 & 4 \\ 0.9 & 0.1 \end{pmatrix} = \begin{pmatrix} 3 & 7 & 11 \\ 0.09 & 0.82 & 0.09 \end{pmatrix}$$

Let $\mathcal{X}_1$ and $\mathcal{X}_2$ be two random variables. The variable $\mathcal{X}_2$ is greater than $\mathcal{X}_1$ if $F_{\mathcal{X}_1}(x) \le F_{\mathcal{X}_2}(x)$, $\forall x$, and we denote by $\mathcal{X}_2 \succeq \mathcal{X}_1$ [LOP 08].

The relation $\succeq$ between random variables can be graphically represented in Figure 2.3 using the CDFs of the variables. Let us note that $F_{\mathcal{X}_1}(x)$ never goes below $F_{\mathcal{X}_2}(x)$. We may note that $\mathcal{X}_2$ and $\mathcal{X}_3$ are not comparable.

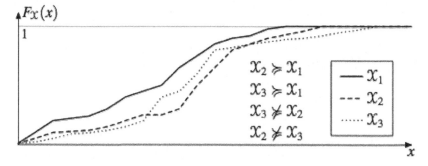

Figure 2.3. *Possible relations between the CDFs of various random variables*

2.3. Modeling a probabilistic real-time system

We consider a system of n tasks $\{\tau_1, \tau_2, \ldots, \tau_n\}$ with simultaneous releases, which needs to be scheduled on a single processor using a fixed-task priority scheduling policy.

Without loss of generality, we consider that τ_i has a higher priority than τ_j for $i < j$. We denote by $hp(i)$ the set of tasks with higher indices than τ_i.

Each task τ_i generates an infinite number of successive jobs $\tau_{i,j}$, with $j = 1, \ldots, \infty$.

The probabilistic execution time (pET) of a job of a task describes the probability that the execution time is equal to a given value.

Every task τ_i is a generalized sporadic task [MOK 83] and is defined by a probabilistic worst-case execution time (pWCET) denoted by $\mathcal{C}_i$ and a probabilistic minimum inter-arrival time (pMIT). These notations are defined below.

The pWCET $\mathcal{C}_i$ of a task is bound on all C_i^j, $\forall j$ and it can be described by the relation $\succeq$ with $C_i \succeq C_i^j$, $\forall j$. Graphically, this implies that the CDF of $\mathcal{C}_i$ remains below C_i^j, $\forall j$.

The pWCET $\mathcal{C}_i$ can be written as:

$$\mathcal{C}_i = \begin{pmatrix} C_i^0 = C_i^{\min} & C_i^1 & \cdots & C_i^{k_i} = C_i^{\max} \\ f_{\mathcal{C}_i}(C_i^{\min}) & f_{\mathcal{C}_i}(C_i^1) & \cdots & f_{\mathcal{C}_i}(C_i^{\max}) \end{pmatrix}, \qquad [2.2]$$

where $\sum_{j=0}^{k_i} f_{\mathcal{C}_i}(C_i^j) = 1$.

For instance for a task τ_i, we can have a pWCET of $\mathcal{C}_i = \begin{pmatrix} 2 & 3 & 25 \\ 0.5 & 0.45 & 0.05 \end{pmatrix}$; then $f_{C_i}(2) = 0.5$, $f_{C_i}(3) = 0.45$ and $f_{C_i}(25) = 0.05$.

Using the same line of thought, we define the pMIT denoted by $\mathcal{T}_i$.

The probabilistic inter-arrival time (pIT) of a job of a task describes the probability that a job will arrive at a given time.

The pMIT $\mathcal{T}_i$ of a task is a bound on the pITs $\mathcal{T}_i^j$, $\forall j$ and it can be described by the relation $\succeq$ with $\mathcal{T}_i^j \succeq \mathcal{T}_i$, $\forall j$. Graphically, this implies that the CDF of $\mathcal{T}_i$ remains below the CDF of $\mathcal{T}_i^j$, $\forall j$.

A task τ_i is therefore defined by a tuple $(\mathcal{C}_i, \mathcal{T}_i)$. A job of a task has to finish its execution before the arrival of the next job of the same task, this indicates that the arrival of the new job represents the deadline of the job currently being scheduled [1] constraint. In conclusion, the deadline of a task can also be represented by a random variable $\mathcal{D}_i$, which may have the same distribution as the pMIT, $\mathcal{T}_i$.

By considering worst-case probabilistic values (pMIT or pWCET), we obtain probabilistically independent random variables in order to express the pMITs and the pWCETs [CUC 13]. This property of independence is obtained through the fact that the values of the pMITs and the pWCETs are bounds instead of values associated with executions of tasks. The property of independence then allows us to use the convolution to calculate the response time of a task, for example.

2.4. Imposed properties

We have thus far talked about the implicit properties of systems, we will now look at properties imposed on real-time systems. A series of constraints ensue from the expected functionalities of the system and the more important metric we use is the *response time*.

The response time of a task is the time between its activation and the end of its execution. We consider jobs with PETs and therefore the response time is also described by a random variable.

---

1. In GMF task analysis this is known as *frame separation*.

The constraints are expressed in the form of a *probability to miss the deadline*, in other words the probability to miss the deadline has to be smaller than or equal to 10^{-9}, or as an optimization function, i.e. minimizing the average probability to miss the deadline for all the tasks of the system.

For a job $\tau_{i,j}$, the probability of failure $DMP_{i,j}$ is the probability that the jth job of a task τ_i misses its deadline and is equal to:

$$DMP_{i,j} = P(\mathcal{R}_{i,j} > D_i).$$ [2.3]

where $\mathcal{R}_{i,j}$ is the distribution of the response time of the jth job of the task τ_i.

If the task studied is periodic, in other words the pMIT distribution has a single value with probability 1, then the probability of the failure of a task can be calculated as being the average of the probabilities of the failure of the jobs activated during the interval $[a, b]$. This could be, for instance, the hyper-period of a scheduling. A worst-case reasoning could only take into account the greatest DMP among the DMPs of all the jobs activated in the interval $[a, b]$.

For a task τ_i and a time interval $[a, b]$, the probability of the failure of a task is calculated:

$$DMR_i(a, b) = \frac{P(\mathcal{R}_i^{[a,b]} > D_i)}{n_{[a,b]}} = \frac{1}{n_{[a,b]}} \sum_{j=1}^{n_{[a,b]}} DMP_{i,j},$$ [2.4]

where $n_{[a,b]} = \lceil \frac{b-a}{T_i} \rceil$ is the number of jobs of a task τ_i activated in the interval $[a, b]$.

2.5. Worst-case probabilistic models

Two probabilistic real-time models have been considered in the literature either using the average values for the task parameters, or using the definitions proposed in section 2.3. We show in this section the interest of using worst-case values (pMIT, pWCET) as they were defined in section 2.3 for calculating the response time. For the sake of presentation, in this section we will focus on an example with pITs.

We will recall, in section 2.5.1, the model proposing an average-based reasoning, followed in section 2.5.2 by a presentation of a comparison between the two models and the consequences for calculating the response time.

2.5.1. *Real-time systems with probabilistic arrivals*

This model was used in articles like [KAC 07, BRO 04].

In this model, for a task τ_i^* the number of possible arrivals $\mathcal{N}_i$ in a time interval of length t_Δ is described by a distribution:

$$\mathcal{N}_i = \begin{pmatrix} N^0 = N^{min} & N^1 & \cdots & N^k = N^{max} \\ f_{\mathcal{N}_i}(N^{min}) & f_{\mathcal{N}_i}(N^1) & \cdots & f_{\mathcal{N}_i}(N^{max}) \end{pmatrix}$$

For example if $\mathcal{N}_1 = \begin{pmatrix} 1 & 2 & 4 \\ 0.4 & 0.3 & 0.3 \end{pmatrix}$ for $t_\Delta = 12$, then the task τ_1^* has at most four arrivals between $t = 0$ and $t = 12$.

2.5.2. *Comparison of the two models*

We will now present the main differences between the worst-case model and the model introduced in section 2.5.1. In our example below, we only take into account the inter-arrival times, which are important for our discussion.

The first model provides a schedulability analysis with information that the second model does not provide

– pMIT: the task τ_1 has at most two arrivals before $t = 7$ (with probability 0.3).

– Probabilistic number of arrivals: it is not possible to estimate the number of times that τ_1^* is released between times 0 and 7. Various situations are possible and two of them are described in Figure 2.4.

Figure 2.4. *The arrivals defined using the number of arrivals in an interval may correspond to different situations*

The first model can provide information that the second model provides to a schedulability analysis

– pMIT: between $t = 0$ and $t = 12$ there are three scenarios for the task τ_1:

- three of the arrivals at $t = 0$, $t = 5$ and $t = 10$ with a probability of 0.21,

- two of the arrivals at $t = 0$ and $t = 5$ with a probability of 0.09,

- two of the arrivals at $t = 0$ and $t = 10$ with a probability of 0.7.

Consequently, between $t = 0$ and $t = 12$ the number of possible arrivals of τ_1 is described by $\begin{pmatrix} 2 & 3 \\ 0.79 & 0.21 \end{pmatrix}$.

– Probabilistic number of arrivals: between $t = 0$ and $t = 12$ the number of arrivals of τ_1^*

$\mathcal{N}_1 = \begin{pmatrix} 1 & 2 & 4 \\ 0.4 & 0.3 & 0.3 \end{pmatrix}$ is provided by this model.

2.6. Probabilistic real-time scheduling

In this section, we present the results concerning fixed-priority scheduling algorithms on a single processor. The tasks studied here have a single parameter described by a random variable, which is the pWCET. We therefore consider a set of n tasks $\tau_i, \forall i \in \{1, 2, \cdots, n\}$ described by (C_i, T_i, D_i, p) with $p \in [0, 1]$ the maximum probability that the task τ_i misses its deadline. We consider that at the end of each hyper-period [2] each job that has not finished its execution is stopped, allowing us to study the scheduling only for the first hyper-period $[0, P]$ where $P = lcm\{T_1, T_2, \cdots, T_n\}$ of the scheduling.

Fixed-priority scheduling algorithm problem (BPAP). This problem requires us to find a priority for each task such that the DMR of each task does not surpass a certain threshold, in other words $DMR_i(\Phi) \leq p_i$. Thus, in the framework of BPAP, we seek to assign priorities to the tasks such that $DMR_i(\Phi^*) \leq p_i, \forall i$.

Non-optimality of the rate monotonic algorithm

The rate monotonic algorithm [LIU 73], which associates the highest priority to the task with the smallest period, is proven to be optimal for every system of tasks with implicit deadlines and simultaneous releases [3] and with all parameters defined in a deterministic way. By switching to systems with pWCETs, we verify whether rate monotonic remains optimal. In that respect, we present a counter-example (in the form of a theorem) of a system that is schedulable using BPAP and for that rate monotonic proposes no solution.

---

2. The hyper-period is the least common multiple of all the periods of all the tasks of the system studied.

3. We mean by tasks with simultaneous releases that the tasks are all active for the first time at $t = 0$.

THEOREM 2.1.– Let $\tau = \{\tau_1, \cdots, \tau_n\}$ be a system of n tasks with simultaneous releases and with pWCETs. For this system, rate monotonic (RM) is not optimal in the sense that there is a feasible assignment of priorities to the tasks, but RM will not necessarily find it.

Proof. Let $\tau = \{\tau_1, \tau_2\}$ be a system with 2 periodic tasks with pWCETs. We have τ_1 defined by $(\begin{pmatrix} 1 \\ 1 \end{pmatrix}, 2, 2, 50\%)$ and τ_2 by $(\begin{pmatrix} 3 & 4 \\ 0.5 & 0.5 \end{pmatrix}, 6, 6, 75\%)$.

The task τ_1 has to satisfy at least 50% of its deadlines and the task τ_2 at least 75% of its deadlines.

By applying RM, τ_1 has the highest priority and τ_2 the lowest priority. In this case, τ_1 will satisfy all its deadlines and therefore the required threshold of 50% is also satisfied. Unfortunately, τ_2 will not satisfy 75% of its deadlines, but only 50% (see Figure 2.5).

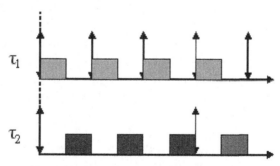

Figure 2.5. *Rate monotonic scheduling*

Let us now consider that τ_2 has the highest priority and τ_1 the lowest priority, then the two tasks will satisfy their respective thresholds. In this case, τ_2 satisfies its deadlines with probability 100% (higher than the requested 75%) and τ_1 will satisfy 50% of its deadlines (see Figure 2.6).

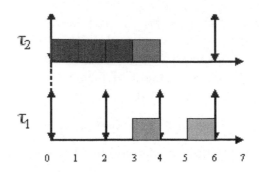

Figure 2.6. *A feasible assignment of priorities*

Given that RM is not optimal in this case, we will look at Audsley's principle. To be able to apply this reasoning to our problem, we have to look at the order of the higher-priority tasks and verify that they have no impact on the response time of a task. The following theorem ensures such a result.

THEOREM 2.2 ([MAX 11] The order of the higher-priority tasks).– Let $\tau = \{\tau_1, \tau_2, \ldots, \tau_n\}$ be a set of n periodic tasks constrained with pWCETs. The tasks are scheduled on a single processor using a fixed-task priority preemptive scheduling policy. If the tasks have fixed and known priorities, then the order of the tasks with higher priorities than a task τ_i (which therefore belong to $hp(i)$) has no impact on the value of $DMP_{i,j}(\Phi)$ for any job j of the task τ_i or on the value of $DMR_i(a, b, \Phi), \forall a, b$.

Theorem 2.2 indicates that if the elements of the sets $hp(i)$ and $lp(i)$ remain unchanged, then the response time $\mathcal{R}_{i,j}$ of any job of τ_i remains unchanged. Likewise, the response time of $\mathcal{R}_i^{[a,b]}$ of the task τ_i is unchanged no matter the order of the priorities in $hp(i)$ and $lp(i)$.

We will now present an example of an algorithm that applies Audlsey's principle (see algorithm 2.1). The algorithm is proven optimal for the BPAP problem in [MAX 11].

Algorithm 2.1. *Optimal algorithm for BPAP: the function* feasibility *verifies that for all* $\forall \tau_i$, $DMR_i < p_i$

Input: $\Gamma = \{\tau_i, i \in 1..n\}$ /* initial set of tasks */
Output: Φ /* ordered set of tasks */

$\Phi \leftarrow ()$;
for $l \in n..1$ **do**
    $assignment \leftarrow FALSE$;
    for $\tau_i \in \Gamma'$ **do**
        /* feasibility function such that $DMR_i < p_i$ */;
        if $feasible(\tau_i, \Phi)$ **then**
            $\Phi \leftarrow \Phi.\tau_i$;
            $\Gamma' \leftarrow \Gamma' \backslash \{\tau_i\}$;
            $assignment \leftarrow TRUE$;
            break;
        end if
    end for
    if $assignment = FALSE$ **then**
        /* no task is suitable for this priority level */;
        break;
    end if
end for

2.7. Probabilistic schedulability analysis

In this section, we consider a set of n tasks with simultaneous releases $\{\tau_1, \tau_2, \ldots, \tau_n\}$ scheduled on a single processor using a fixed-task priority preemptive scheduling policy. Without loss of generality we consider that τ_i has higher priority than τ_j for $i < j$.

We present a response analysis for the calculation of the probability distribution of a task. The scheduler, being fixed-task priority, the response time of a task is not impacted by the lower-priority tasks. Therefore, we consider, without loss of generality, that the studied task τ_n has the lowest priority among the n tasks of the set of tasks.

The analysis described in this section applies to the case of tasks with pWCETs and it has originally been proposed in [DÍA 02]. The response time $\mathcal{R}_{i,j}$ of a job $\tau_{i,j}$ activated at time $\lambda_{i,j}$ is calculated using the following formula:

$$\mathcal{R}_{i,j} = \mathcal{B}_i(\lambda_{i,j}) \otimes \mathcal{C}_i \otimes \mathcal{I}_i(\lambda_{i,j}), \qquad [2.5]$$

where $\mathcal{B}_i(\lambda_{i,j})$ is the accumulation of higher-priority tasks released before $\lambda_{i,j}$ and that have not yet terminated their execution at time $\lambda_{i,j}$. $\mathcal{I}_i(\lambda_{i,j})$ is the sum of the times of the pWCETs of the higher-priority tasks, which arrive after $\lambda_{i,j}$ and can preempt the job $\tau_{i,j}$. We consider the case of tasks with simultaneous releases whose accumulation is equal to $\mathcal{B}_n = \bigotimes_{i \in hp(n)} \mathcal{C}_i$.

Equation [2.5] is solved iteratively and the integration of the new preemptions is done by modifying the distribution of probability $\mathcal{R}_{i,j}$ at every new iteration. The iterations stop either when there are no more preemptions or when the last values are larger than the deadline of the task.

The (probabilistic) independence hypothesis: Equation [2.5] is based on the convolution operation $\otimes$, which requires the (probabilistic) independence between the variables $\mathcal{C}_i, \forall i$.

– The case of pETs. If the random variables $\mathcal{C}_i$ describe the pETs of a task, then the random variables cannot be independent and in this case the current state of the literature does not allow the use of equation [2.5].

– The case of pWCETs. If the random variables $\mathcal{C}_i$ describe the pWCETs of a task τ_i, then the random variables are independent since they are obtained as bounds on the pETs of all the jobs of the task. Equation [2.5] can therefore be used.

We consider the example given in the proof of theorem 2.1. Let $\tau = \{\tau_1, \tau_2\}$ be a system of two periodic tasks with pWCETs. We have τ_1 defined by $\left(\begin{pmatrix} 1 \\ 1 \end{pmatrix}, 2, 2, 50\% \right)$ and τ_2 by $\left(\begin{pmatrix} 3 & 4 \\ 0.5 & 0.5 \end{pmatrix}, 6, 6, 75\% \right)$.

We compute the response time of the first job $\tau_{2,1}$ of the task τ_2 when τ_2 is of lesser priority than τ_1. Using equation [2.5] we therefore calculate

$$\mathcal{R}_{2,1} = \mathcal{B}_2(\lambda_{2,1}) \otimes \mathcal{C}_2 \otimes \mathcal{I}_2(\lambda_{2,1})$$

where $\lambda_{2,1} = 0$. We have $\mathcal{B}_2(0) = \mathcal{C}_1 = \begin{pmatrix} 1 \\ 1 \end{pmatrix}$.

We then obtain $\mathcal{R}_{2,1} = \begin{pmatrix} 4 & 5 \\ 0.5 & 0.5 \end{pmatrix} \otimes \mathcal{I}_2(0)$. We finally obtain $\mathcal{R}_{2,1} = \begin{pmatrix} 5 & 7 \\ 0.5 & 0.5 \end{pmatrix}$ with $\mathcal{I}_2(0)$ that takes into account three possible preemptions from the following job of τ_1: $\tau_{1,2}$ at time $t = 2$, $\tau_{1,3}$ at time $t = 4$ and $\tau_{1,4}$ at time $t = 6$.

2.8. Classification of the main existing results

The first articles published in the real-time community close to the work described in this chapter used terms such as *stochastic analysis* [GAR 99], *probabilistic analysis* [TIA 95a, MAX 11, SAN 07], *statistical analysis* [ABE 98] and *real-time queuing theory* [LEH 90]. Since the publication of [DÍA 02], the concept of *stochastic analysis* of real-time systems spread in the community, no matter the type of technique the analysis is based on. We rather use the concept of *probabilistic analysis* or *statistical analysis* depending on the technique the analysis is based on. A probabilistic analysis will compute the probability of the appearance of an event for a system while a statistical analysis will determine certain properties of a system by studying data (in general large amounts of data) characterizing past events. We consider that the term *stochastic analysis* is only adequate in the context of a model with probabilistic parameters, which evolve with time.

The probabilistic real-time results can be grouped into four classes:

– *Schedulability analysis:* The seminal article by Lehoczky [LEH 96] proposes a schedulability analysis for tasks with pETs. This result, as well as several improvements of this first result [ZHU 02, HAN 02], consider restrained cases of probability distributions for the pETs. Tia *et al.* [TIA 95b] and Gardner [GAR 99] propose specific analyses for some schedulers. Abeni *et al.* [ABE 98] propose probabilistic analyses for isolated tasks and a recent article also proposes models that evolve with time [PAL 12]. The most general analysis for systems with p(WC)ETs is proposed in [DÍA 02]. It does not impose any constraints on the distributions and the schedulers are fixed-job priority. The most general analysis for systems with pWCETs and pMITs is proposed in [MAX 13]. An evolutionary model is also proposed in [MAN 04] and the associated analysis considers the case of several processors. The other results above only concern the case of a single processor.

Schedulability analyses are the most studied of the classes of results for probabilistic real-time systems. This class can be completed by statistical methods for the problems mentioned earlier as it was done in [LU 12, NAV 07]. The statistical methods for these problems have the advantage of enabling the study of more complex task models or architectures without increasing complexity. Comparisons between the probabilistic and statistical approaches will have to be carried out afterward.

– *Sampling with respect to probabilistic worst-case parameters (pWCETs or pMITs):* The probabilistic analyses can have a large complexity directly related to the number of possible values described by the probability distribution. This complexity can be reduced by sampling techniques that ensure its safety, the new response times being bounds on the response times without sampling [REF 10, MAX 12b]. For instance, the analysis of the response time presented in [MAX 13] becomes interesting for systems with a large number of tasks if sampling techniques are used for the pWCETs and pMITs. As indicated in [MAX 12b], there is no optimal sampling technique and therefore each new schedulability analysis has to have its own sampling technique.

– *Estimating the probabilistic parameters:* Ever since the seminal article by Edgar and Burns [EDG 01], various articles [HAN 09, YUE 11, GRI 10, CUC 12, HAR 13, LU 11] have proposed solutions to the problem of estimating the pWCETs. These contributions are all based on statistical approaches. To our knowledge, only one article proposes an estimation of the pETs [DAV 04]. Estimating the pMITs is an open problem and a short article suggests an appropriate method [MAX 12a].

– *Optimal scheduling algorithms:* To our knowledge, there is only one article presenting optimal algorithms and this, only in the case of a single processor [MAX 11]. In the case of models with evolutionary pETs an optimal algorithm is proposed for sets of tasks scheduled on several processors [MAN 04a].

2.9. Bibliography

[ABE 98] ABENI L., BUTTAZZO G., "Integrating multimedia applications in hard real-time systems", *Proceeding of 19th IEEE Real-Time Systems Symposium (RTSS)*, 1998.

[BRO 04] BROSTER I., BURNS A., "Applying random arrival models to fixed priority analysis", *Proceedings of the Work-In-Progress of the 25th IEEE Real-Time Systems Symposium (RTSS)*, 2004.

[BUT 12] BUTTLE D., "Real-time in the prime-time", *Proceeding of the Keynote talk at the 24th Euromicro Conference on Real-Time Systems (ECRTS)*, 2012.

[CUC 12] CUCU-GROSJEAN L., SANTINELLI L., HOUSTON M., *et al.*, "Measurement-based probabilistic timing analysis for multi-path programs", *Proceeding of the 24th Euromicro Conference on Real-time Systems (ECRTS)*, 2012.

[CUC 13] CUCU-GROSJEAN L., "Independence – a missunderstood property of and for real-time systems", *Proceeding of the 60th Anniversary of A. Burns*, 2013.

[DÍA 02] DÍAZ J.L., GARCÍA D.F., KIM K., *et al.*, "Stochastic analysis of periodic real-time systems", *Proceeding of the 23rd IEEE Real-Time Systems Symposium (RTSS)*, 2002.

[DAV 04] DAVID L., PUAUT I., "Static determination of probabilistic execution times", *Proceeding of the Euromicro Conference on Real-Time Systems(ECRTS)*, 2004.

[EDG 01] EDGAR S., BURNS A., "Statistical analysis of WCET for scheduling", *Proceeding of the 22nd IEEE Real-Time Systems Symposium (RTSS)*, 2001.

[GAR 99] GARDNER M., LUI J., "Analyzing stochastic fixed-priority real-time systems", *Proceeding of the 5th International Conference on Tools and Algorithms for the Construction and Analysis of Systems (TACAS)*, 1999.

[GRI 10] GRIFFIN D., BURNS A., "Realism in statistical analysis of worst case execution times", *Proceeding of the 10th International Workshop on Worst-Case Execution Time Analysis (WCET)*, 2010.

[HAN 02] HANSEN J., LEHOCZKY J., ZHU H., *et al.*, "Quantized EDF scheduling in a stochastic environment", *Proceeding of the 16th IEEE International Parallel and Distributed Processing Symposium (IPDPS)*, 2002.

[HAN 09] HANSEN J., HISSAM S., MORENO G.A., "Statistical-based WCET estimation and validation", *Proceeding of the 9th International Workshop on Worst-Case Execution Time Analysis (WCET)*, 2009.

[HAR 13] HARDY D., PUAUT I., "Static probabilistic worst case execution time estimation for architectures with faulty instruction caches", *Proceeding of the 21st International Conference on Real-Time and Network Systems (RTNS)*, 2013.

[KAC 07] KACZYNSKI G., LO BELLO L., NOLTE T., "Deriving exact stochastic response times of periodic tasks in hybrid priority-driven soft real-time systems", *Proceeding of the 12th IEEE International Conference on Emerging Technologies and Factory Automation (ETFA)*, 2007.

[LEH 90] LEHOCZKY J., "Fixed priority scheduling of periodic task sets with arbitrary deadlines", *Proceeding of the IEEE Real-Time Systems Symposium (RTSS)*, 1990.

[LEH 96] LEHOCZKY J., "Real-time queueing theory", *Proceeding of 10th IEEE Real-Time Systems Symposium (RTSS)*, pp. 186–195, 1996.

[LIU 73] LIU C.L., LAYLAND J.W., "Scheduling algorithms for multiprogramming in a hard-real-time environment", *Journal of the ACM*, vol. 20, no. 1, pp. 46–61, January 1973.

[LOP 08] LOPEZ J., DÍAZ J.L., et al., "Stochastic analysis of real-time systems under preemptive priority-driven scheduling", *Real-time Systems*, vol. 40, no. 2, pp. 180–207, 2008.

[LU 11] LU Y., NOLTE T., BATE I., et al., "A new way about using statistical analysis of worst-case execution times", *SIGBED Review*, vol. 8, no. 3, pp. 11–14, 2011.

[LU 12] LU Y., NOLTE T., BATE I., et al., "A statistical response-time analysis of real-time embedded systems", *Proceeding of the IEEE Real-Time Systems Symposium (RTSS)*, 2012.

[MAN 04] MANOLACHE S., ELES P., PENG Z., "Schedulability analysis of applications with stochastic task execution times", *ACM Transactions on Embedded Computing Systems*, vol. 3, no. 4, pp. 706–735, 2004.

[MAN 04a] MANOLACHE S., ELES P., PENG Z., "Task mapping and priority assignment for soft real-time applications under deadline miss ratio constraints", *ACM Transactions on Embedded Computing Systems*, vol. 7, no. 2, pp. 1–34, 2004.

[MAX 11] MAXIM D., BUFFET O., SANTINELLI L., et al., "Optimal priority assignments for probabilistic real-time systems", *Proceeding of the 19th International Conference on Real-Time and Network Systems (RTNS)*, 2011.

[MAX 12a] MAXIM C., GOGONEL A., MAXIM D., et al., "Estimation of probabilistic minimum inter-arrival times using extreme value theory", *Proceeding of the 6th Junior Researcher Workshop on Real-Time Computing (JRWRTC)*, 2012.

[MAX 12b] MAXIM D., HOUSTON M., SANTINELLI L., *et al.*, "Re-sampling for statistical timing analysis of real-time systems", *Proceedings of the 20th International Conference on Real-Time and Network Systems*, pp. 111–120, 2012.

[MAX 13] MAXIM D., CUCU-GROSJEAN L., "Response time analysis for fixed-priority tasks with multiple probabilistic parameters", *Proceeding of the IEEE Real-Time Systems Symposium (RTSS)*, 2013.

[MOK 83] MOK A., Fundamental design problems of distributed systems for the hard-real-time environment, PhD Thesis, Laboratory for Computer Science, Massachusetts Institute of Technology, 1983.

[NAV 00] NAVET N., SONG Y.-Q., SIMONOT F., "Worst-case deadline failure probability in real-time applications distributed over controller area network", *Journal of Systems Architecture*, vol. 46, no. 7, pp. 607–617, April 2000.

[NAV 07] NAVET N., CUCU-GROSJEAN L., SCHOTT R., "Probabilistic estimation of response times through large deviations", *Proceeding of the 28th IEEE Real-Time Systems Symposium (RTSS)*, 2007.

[PAL 12] PALOPOLI L., ABENI L., FONTANELLI D., *et al.*, "An analytical bound for probabilistic deadlines", *Proceeding of the 24th Eumicro Conference on Real-time Systems (ECRTS)*, 2012.

[REF 10] REFAAT K., HLADIK P.-E., "Efficient stochastic analysis of real-time systems via random sampling", *Proceeding of the IEEE Euromicro Conference on Real-Time Systems (ECRTS)*, pp. 175–183, 2010.

[SAN 07] SANTINELLI L., MEUMEU P., MAXIM D., *et al.*, "A component-based framework for modeling and analyzing probabilistic real-time systems", *Proceeding of the 16th IEEE International Conference on Emerging Technologies and Factory Automation (ETFA)*, 2007.

[TIA 95a] TIA T., DENG Z., SHANKAR M., *et al.*, "Probabilistic performance guarantee for real-time tasks with varying computation times", *Proceeding of the 2nd IEEE Real-Time and Embedded Technology and Applications Symposium (RTAS)*, 1995.

[TIA 95b] TIA T., DENG Z., SHANKAR M., *et al.*, "Probabilistic performance guarantee for real-time tasks with varying computation times", *Proceeding of the IEEE Real-Time and Embedded Technology and Applications Symposium (ETFA)*, 1995.

[YUE 11] YUE L., BATE I., NOLTE T., *et al.*, "A new way about using statistical analysis of worst-case execution times", *ACM SIGBED Review*, vol. 8, no. 3, pp. 11–14, September 2011.

[ZHU 02] ZHU H., HANSEN J., LEHOCZKY J., *et al.*, "Optimal partitioning for quantized EDF scheduling", *Proceeding of IEEE Real-time Systems Symposium (RTSS)*, 2002.

3

Control and Scheduling Joint Design

Control systems and real-time computing have for a long time been associated with control systems, with the aim of controlling a process and bringing it toward a state that complies with the objectives specified by the user. The process is often a physical device, for instance, mechanical (rolling mills), electromechanical (DVD player and robots), thermal (internal combustion engines), chemical (reactors), hydraulic (energy production), etc. These can be complex processes associating several of these technologies, for instance in terrestrial, aerial or underwater vehicles. They can also be computing components (scheduling of tasks, network gateway and Website management) or electronic (power supply of a chip and phase-locked loop), or even simulated components (avatar control in a virtual world, "hardware-in-the-loop" real-time simulators).

The increasing complexity of these systems requires reviewing their properties in order to better integrate the control system design and implementation constraints executed on computing systems. The first section will recall the main properties of closed loop control as well as the

Chapter written by Daniel SIMON, Ye-Qiong SONG and Olivier SENAME.

constraints and limitations induced by their digital implementation. Section 3.2 examines how the control task scheduling constraints can be relaxed by exploiting these properties. The design of scheduling controllers can be performed in the formalism of sampled systems (section 3.3), but also in that of weakly hard real-time scheduling (section 3.4). Finally, an example of designing and implementing the scheduling control of tasks in a video decoder will be detailed in section 3.5.

3.1. Control objectives and models

The control objectives can be of varying nature. A control system is useful in regulation, to maintain the output of the controlled process at a constant value, for instance the speed of a vehicle subject to a speed regulator. It can also be used to track an objective variable in time, for instance the orientation of a radar antenna that keeps the observed mobile in the active zone of the antenna.

In every case, the control processes are never perfectly known. They are too complex for their behavior to be perfectly detailed, this behavior can only be approached by a simplified *model* of reduced size, in which we have for instance omitted the very uncertain fast dynamics of components. The dispersion of the manufacturing tolerance within a series of seemingly identical components is another source of uncertainty. Moreover, the behavior of a physical component varies in time in a hardly predictable manner, for instance due to its usage or overheating.

These processes are also subjected to disturbances from their environment, in themselves little known, which are not entirely measurable or even controllable. It is, therefore, meaningless to try to control a system through a perfectly detailed and understood knowledge of its behavior. To the contrary, a good controller will allow us to satisfy the specified control objectives despite an approximative knowledge of the process and the disturbances it is subject to. The principle of the *closed loop* control allows us to partly overcome these uncertainties (see, for example, [GOO 01] for a very complete presentation).

3.1.1. *Closed loop control*

In a closed loop controller (also called feedback loop), the process is controlled, in a continuous (or repetitive) manner, from an error signal resulting from the difference between the observed output (or the estimated state [1]) of the process and the ideal state corresponding to the objective of the specified control (Figure 3.1). The controlled process must, therefore, include actuators allowing us to act on its state, but also sensors that allow us to observe it in a continuous way. The action of control is repeated indefinitely, with control signals permanently refreshed depending on the observations, in a "sufficiently fast" rhythm compared to the proper dynamics of the controlled process.

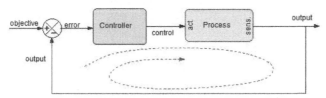

Figure 3.1. *Principle of feedback control*

Compared to the "open loop" approach, based only on a precise knowledge of the process model, the closed control loop approach is distinguished by many characteristic advantages:

– *Stability:* this allows us to stabilize naturally unstable processes. This is the case, for instance, with modern aircraft,

---

1. The state of the process is a set of variables allowing us to predict its evolution from the initial state and the applied controls.

which is aerodynamically unstable and can only be piloted with the assistance of a closed control loop.

– *Robustness:* this allows us to perform correct commands on uncertain processes. The permanent control error correction, associated with a fast repetition rate faced with the inertia of the process, allows us to obtain a robust control whose performance and stability are relatively insensitive to the uncertainties related to the structure and parameters of the controlled process.

– *Precision:* this guarantees the achievement of control objectives over a broad range of operating points with specifiable and configurable precision, rapidity and tolerance to external perturbations.

In turn, a badly designed controller, for instance with a too large amplification in a poorly chosen frequency band, or even reacting too slowly with respect to the proper dynamics of the process, can lead to a dangerous *instability* of the system. Therefore, a controller has to be designed and implemented carefully in order to take into account the characteristics of the controlled process.

The principle of control by feedback has been known for a long time, first by using hydraulic energy (water clocks), mechanical energy (centrifugal governor) and fluid pressure energy (steam actuator supply) both for actuation and error correction. Continuous supply using analog electronics appeared during the 20th Century and has encouraged the first scientific analysis of control systems.

Control devices have been quickly associated with digital technologies, in particular due to the first industrial minicomputers and associated real-time operating kernels [ÅST 97]. The programmed controllers in particular allow us to execute controllers with an algorithmic complexity that is impossible to perform with analog ones, for instance for nonlinear control. The unending miniaturization of increasingly powerful and less and less costly digital computing components now allows for the presence of digital control loops embedded and hidden within a very large number of everyday items, for instance in mobile phones. The availability of communication networks, wired or wireless, has on the other hand allowed for the deployment of distributed control systems associating sensors, actuators and computer components in numerous fields, such as, for example, in industry and transport (we then refer to network controlled systems [MUR 03], or cyber-physical systems [LEE 07]).

3.1.2. *Control and temporal parameters*

A digital control loop allows us to control a process, most of the time continuous, by a central processing unit (CPU) operating in discrete time with sampling and conversion processes between continuous and discrete data. The components of a distributed digital control loop are summarized in Figure 3.2.

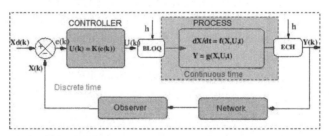

Figure 3.2. *Digital implementation of a control loop*

– The measurements performed on the output of the continuous process $Y(t)$ are filtered, sampled (over a clock h_e) and digitized by an analog/digital converter (series of values Y_k), the current quantization going from 8 to 16 bits.

– In the case of a system deployed on a network, these pieces of data are encoded and inserted into the frames whose format is characteristic of the transmission protocol used.

– It is often necessary to use an observer to reconstruct the internal state X_k of the process from measurements of the outputs Y_k.

– The controls U_k are calculated over a clock h_c from the discrete series of measurements and objective values. More and more often, the execution of these computations is regulated by a real-time scheduler, allowing us to share the computing resource between several activities.

– The sequence of computed controls is converted into continuous signals $U(t)$ by a digital/analog converter, and is blocked between the sampling times (often at a constant value) in order to maintain a continuous action at the input of the actuators.

With respect to the schematic principle of Figure 3.1, the digital implementation of the control of a continuous process introduces a certain number of new elements relative to the implementation:

– *Modeling:* Except the academic case of a continuous linear model sampled by a constant clock, the discretization of realistic (nonlinear) models, and/or the utilization of a non-equidistant sampling adds modeling approximations to the uncertainties relative to the continuous model. It makes the synthesis of the controls based on the model more delicate.

– *Delays:* The sources of delays in the loop are numerous: non-negligible computation time variable in the CPUs, interruption of the execution due to preemption, waiting in the network gateways,... The random loss of data is also possible in the case of network transmission, in particular in wireless links.

– *Clocks:* A digital control system can be regulated by various sources of synchronization. The execution of the calculations can, for instance, be triggered by the arrival of a new measurement at the input of the CPU, and therefore by the clock linked to the sensors h_e polluted by the delay and jitter (temporal dispersion of the signal) due to the transmission canal. Similarly, the variable computing time will induce additional delays and jitters on the emission times of new controls, even if their triggering was regulated by a perfectly periodic clock h_c.

For a given control algorithm, the performances of the controller depend on its implementation, and in particular on several essential temporal parameters, which are function of the dynamics of the controlled process:

– The *sampling interval* has to be small enough compared to the smallest time constant of the closed loop system. In the case of a linear system and a constant clock of period h, a first approach to choosing the sampling period can be the interval [ÅST 97]: $\omega_c.h \in [0.15 \dots 0.5]$, where ω_c is the desired pulsation of the closed loop. It is unnecessary to sample faster, the gain in performance being negligible whereas the cost of computation grows linearly with the frequency of execution. A far too fast sampling rate can even lead to system instability. A too slow sampling rate leads first of all to a degradation of performance, followed by inevitable instabilities (loss of system controllability). The analog signals have to be preprocesses before the sampling, since the high frequencies need to be eliminated from the measurements by filtering in order to avoid frequency aliasing [GOO 10].

– The input/output *latency* is the interval separating the time of taking a measurement on the output of the process and the time when the control using this measurement is applied to the actuators (it gathers all the delays in the loop). Generally, the significant latencies degrade the control performance, up to the point of system instability due to the phase shift created by the delay. Large latencies, whose value may be significantly higher than the sampling interval, can be introduced by the communication network in the case of distributed networks. Control algorithms specific to delayed systems can attenuate the influence of delays in the control loop [RIC 03, NIC 01], however, it is desirable to minimize these latencies as much as possible.

– The *jitter*, due to the contingencies in computing time and transmission, disrupts the regularity of the sampling intervals. It is also likely to degrade the performances of a control loop.

– *Losses* of samples can appear in the case of non-compliance with deadlines or corruption of the message. This is generally not catastrophic, since a new control will be generated at the next interval, and the effect of the induced disturbance can be minimized due to the robustness of the closed loop. We could, for instance, assimilate the loss of a sample to a temporary doubling of the interval or to an isolated increase of the latency. It is, however, essential that this situation is correctly handled by the computer system, for example, by jumping a clock tick instead of indefinitely waiting for the lost piece of data or generating a fatal exception.

Generally, we can say that obtaining good performances for a control loop will be encouraged by small execution times and delays compared to the system time constants, whereas too high values for these parameters will not even allow us to stabilize the control loop.

The stability and performances of a control loop can only be ensured by the coherence between the temporal parameters used for the design and the configuration of the control law as well as the effective execution parameters. The distortions of temporal parameters due to the implementation are often non-measurable and are hard to predict [WIT 01]. It is more realistic to evaluate uncertainty intervals concerning the temporal parameters of effective execution, on which robust controls may be built [BAI 07].

A digital control will only be able to operate correctly if its execution complies with the timing constraints required by the dynamics of the controlled process and the control law used: this is the commonly accepted definition of a real-time system.

3.2. Scheduling of control loops

The aim of a control system is to ensure a level of performance, specified, for example, in terms of objective precision or response time. It has been noted very early (at a time when the computing power of digital machines was pathetically low) that equidistant sampling is not necessarily the most economical in CPU cycles in order to obtain a given control performance [DOR 62]. It can sometimes be useful to sample the control faster during the fast transitions of the system, whereas a more spaced sampling could suffice to stabilize the state of equilibrium once it is reached. In other cases, a strong requirement of disturbances rejection near the equilibrium will need a sampling rate faster near this equilibrium than during the approach trajectory. A certain number of adaptive sampling control methods have, therefore, been proposed [HSI 74], at the expense of an analysis notably more complex than for periodic controls. These have been forgotten when the availability of powerful processors has made these optimizations unnecessary.

Thus, control systems have for a long time been considered as having to be perfectly periodic, as much from a design point of view as from that of their implementation on real-time computers. One of the reasons without doubt is the simplicity of design and analysis of the system: indeed, a continuous linear model sampled with an equidistant clock produces a linear discrete model. A theory of fixed-step discrete linear control systems, with negligible or constant computing delays, has been developed quickly and very widely employed in these last decades. [ÅST 97]. The implementation of such a controller in real-time multitask systems naturally involves the schedulability analysis of periodic task systems, initialized by [LIU 73] and then generalized as summarized by [SHA 04].

The aim of these scheduling algorithms is to verify the schedulability of the task system and to ensure that every one of them will be able to execute before their temporal deadline (assuming the classical hard real-time hypothesis). These algorithms are based on the *a priori* knowledge of the execution time of the tasks. Being variable from one execution to another, we use this as an upper bound of the worst-case execution time (WCET). The waste is getting worse and worse when the ratio between the average execution time and the WCET is getting smaller.

This approach was for a long time used on small size systems, executed on relatively deterministic dedicated processors with a low dispersion of execution times. However, the new generations of processors have a less deterministic architecture that makes it difficult to predict the execution times and the precise determination of the WCET [PUS 08, BEN 11]. Modern processors, equipped with speculative execution mechanisms, present an increasing spread of the probability curve of the execution time of a given task (Figure 3.3). Assuming that the determination of the WCET is solved, this scheduling approach is conservative anyway: reaching an execution time close to the WCET is large compared to the average execution time, and the waste of CPU cycles is then unacceptable. The chronic underutilization of the available resources correlatively leads to a costly oversizing (in the price of the materials as well as in weight and consumed energy) of the computing and communication capacities.

It appears that a joint design approach, taking into account from the beginning the sometimes contradictory constraints between control and real-time computing, allows us to obtain more efficient and safer methods.

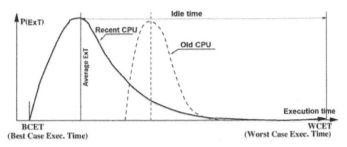

Figure 3.3. *Probability distribution of the execution time of a task*

Among the pioneering works in the field, [EKE 00] re-examines the traditional hypotheses through a study of processor sharing between several feedback control tasks. More precisely, the global control performance has to be optimized (sum of the individual performances of the controllers), under the constraint of not overshooting a specific utilization rate of the CPU. The execution times of the tasks and the CPU load are assumed to be measured and made available by the operating system. The control variables used to handle processor load are the activation intervals of the control tasks. Several concepts of interest emerge from this approach:

– The controllers are not necessarily periodic, the interval of execution of the control laws can be variable. It can even be used as a control variable, dependent on the objectives to reach (objective load of the CPU), on the measurements performed in real-time on the controlled process (control performance criteria) and on the execution resource (CPU load). The stability of these control laws of course has to be ensured despite the variable sampling.

– A closed loop control can be applied to a computer process. A new kind of controller appears, *feedback scheduler*, using measurements of the activity of the computer system (for instance, the CPU load) in order to produce, as control variables, scheduling parameters of the controlled activities (for instance, the sampling interval). Thus, the computer processes can benefit from the adaptability and robustness properties that are characteristics of closed control loops.

This preliminary work [EKE 00] results in the analytic formulation of the feedback scheduler solving the problem of joint optimization of the control performances and of computing resource usage. Let us note that this is still a very academic case of a linear system without uncertainties and disturbances. However, even in this simple case, the theoretical solution is far too costly to implement in real-time in order for the concept of optimal utilization of the computing resource to still have a meaning.

Luckily, the simpler formulation of problems using these new perspectives has lead to the development of fruitful case studies, declining the association between control systems and real-time computing in a more or less integrated manner:

– Feedback schedulers can be linked to the control of physical processes, but they can also directly handle computer-like processes, such as, for example, the management of web server overloads or the electrical consumption of digital components (for a detailed example see section 3.5).

– The control laws can be designed to be especially robust to the uncertainties of temporal execution, or even to be adaptive by using the scheduling parameters as new control variables (section 3.3).

– The integration between control and real-time scheduling can be even more comprehensive if we can directly express the control performances in function of the temporal execution parameters (see the example in section 3.4.3).

3.2.1. *Robustness and relaxation of hard real-time constraints*

In a distributed control system, the computation and communication resources have to be shared between a number of controllers. It could be interesting to optimize the functioning of the system by permanently adapting the allocation of resources in function of the variable needs of the autonomous mobile systems, in which the embedded energy source is of limited capacity. The computing power provided by a processor being a function of its electric consumption, the adaptation of the computing task frequency allows us to optimize the operating time of the device. These emerging needs have called into question the hypothesis of periodicity of the control algorithms, implemented under a hard real-time assumption.

Currently, control systems, such as flight or brake controls, are most often considered to be hard real-time systems, and it is assumed right from the design phase that the software tasks will have to be executed in a strictly periodic manner. Prefixed time slots are allocated to the control tasks, and deadline misses as well as the phenomenon of jitter are forbidden. We consider that every deviation from this ideal scheduling is an operational failure of the system, leading to the halt of the faulty processor and the activation of a backup processor. The knowledge (which is assumed to be safe) of the WCETs is used to design the system.

The distribution of the execution time (Figure 3.3) for an embedded processor shows that an execution close to the WCET is quite a rare event. A scheduling based on an average occupation of the CPU instead of the worst case can produce substantial gains in terms of the design of the embedded equipment. The validity of the usual hard real-time hypothesis, therefore, deserves to be closely re-examined by taking into account the robustness of the feedback control systems.

One idea, analyzed in [AND 11], consists of allocating an execution time slot T_{slot} for a control task within the interval (best case execution time (BCET) and WCET) (Figure 3.4a). When the effective execution time of the task is lower than

T_{slot}, the control is computed and sent normally to the actuators. Let us note that in this case, the input/output latency is reduced by a value of $WCET - T_{slot}$, which allows us to improve the nominal performances of the control.

It can also happen that the computation time is higher than the allocated time slot T_{slot}. In order to handle missing the deadline, we can freeze the current value of the controller's output, and let the computation finish within the next allocated interval, or even terminate the current computation and restart the task with new measurements. These sporadic sample losses induce variable delays and disturb the control loop. The stability and performances of the control result from the compromise between reduction of the average latency and perturbations due to losses, specified by the ratio between the worst case and the allocated interval $\epsilon = \frac{T_{slot}}{WCET}$.

The stability analysis of these disrupted control loops was performed by using recent theories on the control stability of uncertain sampled and delayed systems [SEU 11]. More particularly, in order to design the system, the maximum number of consecutive samples that can be lost before destabilization has to be computed. It has been shown by this method that the elevator control of an F16 aircraft (unstable in open loop) could lose a large number of successive samples while remaining stable: up to 24/25 if the aircraft is perfectly known, and even 3/4 for an uncertain model at 50% (Figure 3.4(b)).

This example clearly shows that the hard real-time hypothesis is unnecessarily constraining for closed loop controls. In order to fully exploit the robustness of these controls, we could use *weakly hard* scheduling methods to our benefit, such as those defined in [BER 01]. In this context, deadline misses are considered to be legal, subject to admissible faulty patterns and error rates dependent on the application being executed. The (m,k)-firm scheduling presented in section 3.4, where we have to ensure at least m correct executions of a task on each window of k consecutive instances, is of this type.

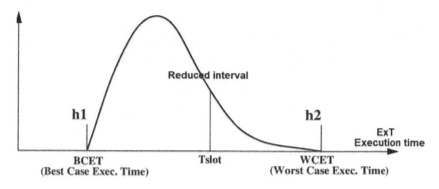

a)

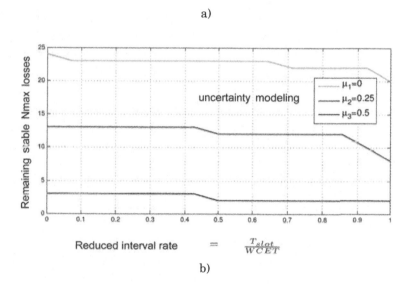

b)

Figure 3.4. *a) Relaxation of constraints b) Stability and sample losses*

Generally, the performance criteria allowing us to specify and configure the control loops can be formulated as

Quality-of-Service   (QoS)   criteria,   merging   together
measurements of the quality of controls (for instance, in
terms of response time and following errors, etc.) and others
related to characteristic measures of the execution platform
(for instance, CPU load, ratio of deadline misses, electric
consumption, etc.). Thus, the QoS allows us to formulate
control issues under execution resource constraints and
implement control systems tolerant to errors, with a gradual
degradation of performances in case of overloads [LI 06]. The
management of computing and communication resources can
then be formulated in the framework of control systems such
as in the following section, or in the framework of real-time
scheduling with relaxed constraints as in section 3.4.

3.3. Continuous approach: regulated scheduling

An emerging concept of the pioneering works of control
systems engineers [CER 02] and computer scientists [LU 02],
is that of the *feedback scheduler*: the operation of a digital
procedure, and in particular that of a scheduler, can be the
object of a control loop on the same basis as the physical
processes usually employed in control systems. Thus, a
digital object controlled in closed loop can benefit from the
properties   of   adaptability   and   robustness   that   are
characteristics of feedback loops.

3.3.1. *Architecture, sensors and actuators*

Speaking of sensor/controller/actuator loops, the composing
elements of these controls have to be identified and chosen
in accordance with the aim to attain and the technology
available. The general architecture is given in Figure 3.5, with
a hierarchy of control layers controlling objectives of various
levels [ROB 07]:

– The internal loops (bottom side) are physical process controls, designed and parametrized to be compatible with variable scheduling parameters.

– The external loop (top side) is the scheduling regulation loop calculating, in a cyclical manner, new scheduling parameters depending on the measures of computing activity (and possibly on performance estimates of the process controls).

– Higher level layers (manager) are concerned with the safety of operation of the system and the handling of exceptions, by managing the changes in the operating mode and the reconfiguration of the system when it is necessary to switch between control laws.

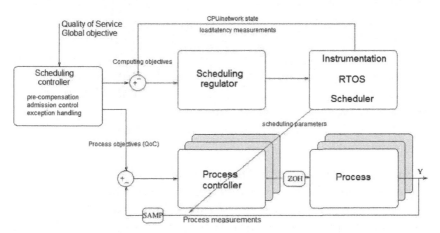

Figure 3.5. *Control architecture with regulated scheduling*

In order to build a control law from specified objectives, the variables to be measured have to be defined, specifically related to the quantity to control, and the usable action variables need to be determined in order for the process to act efficiently on it. The sensors and actuators used in a scheduling regulator will often be software components, or possibly material components buried in silicon.

3.3.2. Sensors

The measured signals have to allow the characterization of the activity of the execution platform with relation to the control objective to attain.

– *CPU load*: One of the main aims of a scheduling regulator is to manage the computing load (or the communication load) of an executing computing resource, it is, therefore, almost always necessary to evaluate the workload of the resource. In the case outlined by Figure 3.5, where the controlled actions are periodic commands over time windows (between two execution parameter updates), the estimation of the computing load induced by a task i during a period h_s of the scheduling loop is [ROB 07]:

$$\hat{U}_{kh_s} = \lambda \, \hat{U}_{(k-1)h_s} + (1 - \lambda) \, \frac{\overline{c}_{kh_s}}{h_{(k-1)h_s}} \qquad [3.1]$$

where h is the execution period of the task i during the interval in question of length h_s, k is the discrete measuring time, $\overline{c}$ is the average of the execution times measured for this task and λ is the gain of a low-pass filter allowing us to smooth the measurements.

We may note that the measure of the CPU load is only meaningful over a time window: a small window will allow the system to be more reactive, at the cost of a significant noise level. This window corresponds here to the execution time of the scheduling loop, which we generally choose to be large in front of the periods of process control tasks in order to obtain stable measurements.

– Deadline overruns are events that are easy to detect; however, the ratio of exceeded deadlines only gives a significant measure in case of CPU overload. They can nevertheless be used as a complement to the estimation of the load, which precisely does not give any more usable quantitative estimation in the case of a CPU overload. Let us note that a deadline overrun must be associated with an error recovery policy.

– The slackness of the tasks (time left between the end of execution of an instance and the activation time of the following instance) can also be seen as an indicator of the load of the system, which is a quantitative measure that sometimes allows us to detect trends.

– In the case of a distributed system, the same kind of measure can be transposed to the case of a network.

Measurements can be obtained using software sensors, programmed into functions of the operating system or into middleware libraries. For instance, the real-time portable operating system interface for uniX (POSIX) library provides tools that allow the instrumentation of a piece of source code and, for example, to retrieve very precise measurements on the execution time passed between two beacons.

3.3.3. *Actuators*

Here, actuators are scheduling parameters, acting on the execution of lower level tasks, including those related to the management of the processor.

– *Execution interval:* the computational load of a CPU appears almost always in the specification of a scheduling controller, either as the main objective (load regulation), or as a constraint (performance optimization). The computational load induced by n tasks of duration c_i and period h_i is $U = \sum_{i=1}^{n} \frac{c_i}{h_i}$. It is, therefore, immediately noticeable that the activation interval of the tasks will be the essential actuator allowing us to regulate the CPU load (or the network by acting on the transmission rate of messages). The actuator is then a programmable and variable clock generator, allowing us to trigger the lower level tasks at the times computed by the feedback scheduler.

– *CPU clock:* numerous current CPUs, in particular those used in nomadic devices, are equipped with digital voltage and frequency scaling (DVFS), allowing us to permanently adapt the computing capacity and correlatively of the electric consumption of the chip. This actuator is to be used when the electric consumption of the system is part of the control objectives. At least one part of the actuator is integrated within the silicon, which interfaces with the operating system (see, for example, the case study in section 3.5).

– *Variable-cost computations:* during the convergence of a recursive function, for instance in an optimization process, we can choose to halt the computation at a given precision level in order to limit the computing latency of the task in consideration [HEN 02]. We can also consider tasks composed of compulsory part and an optional part, the latter only being executed if the computing resources are sufficient [LIU 94]. Finally, the same functionality may be executed by several variants of an algorithm, the most complex ones giving the most precise results at the expense of more significant computing costs. The use of the least costly variants can cause a gradual degradation of the system in case of temporary overload. The {cost and precision} models of these variants have to be integrated into the QoS criterion of the system.

– *Priorities:* the priority of the tasks does not have a direct impact on the load of the processor, but influences the interleaving of the executions (that may potentially cause troublesome variable delay issues for the stability of control loops). In contrast with classical scheduling problems, where the selection of priorities is itself the study objective, this is not an efficient actuator to implement control laws under constraints of non-saturation of execution resources. We may on the other hand use a fixed-priority scheduler in order to classify the control tasks following an order of importance (as in the robot controller [SIM 05]). This allows us to manage the operating safety of the system by preserving the execution of critical tasks in case of overload, the role of priorities is thus well-separated from the control of the computing load, delegated to the scheduling regulator using the activation intervals.

3.3.4. *Control laws*

The control engineer's toolbox is full of a large number of algorithms, adapted to different types of processes and control objectives, many of them can be applied to feedback schedulers and other digital processes [PAT 12]. If we observe the activity of a control system, the cost of the feedback scheduler has to be integrated into the CPU load balance. Insofar as a feedback scheduler is often intended to optimize, or at least increase, the use of an execution resource, the complexity as well as the cost of the control law used will have to be limited in order for the problem to remain meaningful.

Digital processes often have simple dynamics. Computer tasks do not have inertia and can be halted and resumed instantaneously. Measurement filters, such as [3.1], provide the essentials of the system's dynamics, the other part coming from the queues of the tasks or messages that have simple, integrator-type dynamics. The analogy with storage units (server), valves (processor) and throughputs (request flows) has allowed the establishment of "fluid" models, first linear [HEL 04], adapted to the synthesis of simple controls. A bit more complex, nonlinear models allow for instance to take breakdown phenomena into account under heavy loads [MAL 11]. In each case, the relatively simple dynamics of digital processes allows the utilization of control laws, themselves having a simple structure and low implementation cost.

Let us name several examples of closed control loops applied to digital processes:

– The proportional-integral-derivative (P.I.D.) controller, very widely used in numerous industrial applications, is adapted to single-input/single-output control systems. One of its many versions is given by

$$u_k = u_{k-1} + K[e_k - e_{k-1}] + \frac{K \cdot T_d}{T_s}[e_k - 2e_{k-1} + e_{k-2}]$$

$$+\frac{K \cdot T_s}{T_i}e_k \qquad\qquad [3.2]$$

where u_k is the control signal composed of a term proportional to the error e_k (rise time control), of a derivative term to control the damping of the control and of an integral term to cancel out the static error. K, T_i and T_d are adjustment gains of the control, and T_s is the sampling period. This type of controller was one of the first ones to be tested for the handling of web server overloads [LU 02], with an admission control as main actuator. It is easy to adjust, but its simplicity limits its performance and robustness.

– Nonlinear models, allowing us to model the breakdown due to the overhead of parallelism, have been successfully associated with *predictive* controllers to handle the load of computer servers: a small number of adjustment parameters allow us to manage the balance between the response time to requests and the number of clients simultaneously served [MAL 11]. The same kind of controller can be used for managing the computing power/consumption compromise of a multicore chip [DUR 11]. [HEN 02] presents an example of a predictive control in which the temporal optimization horizon (deadline) is adjusted online in function of an estimation of the error due to the computing latency.

– *Linear quadratic*-type optimal controls allow us to specify the performance/computing cost compromise in the form of a mathematical criterion to optimize [EKE 00]. The general problem is too complex to be implemented in real-time, but restrictive hypotheses allow the implementation of particularly simple scheduling regulators [HEN 05]. When the cost functions that relate control performance to sampling intervals can be identified by quadratic functions, their convexity properties allow us to compute the optimal values (in the sense of linear quadratic (LQ)) of the sampling intervals [BEN 08].

– *Robust* controls are dedicated to the control of uncertain systems, they are, therefore, particularly well-adapted to systems combining uncertainties on the physical model of the process and uncertainties on the temporal execution parameters. A robust control H_∞ was synthesized in order to control the sampling of control functions of the the arm of a robot under the constraint of processor saturation [SIM 05], which was then improved in [SEN 08] where the variable parameters of the systems are functions of the control performance. This same type of robust control can also be used for controlling physical processes themselves, in order to make them adaptable to the variable sampling rate resulting from the feedback scheduler [ROB 10, ROC 11]. The sampling interval of the control laws is then considered, at the same time, to be a varying parameter of the sampling model and a control variable of the computing load and QoS of the system [SIM 12].

3.4. Discrete approach: scheduling under the (m,k)-firm constraint

There are numerous real-time applications in which the respect of the temporal constraint of each instance is not as strict as in hard real-time for ensuring the correct operation of the system. For such applications, it is enough that a sufficient number of task instances (or jobs if we consider an application distributed around a network) end their execution (or their transmission) before their deadline. This kind of application, tolerant in a certain way of the non-compliance with the temporal constraint linked to the deadline, is traditionally called a soft real-time system.

However, the concept of soft real-time is not suitable for most control systems, for which the admissible ratio of instance losses has to be explicitly specified. Let us take the example of the control of an inverted pendulum: the control task periodically computes the next action to take in order to maintain the pendulum in the stable position of equilibrium (an elongation of 180°). Occasionally, missing a couple of deadlines for this task can be tolerated due to the robustness of the control loop (the pendulum remains around the point of equilibrium, but with more vibrations). However, if the number of consecutive instances of this task that miss their deadline becomes too large, then the pendulum may fall.

In this case, the weakly hard real-time model [BER 01], whose representatives include the (m,k)-firm model, can be used to better specify the degree of tolerance of the control task to the non-respect of deadlines.

3.4.1. *(m,k)-firm model*

The (m,k)-firm model was proposed by Hamdaoui and Ramanathan [HAM 94] to describe in a precise manner the level of temporal guarantee offered to real-time applications tolerating deadline misses of certain instances. The (m,k)-firm model is characterized by two parameters m and k. More formally, an application is said to be under an (m,k)-firm temporal constraint if at least m instances, among k consecutive instances, must be executed by respecting their temporal deadline. Having said this, if the (m,k)-firm temporal constraint of an application is respected, then in any window of k consecutive instances, there are at least m instances that respect their deadlines.

A task under an (m,k)-firm constraint is said to be in a state of dynamic failure at time t, if at this time there are more than $(k-m)$ instances having missed their deadlines among the last k instances. Thus, a task under (m,k)-firm constraints can be in one of two states: normal or dynamic failure. The knowledge of its state at time t depends on the processing history of the k

last instances. If we associate "1" to an instance that respects its deadline and "0" to an instance missing its deadline, then this history is entirely described by a series of "0"s and "1"s of k bit length called an (m,k)-pattern. Figure 3.6 gives an example of a state-transition diagram of the (m,k)-patterns of a task under a (2,3)-firm constraint. By convention, the movement of bits in an (m,k)-pattern is done from the right to the left.

Let us note that this model generalizes the hard real-time model by being more flexible in order to describe the temporal constraint of a real-time application. The case when $m = k$ represents the strict temporal constraint. The (m,k)-firm constraint with $m < k$ could be used to represent the soft real-time constraint with a maximum allowed loss rate equal to $\frac{k-m}{k}$. Thus, the (m,k)-firm constraint allows us to describe the intermediate levels between hard real-time and soft real-time. This is also called *firm* real-time.

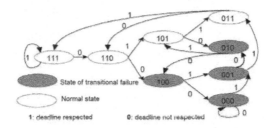

Figure 3.6. *State-transition diagram of a task with (2,3)-firm*

Furthermore, the (m,k)-firm model allows us to explicitly specify the patterns of rejection (or non-compliance with the deadlines). Due to the characteristics of the (m,k)-firm model, it is appropriate to model the way in which the control system tolerates the non-respect of its temporal constraint. It is important to note that there is a fundamental difference between firm real-time and soft real-time, related to the way of handling instances that cannot comply with their deadline in case of a system overload. In particular, in a firm real-time system, (this is the case of (m,k)-firm), every instance that cannot respect its deadline will simply not be executed (and consequently will be rejected by the system). This point is of particular importance in the handling of an overload of the system, since it allows us to apply the concept of selective rejection that we can see in the example presented in section 3.4.3.

3.4.2. Scheduling under the (m,k)-firm constraint

With respect to the classical real-time task model of Liu and Layland [LIU 73], two new parameters characterizing the (m,k)-firm constraint are added:

– m_i and k_i: (m,k)-firm constraint of τ_i with $m_i <= k_i$;

– The (m,k)-pattern Π_i: the character string $\Pi_i = \Pi_i(1)\,\Pi_i(2)\,...\Pi_i(n)$ such that $\sum_{j=l}^{l+k_i-1}\Pi_i(j) = m_i$ for $l \in [1..n]$ and that the jth instance of τ_i has to be executed by the processor if $\Pi_i(j-1) = 1$, or can be ignored if $\Pi_i(j-1) = 0$.

There are mainly two families of algorithms that calculate the priority of the tasks while taking into account the (m,k)-firm constraints:

– Static (for instance, enhanced fixed priority (EFP) or rate monotonic (RM)) in which the priority assignment is determined in function of a fixed parameter (for example, the $\frac{m}{k}$ ratio).

– Dynamic (for instance, distance-based priority (DBP)), in which the priority assigned to each instance (or message) is dynamically adjusted depending on the current state of the system.

Dynamic scheduling algorithms allow a dynamic adaptation to the change of the system load. Static scheduling algorithms are less flexible but allow an offline verification of the system. In the following, we present two algorithms representative of the dynamic and static scheduling algorithms proposed in the literature.

– EFP

According to EFP [RAM 99], the instances of each task are classified into two categories: critical instance and optional instance. Every critical instance is scheduled according to its fixed priority, whereas optional instances are assigned the lowest priority. It has been shown that if all the critical instances terminate their execution before the deadline, then the (m, k)-firm constraint is satisfied.

The classification of the instances of a task τ_i according to its (m_i, k_i)-firm constraint is given by the following law: the ath instance of the task, with $(a = 0, 1, ...)$, is marked as critical (i.e. $\Pi_i (a - 1) = 1$) if a verifies:

$$a = \left\lfloor \left\lceil \frac{a \cdot m_i}{k_i} \right\rceil \cdot \frac{k_i}{m_i} \right\rfloor \qquad [3.3]$$

– DBP

The aim of the dynamic scheduling algorithm under the (m,k)-firm DBP constraint [HAM 95] is to reduce the probability of a dynamic failure. DBP defines the concept of distance between the current state of a task at time t and a state of dynamic failure. For an (m,k)-pattern in a normal state at time t, this distance is defined by the number of consecutive "0" bits that can be added to the (m,k)-pattern to be in a state of dynamic failure.

As a result, the priority assigned by DBP to the various tasks is inversely proportional to the distance separating the current state and the dynamic failure. If a task is already in a state of dynamic failure, in other words if there are less than m deadlines respected in the (m,k)-pattern, the highest priority "0" is assigned to this task.

Formally, the priority of the $(i + 1)^{th}$ instance of τ_j is given by:

$$DBP_{i+1}^j = k_j - l_j(m_j, s) \qquad [3.4]$$

where $s_i \left(\delta^j_{i-k_j+1}, ... \delta^j_{i-1}, \delta^j_i \right)$ is the (m,k)-pattern of the task τ_i with $\delta^j_i \in \{0, 1\}$ represents the execution state of the ith instance, and $l_j(n, s)$ is the position (counting from the right) of the nth deadline respected in s. Let us note that when there are less than m_j "1" symbols in s_j, then $l_j(m_j, s_j) = k_j + 1$ in order for the highest priority (zero) to be affected. This dynamic-priority affectation policy can easily and efficiently be implemented within the material, since the history of each source can be stored in a register of k_j bits. In case of two or more tasks having the same priority, the EDF scheduling policy is used to choose the next instance to process.

3.4.3. *Regulated (m,k)-firm scheduling*

The previous algorithms (EFP and DBP) are only based on quantities relative only to the computer system and use the priority of the tasks as a metric of action, but remain in open loop with respect to the control application. It is possible to make the (m,k)-firm scheduler sensible to the control performance and active on the computing load using a regulation loop, as in the following example (the details concerning the design of a controller and its implementation can be found in [FEL 10] and [SIM 11]).

The case study concerns the in-flight attitude stabilization of a quadri-rotor mini-drone described in [GUE 09] and outlined in Figure 3.7. The drone has to be stabilized around the roll Φ, pitch Θ and yaw Ψ axes using four propellers $[Q_1, ..., Q_4]$. The controls are computed from an estimate of the attitude measured by an embedded inertial sensor. The attitude controller, the sensors and the actuators communicate through a controller area network (CAN) bus whose low bandwidth limits the sampling rate.

The scarce embedded execution resources do not always allow us to execute the attitude controller at its maximum rate. An (m,k)-firm scheduling allows us to guarantee a sufficient access to the resources in order to stabilize the drone, even in the worst case of rejection of instances of the control task. However, it has to be ensured that the associated control law stabilizes the drone for all possible patterns in the (m,k)-pattern.

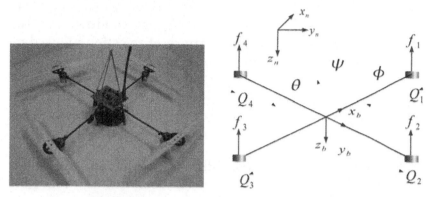

Figure 3.7. *Drone – axes and coordinate system*

The proposed control law is a classical LQ control [3.7] synthesized from a linearized and discretized model of the drone [3.5]–[3.6]:

$$x_{i+1} = \Phi(h_n)x_i + \Gamma(h_n)u_i \qquad [3.5]$$

$$y_i = C_d(h_n)x_i + D_d(h_n)u_i \qquad [3.6]$$

$$u_i = [\tau_\Phi \tau_\Theta \tau_\Psi]^T = [L_\Phi L_\Theta L_\Psi]x_i^T \qquad [3.7]$$

where x is the state vector (positions and speeds) of the drone, y is the vector of measured outputs and u is the vector of couples generated by the propellers on the axes of the engine. h_n is the nominal sampling period of the controller, and Φ, Γ, C_d and D_d are matrices dependent on the nominal sampling period.

The major difficulty, with respect to a standard controller with equidistant sampling, is to calculate the gains $[L_\Phi L_\Theta L_\Psi]$ of the controller allowing us to guarantee the stability of the drone during the rejection of certain instances of the control task by the scheduler and this, for every rejection sequence allowed in the (m,k)-pattern. We can consider that the rejection of instances creates a discrete number of sampling periods, multiples of the nominal period h_n, whose concatenation creates a family of real-time switched discrete systems. The computation of a sufficient condition for the stability of the system for any pattern of rejection allowed by the scheduler can be performed (among other synthesis methods) by using the properties of convexity of this set [FEL 98], which leads to an explicit computation of the gains $[L_\Phi L_\Theta L_\Psi]$, variable in function of the position of the current instance in the (m,k)-pattern and in function of h_n.

We may note that, if the offline synthesis of a controller stabilizing the switched system is complex, its real-time implementation, in the case of a control subjected to an (m,k)-firm scheduling, is particularly simple. In the case in which a scheduler decides to reject an instance of a control task, it is sufficient to avoid propagating the clock signal relative to this particular instance, which maintains the task in an idle state, waiting to be executed and does not waste any CPU cycles.

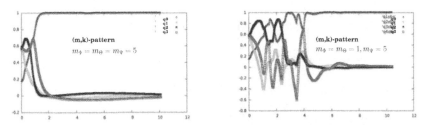

Figure 3.8. *Stabilization of the axes a) without loss b) with controlled losses*

Figure 3.8 shows the components of the attitude quaternion of the drone, simulated with a (1,5)-firm scheduler. Compared with the ideal case without rejection (a), we can note in Figure (b) that if the degradation of performance is significant, the control is still stable in the case of maximum rejection, in which only 1 instance out of the 5 is executed for the roll and pitch axis controls. We can, therefore, see (as in the example of section 3.2.1) that even for an unstable flying engine in open loop, the hard real-time assumption is no longer justified as soon as the control law used is designed to adapt to the specified temporal disturbances.

Finally, it is possible to integrate into a chip the optimization of parameters, some of them being related to the control performance and others being related to the computing activity of the system. This is, for instance, the case of [GAI 09] where a predictive controller allows us to select online the instances of tasks to be rejected depending on the available CPU (or network) capacity, and of [FEL 10] where it is shown that the patterns of the particular rejections can be chosen in the (m,k)-pattern in order to maximize the control quality.

3.5. Case study: regulated scheduling of a video decoder

Numerous nomadic devices, such as laptops, mobile phones tablets and personal assistants, embed computer systems in mobile and autonomous devices. These devices benefit from increasingly powerful processing powers, in particular graphical ones, allowing the implementation of multimedia applications. For this, they are equipped with multicore processors operating at relatively high clock frequencies, and are therefore energy-hungry. However, they are powered by batteries, with as limited capacities as the device is miniature. Handling the conflicting constraints of application performance and energy consumption is related to a QoS optimization approach.

The electrical power consumed by a complementary metal-oxide-semiconductor (CMOS) chip is approximatively proportional to the clock frequency and to the square of the supply voltage by [3.8].

$$P_{avg}(t) \propto f_{clk}(t)V_{dd}(t)^2 \qquad [3.8]$$

$$E(t) \propto V_{dd}(t)^2 \qquad [3.9]$$

The supply voltage V_{dd} itself has to be approximatively proportional to the clock frequency f_{clk}, in order to adjust the propagation time of the signals in function of the increase in frequency. The energy consumed by the chip during a given time interval is, therefore, significantly proportional to the square of the supply voltage V_{dd} [3.9].

Reducing the computing speed of the circuit to the minimum required value for the execution of a task in the given deadline allows us to avoid a waste of embedded energy, increase the lifetime between recharges of the battery and decrease the heating up of the components. Numerous current processors, in particular those used in nomadic devices, are equipped with a capacity of dynamic variation of the clock frequency and of the corresponding supply voltage (DVFS) [ISH 98]. A closed control loop approach can provide an elegant solution to the problem of real-time adaptation of the processing speed to the application needs, as in the following example describing an embedded video decoder on a multicore chip [DUR 13].

It is an H.264 decoder with scalable video coding (SVC) extensions, where a certain number of quality parameters (image resolution, decoding rate and contrast quantification) are variable, and can be used to meet the objectives of the QoS. The effective actions are performed by control loops, layered from the application software down to the silicon with increasing activation frequencies. The embedded control architecture (Figure 3.9) is composed of a hierarchy of control loops, intended to (starting from the material layer and going up toward the software layer):

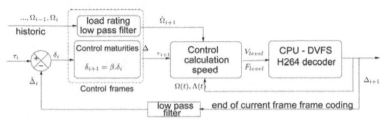

Figure 3.9. *Frame controls and computing speed*

– Handle frequency and power voltage transitions, by minimizing the consumed energy during the transitions. Here, the controllers and the actuators are power transistor and delay lines embedded within the silicon.

– Adapt the instantaneous computing speed to the variable needs of the decoder, by generating objective computing frequencies and supply voltages. This computing speed controller is generic, it is also integrated into the silicon.

– Evaluate the computing speed necessary for the decoding of the current frame, in the form of a computing load to execute before the processing deadline of the frame. The corresponding controller is specific to the type of the application, it can be a middleware module on top of an operating system.

– Handle a QoS criterion between the decoding quality and the lifetime of the battery by using the SVC quality parameters. This controller is part of the application layer.

Low-level loops allow us to take into account the dispersion of performance between the CPUs due to the uncertainties of chip fabrication [ZAK 10]. The supply voltage has to be stable despite the uncertainties on the impedance and the consumption of the receiving circuits [ALB 10]. The maximum computing frequency can, therefore, be different between cores of a same silicon wafer, it can also vary in function of the temperature. The speed controller permanently adjusts, depending on the observed progress of the calculations, the objective voltages and frequencies necessary for the accomplishment of the decoding task within the given time limit [DUR 11]. These controllers, integrated into the silicon, provide the application layer with idealized computing units that are robust to the uncertainties of fabrication and execution.

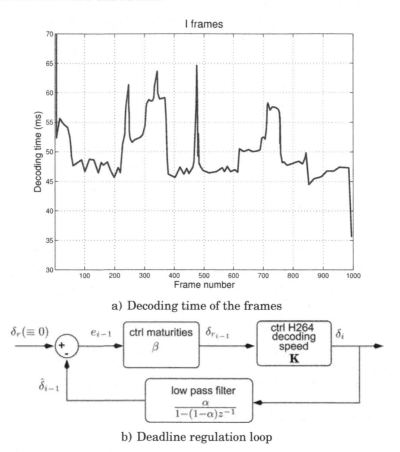

a) Decoding time of the frames

b) Deadline regulation loop

Figure 3.10. *Frame control*

The role of the *frame controller* is to evaluate in real-time the objective computing speed necessary for the decoding of the incoming frame. In practice, this speed is specified using the couple $\{\hat{\Omega}, \Delta_r\}$, composed of an approximation of the number of computing cycles to perform $\hat{\Omega}$ and of the temporal deadline required for decoding the frame Δ_r. The display rate of the frames is fixed, for instance at 40 ms for video. On the other hand, the order of the frames in the incoming stream is different than the final display order, since the type I master frames need to be decoded first. The decoding is, therefore, performed several frames upstream of the display time, it is thus necessary that the decoding be performed *on average* at the rate of display, the jitter being removed during the final sequencing of the frames before being displayed.

In a sequence of video frames, the computational load to be performed for the decoding of the incoming frame is not known beforehand, we, therefore, need an approximation model. Measurements performed on the various types of frames of a video sequence encoded with H.264 show that the computing times are grouped into ranges of relatively uniform noisy values, separated by isolated peaks whose amplitudes can go up to three times the average value (Figure 3.10). An approximation of the load based on the worst case would, therefore, be around three times more conservative than necessary on average.

The model chosen to predict the decoding time $\hat{\Omega}_{i+1}$ can simply be the value measured at the previous frame Ω_i, or even better a value filtered from the previous approximations:

$$\hat{\Omega}_{i+1} = \alpha\hat{\Omega}_{i-1} + (1 - \alpha)\Omega_i \qquad\qquad [3.10]$$

where $0 \le \alpha \le 1$ determines the bandwidth of the low-pass filter aimed at smoothing the noise. This model is of course grossly false in case of a peak load: in this case, a buffer big enough to store three frames temporarily absorbs the data waiting to be decoded. The peak loads being isolated, the deadline miss consecutive to the overload is regulated by a control loop in order to progressively return the required deadline to the theoretical schedule $\{..., \tau_{i-1}, \tau_i, \tau_{i+1}, ...\}$ regularly spaced according to the video rate.

The control objective is, therefore, to regulate the deadline command Δ_{r_i} to the ideal value τ_i. Due to decoding time fluctuations, the end of the measured calculation will be different than the objective, hence an observed deadline $\Delta_i = \tau_i + \delta_i$. In case of overshoot ($\delta_i > 0$), we terminate the computations, and the untreated data are stocked in the buffer. We formalize the control objective by an exponential decay of the deadline error:

$$\delta_{i+1} = \beta \, \delta_i \text{ with } 0 < \beta \leq 1. \hspace{2cm} [3.11]$$

which leads, by using a filtered measurement of δ_i, to the scheduling regulator:

$$\Delta_{r_{i+1}} = \tau_{i+1} + \beta \, \hat{\delta}_i = \tau_{i+1} + \beta \, (\alpha \hat{\delta}_{i-1} + (1 - \alpha)\delta_i) \hspace{1cm} [3.12]$$

whose output is the objective deadline sent to the computing speed controller. The dynamic behavior of this loop only depends on the gains of filtering α and of control β, and the conditions of stability and robustness are easily computed [DUR 13].

These controllers were easy to program and integrate into the source code of an H.264 decoder, running on a standard Dell E6400 DuoCore2 laptop and a Linux symmetric multi processing (SMP) kernel. The thread encapsulating the frame controller is executed on one core and the decoder on another. The computing speed controller is implemented as a modified version of the middleware module *cpufrequtils*, which allows us to control the frequency of the CPUs in the set of the three discrete values $[800, 1600, 2535]$ MHz, the supply voltage is automatically adjusted in function of the required frequency by the clock generation component. The instrumentation of the measure and the operation uses functions from the real-time POSIX library.

The tests were carried out on a video sequence of 1000 frames. At the highest possible level of decoding quality, the average processing time of a frame is around 50 ms. The compliance with the display rate of 40 ms, without loss of frame, is, therefore, only possible with a real-time control of the decoding quality and scheduling parameters. These tests allow us to observe an excellent control or the average decoding rate, whereas in absence of any regulation the processing end times inexorably drift until a loss of frame occurs. Thus, the quality of the decoding is better than in the absence of control, while the estimated gain in energy consumption (from model [3.9]) may reach 25% of the nominal energy consumed by the non-regulated decoder (Figure 3.11).

a) Deadline error with regulation

b) Deadline error without regulation

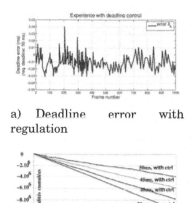

c) Penalty function

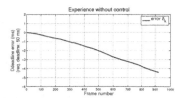

	Normalised energy consumption	
Deadline	Speed control only	Speed and frame control
40	1	0.76
45	1	0.81
50	1	0.86
55	0.92	1.01
60	0.78	0.91
65	0.65	0.77

d) Energy gain

Figure 3.11. *Experimental results*

We may note that the gain of quality and electric consumption of the decoder is obtained for a negligible computing cost faced with the cost itself of decoding. As is often in regulated schedulers, the associated control algorithm and stability analysis are very simple, due to the low dynamic complexity of the controlled computer process. In fact, the dynamics of a computer process mainly come from measurement filters as well as from queues with simple integrator behavior. Finally, the sensors and actuators are programmed with software probes and system calls, easily reproducible and a lot cheaper than the material sensors and actuators necessary for controlling physical processes. It appears that the cost of design and programming of a computer component regulator can be very low relative to the gains in performance and consumption that can be achieved.

3.6. Conclusion

The design of efficient control systems requires understanding and integrating the characteristics of control procedures, the properties of control algorithms and the computing and communication constraints as soon as possible. Traditionally, control systems are implemented under hard real-time hypotheses, leading to a significant waste of execution resources. The exploitation of the robustness of closed loop controls allows us to relax the real-time constraints and make better the use of resources while guaranteeing the stability and the level of performance of the controls.

On the other hand, the use of control loops to manage computer components themselves allows them to efficiently adapt to load and environment fluctuations as well as to automatically adjust the computing capacity and the level of energy used for the immediate requirements of the application. This is an essential tool for reaching the autoadministration of computer systems.

3.7. Bibliography

[ÅST 97] ÅSTRÖM K., WITTENMARK B., *Computer Controlled Systems: Theory and Design*, Prenctice Hall Information and System Science Series, 3rd ed., 1997.

[ALB 10] ALBEA-SANCHEZ C., Control design for electronic power converters, Thesis, Institut National Polytechnique de Grenoble – INPG and Universidad de Sevilla, September 2010.

[AND 11] ANDRIANIAINA P.-J., SEURET A., SIMON D., "Robust control under weakened real-time constraints", *50th IEEE CDC/ECC*, Orlando, USA, December 2011.

[BAI 07] BAILLIEUL J., ANTSAKLIS P.-J., "Control and communication challenges in networked real-time systems", *Proceedings of the IEEE*, vol. 95, no. 1, pp. 9–28, 2007.

[BEN 08] BEN GAÏD M.E.M., SIMON D., SENAME O., "A convex optimization approach to feedback scheduling", *16th Mediterranean Conference on Control and Automation, MED'08*, Ajaccio, France, Mediterranean Control Association/IEEE, 2008.

[BEN 11] BENHAMAMOUCH B., Calcul du pire temps d'exécution: Méthode formelle s'adaptant à la sophistication croissante des architectures matérielles, PhD thesis, Université de Grenoble, 2011.

[BER 01] BERNAT G., BURNS A., LLAMOSÍ A., "Weakly hard real-time systems", *IEEE Transactions on Computers*, vol. 50, no. 4, pp. 308–321, 2001.

[CER 02] CERVIN A., EKER J., BERNHARDSSON B., *et al.*, "Feedback-feedforward scheduling of control tasks", *Real-Time Systems*, vol. 23, nos. 1–2, pp. 25–53, July 2002.

[DOR 62] DORF R., FARREN M., PHILLIPS C., "Adaptive sampling frequency for sampled-data control systems", *IEEE Transactions on Automatic Control*, vol. . 7, no. 1, pp. 38–47, 1962.

[DUR 11] DURAND S., MARCHAND N., "Fully discrete control scheme of the energy-performance tradeoff in embedded electronic devices", *18th IFAC World Congress*, Milano, Italy, pp. 3298–3303, 2011.

[DUR 13] DURAND S., ALT A.-M., SIMON D., *et al.*, "Energy-aware feedback control for a H.264 video decoder", *International Journal of Systems Science*, Taylor&Francis, pp. 1–15, available at http://dx.doi.org/10.1080/00207721.2013.822607, 2013.

[EKE 00] EKER J., HAGANDER P., RZÉN K.-E., "A feedback scheduler for real-time controller tasks", *Control Engineering Practice*, vol. 8, no. 12, pp. 1369–1378, January 2000.

[FEL 98] FELICIONI F., JUNCO S., "A lie algebraic approach to design of stable feedback control systems with varying sampling rate", *17th IFAC World Congress*, Seoul, Korea, July 1998.

[FEL 10] FELICIONI F., JIA N., SIMONOT-LION F., *et al.*, "Overload management through selective data dropping", in *Co-design Approaches for Dependable Networked Control Systems*, ISTE, London and John Wiley & Sons, New York, 2010.

[GAI 09] GAID M.-M.B., CELA A., HAMAM Y., "Optimal real-time scheduling of control tasks with state feedback resource allocation", *IEEE Transactions on Control Systems Technology*, vol. 17, no. 2, pp. 309–326, 2009.

[GOO 01] GOODWIN G., GRAEBE S., SALGADO M., *Control System Design*, Prentice Hall, New Jersey, 2001.

[GOO 10] GOODWIN G., YUZ J., AGÜERO J., *et al.*, "Sampling and sampled-data models", *American Control Conference*, Baltimore, USA, 2010.

[GUE 09] GUERRERO-CASTELLANOS J.-F., BERBRA C., GENTIL S., *et al.*, "Quadrotor attitude control through a network with (m-k)-firm policy", *10th European Control Conference (ECC'09)*, Budapest, Hungary, 2009.

[HAM 94] HAMDAOUI M., RAMANATHAN P., "A service policy for real-time customers with (m,k)-firm deadlines", *Fault-Tolerant Computing Symposium*, Austin, TX, pp. 196–205, April 1994.

[HAM 95] HAMDAOUI M., RAMANATHAN P., "A dynamic priority assignment technique for streams with (m,k)-firm deadlines", *IEEE Transactions on Computers*, vol. 44, no. 12, pp. 1443–1451, December 1995.

[HEL 04] HELLERSTEIN J., DIAO Y., PAREKH S., *et al.*, *Feedback Control of Computing Systems*, Wiley-IEEE Press, New York, 2004.

[HEN 02] HENRIKSSON D., CERVIN A., KESSON J., *et al.*, "On dynamic real time scheduling of model predictive controllers", *41st IEEE Conference on Decision and Control*, Las Vegas, NV, December 2002.

[HEN 05] HENRIKSSON D., CERVIN A., "Optimal on-line sampling period assignment for real-time control tasks based on plant state information", *44th Conference on Decision and Control*, Seville, Spain, December 2005.

[HSI 74] HSIA T., "Analytic design of adaptive sampling control law in sampled-data systems", *IEEE Transactions on Automatic Control*, vol. 19, no. 1, pp. 39–42, 1974.

[ISH 98] ISHIHARA T., YASUURA H., "Voltage scheduling problem for dynamically variable voltage processors", *International Symposium on Low Power Electronics and Design*, Monterey, CA, pp. 197–202, 1998.

[LEE 07] LEE E. A., Computing foundations and practice for cyber-physical systems: a preliminary report, University of California, Berkeley, May 2007.

[LI 06] LI J., SONG Y., SIMONOT-LION F., "Providing real-time applications with graceful degradation of QoS and fault tolerance according to (m,k) firm model", *IEEE Transactions on Industrial Informatics*, vol. 2, no. 2, pp. 112–119, IEEE, 2006.

[LIU 73] LIU C., LAYLAND J., "Scheduling algorithms for multiprogramming in hard real-time environment", *Journal of the ACM*, vol. 20, no. 1, pp. 40–61, February 1973.

[LIU 94] LIU J.W. S., SHIH W.-K., LIN K.-J., *et al.*, "Imprecise computations", *Proceedings of the IEEE*, vol. 82, no. 1, pp. 83–94, 1994.

[LU 02] LU C., STANKOVIC J.-A., TAO G., *et al.*, "Feedback control real-time scheduling: framework, modeling, and algorithms", *Real Time Systems*, vol. 23, no. 1, pp. 85–126, 2002.

[MAL 11] MALRAIT L., BOUCHENAK S., MARCHAND N., "Experience with ConSer: a system for server control through fluid modeling", *IEEE Transactions on Computers*, Automatics Department, vol. 60, no. 7, pp. 951–963, 2011.

[MUR 03] MURRAY R.M., ÅSTRÖM K.J., BOYD S.P., *et al.*, "Future directions in control in an information-rich world", *IEEE Control Systems Magazine*, vol. 23, no. 2, pp. 20–33, April 2003.

[NIC 01] NICULESCU S.-I., *Delay Effects on Stability, A Robust Control Approach*, LNCIS 269, Springer, Heidelberg, 2001.

[PAT 12] PATIKIRIKORALA T., COLMAN A., HAN J., *et al.*, "A systematic survey on the design of self-adaptive software systems using control engineering approaches", *ICSE Workshop on Software Engineering for Adaptive and Self-Managing Systems (SEAMS), 2012,* Zurich, Switzerland, 2012.

[PUS 08] PUSCHNER P., SCHOEBERL M., "On composable system timing, task timing, and WCET analysis", *8th International Workshop on Worst-Case Execution Time (WCET) Analysis*, Prague, Czech Republic, July 2008.

[RAM 99] RAMANATHAN P., "Overload management in real-time control applications using (m,k)-firm guarantee", *IEEE Transactions on Parallel and Distributed Systems*, vol. 10, pp. 549–559, June 1999.

[RIC 03] RICHARD J., "Time-delay systems: an overview of some recent advances and open problems", *Automatica*, vol. 39, no. 10, pp. 1667–1694, Elsevier, 2003.

[ROB 07] ROBERT D., Contribution à l'interaction commande/ordonnancement, PhD thesis, Institut National Polytechnique de Grenoble, 2007.

[ROB 10] ROBERT D., SENAME O., SIMON D., "An H_∞ LPV design for sampling varying controllers: experimentation with a T inverted pendulum", *IEEE Transactions on Control Systems Technology*, vol. 18, no. 3, pp. 741–749, 2010.

[ROC 11] ROCHE E., Commande à échantillonnage variable pour les systèmes LPV: application à un sous-marin autonome, PhD thesis, University of Grenoble, 2011.

[SEN 08] SENAME O., SIMON D., BEN GAID M., "A LPV approach to control and real-time scheduling codesign: application to a robot-arm control", *47th IEEE Conference on Decision and Control, 2008*, pp. 4891–4897, 2008.

[SEU 11] SEURET A., "Stability analysis of networked control systems with asynchronous sampling and input delay", *IEEE American Control Conference*, San Francisco, CA, 2011.

[SHA 04] SHA L., ABDELZAHER T., RZÉN K.-E., *et al.*, "Real-time scheduling theory: A historical perspective", *Real-Time Systems*, vol. 28, nos. 2–3, pp. 101–155, November 2004.

[SIM 05] SIMON D., ROBERT D., SENAME O., "Robust control/scheduling co-design: application to robot control", *11th IEEE Real-Time and Embedded Technology and Applications Symposium RTAS'05*, San Francisco, CA, 2005.

[SIM 11] SIMON D., PLANCHET K., ROCHE E., *et al.*, Feasibility mock-ups of feedback schedulers, Deliverable D04.05, FeedNetBack, E.U. project FP7 INFSO-ICT-223866, December 2011.

[SIM 12] SIMON D., SEURET A., SENAME O., "On real-time feedback control systems : requirements, achievements and perspectives", *1st International Conference on Systems and Computer Science (ICSCS 2012)*, Villeneuve d'Ascq, France, August 2012.

[WIT 01] WITTENMARK B., "A sample-induced delays in synchronous multirate systems", *European Control Conference*, Porto, Portugal, pp. 3276–3281, 2001.

[ZAK 10] ZAKARIA H., DURAND S., FESQUET L., *et al.*, "Integrated asynchronous regulation for nanometric technologies", *First European Workshops on CMOS Variability VARI'10*, Montpellier, France, pp. 86–91, 2010.

4

Synchronous Approach and Scheduling

We start this chapter by explaining how modeling needs of the real-time community led to the introduction of synchronous languages in the early 1980s. We present the characteristics of these languages as well as their limitations. We then propose a classification of synchronous languages and of the languages related to them. This introduces a description of the main synchronous languages Signal, Lustre and Esterel by highlighting their similarities and differences. We follow by describing the main techniques that allow us to perform real-time scheduling from these synchronous languages. Finally, we present a few extensions of these languages allowing us to perform real-time scheduling more easily.

4.1. Introduction

As evidenced by the publication record, the first synchronous languages are a product of the 1980s real-time community [BER 83, BER 85, LEG 87]. They were introduced

Chapter written by Yves SOREL and Dumitru POTOP-BUTUCARU.

to facilitate the non-ambiguous specification of the functionalities of complex control systems subjected to strict (hard) time constraints, which are also called *critical real-time systems*.

In the design of critical real-time systems, two levels of representation are particularly important: real-time task models, which serve to perform the real-time scheduling analysis, in other words the feasibility or schedulability analysis, and the low-level code, provided in languages such as C or assembly. The designers of synchronous languages had two objectives in mind. The first objective was to offer a way to describe complex algorithmic control structures, which the task models such as those of Liu and Layland [LIU 73] and their derivatives [BAR 03] hide within the tasks and therefore do not allow us to analyze. The second objective was to offer a higher level of abstraction than low-level programming. Taking into account low-level platform detail allows the implementation of very efficient execution mechanisms, but has the major drawback of complicating both the specification and the correctness proof of the implementation, mainly because the functional requirements are closely intertwined with the platform-related requirements. This complicates the analysis of scheduling and synchronization issues. On the contrary, synchronous languages, by moving away from the implementation, simplify these scheduling and synchronization problems, which are handled in vast majority by the compiler instead of the programmer.

A critical real-time system aims to control, in the sense of automatic control theory, a physical process in order to lead it toward a given state. The physical process and the control system to provide continuous input to the physical process, which form a closed loop [DOY 90], are specified in continuous time at the beginning in order to be simulated. Then, the control system is *discretized* in order to allow its implementation on the embedded execution platform. Figure 4.1 describes the interactions between the discrete control system and the physical process. The interactions are made using sensors equipped with analog-digital converters that produce numerical values for the control system and actuators equipped with digital-analog converters that use the numerical values coming from the control system to provide continuous input to the physical process. These interactions can be implemented using event-driven or periodic sampling (time-triggered) mechanisms.

Synchronous languages were introduced in order to specify discretized control systems. The main characteristics of these systems are *reactivity* and *real-time*. Reactivity means that the execution of such systems can be described as the set of interactions between the system and the physical process. Each acquisition of data by the sensors is followed by a *reaction* of the control system, which consists of performing some computations and then updating the actuators. Control systems are therefore part of the larger family of *reactive systems* [HAR 85, HAL 93]. Multiple reactions may be executed at the same time, competing for the same execution resources, a property known as *concurrency*.

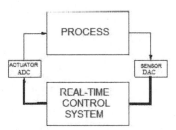

Figure 4.1. *Interaction between processes and the control system*

Control systems are real-time systems, since they are subject to timing constraints. These constraints are determined by the control engineers who have designed the discretized control system. The constraints may concern the sampling periods of the sensors and actuators and/or the latencies (end-to-end delays) of the reactions. The sampling constraints on the sensors and actuators determine the periods of the computation functions that depend on or drive sensing and actuation. The latency constraints are applied to chains of computation functions, which may have a sensor or an actuator as extremity. A deadline is a particular case of latency constraint that is applied to a single computation function, for instance the code controlling a sensor or a digital filter.

Reactive and real-time control systems have particular specification needs. To describe the reactive aspects, synchronous languages offer syntactical constructs allowing the specification of order (*dependency, sequence*), *concurrency (parallelism), conditional execution* and *simultaneity* relations between *operations* of the system (data acquisitions, computation functions, data transfers and actuator updates).

For the non-functional specification of the real-time aspects, the synchronous languages define or allow the definition of one or more discrete time bases, called *clocks*. A clock describes a finite of infinite sequence of events in the execution of the system. Thus, each clock divides the execution of the system into a series of execution steps, which are sometimes called *logical instants*, *reactions*, or *computation instants*. We can associate a clock with each periodic event (for instance a periodic timer), sporadic event (for instance top dead center (TDC) of a piston in a combustion engine), aperiodic event (for instance a button press), or simply with an internal event of the control system, which is built from other internal or external events and therefore other clocks.

Clocks are so-called *logical* time bases. This means that the synchronous languages allow the specification of order relations between events associated with these clocks, but do not offer support for the analysis of the relations between physical quantities they may represent. Clocks associated with physical quantities are called *physical clocks*. For instance, an engine control system may have a clock associated to a timer and a clock associated with the the TDC event. By taking into account the maximum speed of the engine, we can determine the maximal duration (in time) between two events of the TDC clock, thus relating events of the two clocks. Note that our analysis requires the application of physical theories. Also, note that physical clocks are not necessarily linked to time, nor necessarily periodic as shown by the the example above and the example of section 4.5.5. The execution of every operation of the system has to be synchronized with respect to at least one clock. This synchronization is the way of associating real-time information coming from the control specification (periods, deadlines, latencies) to the various operations.

As shown in Figure 4.2, the specification of a real-time implementation problem does not only include the platform-independent part provided under the form of a synchronous program, but also the non-functional constraints related to the implementation of the control system on an embedded execution platform. This platform-dependent specification includes the definition of the resources of the platform, the worst-case execution times (WCETs) of computation on the CPUs, the worst-case communications times (WCCT) over the buses, the allocation constraints, etc. Platform-dependent information is not part of the discrete automatic control specification, and thus synchronous languages are not meant to represent them. Thus, synchronous languages do not allow the specification of all the aspects of a real-time embedded implementation problem. Some synchronous languages allow the specification of platform-related properties through extensions that we will discuss later on in this chapter.

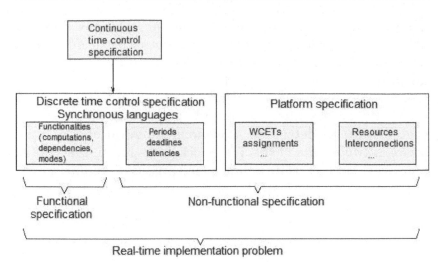

Figure 4.2. *Scope of application of synchronous languages for the specification of a real-time implementation problem*

Ignoring platform-related constraints is one of the key points of synchronous languages. In particular, ignoring the execution times means that we may assume the computations and data transfers to be infinitely fast, in such a way that the arrival of inputs of a computation and the production of results are simultaneous (*synchronous*) in the discrete time scale defined by the clock associated with the computation. This *synchrony hypothesis*, used implicitly in continuous-time modelings, is naturally inherited in synchronous specifications. At the same time, implementing such a specification means solving a scheduling problem which ensures that the resources of the execution platform allow to terminate the execution of each reaction before its results are used by other operations and by satisfying the period and model latency constraints.

Under the synchrony hypothesis, all computations of a reaction are synchronous, in the sense that they are not ordered in the discrete time scale defined by the clock of the reaction. However, their execution has to be *causal*: each variable has to be written at most once during a reaction and, if it is written, then it can only be read after the write operation is completed. Causality ensures *functional determinism* in the presence of concurrency. More precisely, executing the computations and communications of a reaction will produce the same result, for any scheduling of the operations that satisfies the data and control dependencies. In a causal system a set of inputs will always produce the same set of outputs. This property is important in practice, since it simplifies the costly activities of verification and validation (test, formal verification, etc.). The synchronous formalisms have natural interpretations in synchronous digital circuits and synchronous Mealy machines. This provides access to a wide range of analysis and verification algorithms.

The synchrony hypothesis also requires that a reaction has a *bounded* number of operations. This assumption ensures that, independently of the execution platform, the computation of a reaction is always completed in bounded time, which allows the application of real-time schedulability analyses.

The remainder of this chapter is organized as follows. First, we propose a classification of synchronous languages and related formalisms. Then we present these languages and formalisms, explaining how to perform real-time scheduling (real-time schedulability analysis and embedded code generation) with them. Finally, we discuss how various extensions of these languages facilitate real-time scheduling analysis.

4.2. Classification

4.2.1. *Synchronous languages*

Section 4.1 intuitively introduced the ingredients of the synchronous model: clocks, the synchrony hypothesis, causality and functional determinism. These ingredients provide a unique formal base, given that every synchronous language may be interpreted in the mathematical models of synchronous automata and synchronous digital circuits.

From a syntactical point of view, every synchronous language provides a certain number of constructions facilitating the description of complex systems: concurrency, conditional execution and/or modes of execution, dependencies and clocks allowing to describe complex temporal relations such as multiple periods. This allows the incremental (hierarchical) specification of complex behaviors from elementary behaviors (computation functions without side effects and with bounded durations). The concision and the deterministic semantics of synchronous specifications make them a good starting point for design methodologies for safe systems, where a significant part of the time budget is devoted to formal analysis and testing.

However, beyond these aspects, each of the synchronous languages has original points and particular uses, and therefore a classification is required. Table 4.1 summarizes this classification.

Depending on the *programming paradigm* used, synchronous languages are divided into two classes: declarative data-flow languages and imperative languages. Declarative languages, which include data-flow languages, focus on the definition of the function to be computed. Imperative languages allow the definition of the sequence of operations that computes this function (computations, decisions, inputs/outputs, state changes). Among the synchronous languages, ESTEREL, SYNCCHARTS, PSIC, and the "Embedded Code" formalism are classified as imperative, while the LUSTRE/SCADE, SIGNAL, SYNDEX, GIOTTO, and PRELUDE languages are classified as data-flow. The SCICOS and ZÉLUS languages are data-flow languages, with the particularity of being hybrid languages, which allow the representation of both continuous-time and discrete-time control systems.

Language	I/DF	Base clock(s)	"Physical" times	Real-time analyses
Esterel/SSM	I(+DF)	Single	–	
Lustre/Scade	DF(+I)	Single	–	
TAXYS	I	Single	APODW	WCRT, sched
Lucy-n	DF	Refined	–	
SynDEx	DF	Refined	PW (D=P)	WCRT, sched
Giotto	DF	Refined	P (D=P)	
Prelude	DF	Refined	PODW	WCRT, sched
Signal	DF(+I)	Multiple	–	
EmbeddedCode	I	Multiple	AD	
PsiC	I+DF	Multiple	APODW	WCRT, sched
SciCos	DF	Multiple	C	
Zélus	DF	Multiple	C	

Table 4.1. *Classification of synchronous languages following their characteristics. I = Imperative, DF = data-flow, P = periodic activations, A = aperiodic activations, D = deadlines, O = offsets, W = durations, C = continuous-time. WCRT = worst case response time analysis, sched = schedulability analysis*

Data-flow languages are syntactically closer to synchronous digital circuits or real-time dependent task models. In these languages, the concurrency between operations is only constrained by explicit data dependencies. Data-flow languages are used to highlight the computational aspects of an application or its structuring into tasks.

Imperative languages are syntactically closer to (hierarchical) synchronous automata. They are generally used when the aim is to represent complicated control structures, such as those of an operating system scheduler. Besides concurrency, they allow the specification of operation sequencing and offer hierarchical constructs allowing to stop a behavior in response to an internal or external signal. The data dependencies are often represented using shared variable instead of data-flows.

The first synchronous languages were easily classifiable as imperative (ESTEREL) or data-flow (LUSTRE, SIGNAL). The successive evolutions of these languages have however made this classification more difficult. The data-flow language SCADE/LUSTRE for instance has incorporated imperative elements, such as the SAFE state MACHINES formalism, whereas an imperative language such as ESTEREL has incorporated declarative elements such as the "sustained emit" instruction. This is why, in our table, some languages belong to both classes.

A second criterion of classification of synchronous languages is related to the *number of time bases* that the language allows to define. In the LUSTRE/SCADE and ESTEREL languages, which we call *single-clock*, a single logical time base exists, called *global clock* or *base clock*. All other time bases (clocks) are derived from the base clock by sub-sampling.

The SIGNAL and PSIC languages do not have this limitation. They allow the definition of several logical time bases. For example, an automotive engine control application may have two base clocks, one corresponding to time and the other to the rotation of the engine (TDC), and these two clocks cannot be defined from one another. Having two base clocks allows the operations to be ordered with respect to events of two different discrete time bases, which may facilitate both modeling an analysis.[1] The languages allowing the definition of multiple, independent clocks are called *polychronous* or *multi-clock*.

---

1. Buiding a single-clock model of an application is always possible [HAL 06], but analysis may be more complicated.

Between single-clock languages and multi-clock languages, we identify an intermediate class of languages that allow the definition of several time bases, but require that as soon as two clocks are used by a same operation, they become linked by a relation allowing to order their logical instants in a unique way. Therefore, a global clock can be built unambiguously for every program from the time bases specified by the programmer.[2] However, it is often more interesting to not build this global clock and apply specific analyses directly on the clocks specified by the programmer. For instance, the languages GIOTTO, LUCY-N, PRELUDE and SYNDEX allow to build *refined clocks* whose computation times are linked in period and phase (offset) by *affine* relations. These languages allow a more direct description of periodic real-time task systems with different periods [PAG 11, CUR 05, KER 07].

The third classification criterion we use is the presence (or not), in the language, of extensions allowing the description of *"physical" time*. This concept appears naturally in continuous system specification languages, such as SCICOS or ZELUS [CAM 10, BOU 13]. However, we are more interested here by languages in which these extensions aim directly at the specification of a real-time implementation problem. This problem requires concepts such as *periodic* and *aperiodic activations*, *deadlines*, *offsets* and *execution times*. These extensions allow to apply real-time analyses of several types: worst-case response time analysis, schedulability analysis, or even the synthesis of schedulings or the parameter adjustment of the scheduler of a real-time operating system.

Our final classification criterion concerns the enforcement of the *synchrony hypothesis*. The ESTEREL, LUSTRE, SIGNAL, SYNDEX languages require strict adherence to it.

---

2. More precisely, we can build such a clock if the program cannot be divided into completely independent parts.

The computation and data transfer operations are *semantically* infinitely fast, so that a reaction always terminates before the beginning of the next one. The execution of the system can therefore be seen as the *totally ordered* sequence of reactions. [3] In particular, every operation (computation or communication), independently of its clock, can be and must be terminated in the clock cycle where it began, before the beginning of the next clock cycle. If we associate real-time periods to logical clocks, this assumption implies that an operation (computation or communication) cannot have a duration longer than the greatest common divisor (GCD) of the periods of the system.

However, the description of real-time systems often implies so-called "long tasks" with a duration longer than the GCD of the periods. Representing such tasks in a synchronous formalism requires constraining the synchronous composition to ensure that an operation to take more than one logical instant. One way to do it is by systematically introducing explicit delays after the end of an operation and the operations depending on it. These delays explicitly represent the time (in clock cycles) reserved for the execution of the operation. Introducing such delays manually may be tedious, and some languages, such as GIOTTO [HEN 03], PRELUDE [PAG 11] and SYNDEX [GRA 03] have proposed dedicated constructs with the same effect. In GIOTTO, the convention is that the outputs of a task remain available during the clock cycle following the one where the operation started, in the time base given by the clock associated with the task. In PRELUDE, delays shorter than one clock cycle can be defined by refining the clock of the operation and then working in this refined time base. SYNDEX proposes an intermediate solution.

---

3. Even for multi-clock languages.

4.2.2. *Related languages*

Synchronous languages are only one of the families of formalisms dedicated to the representation of embedded control systems. Among the others we only mention the following:

– The task models used by the real-time scheduling community [LIU 73, BAR 03]. These are not designed as full-fledged programming languages, focusing only on the definition of properties that will be exploited during the schedulability analysis. Among these properties: the organization of computations into tasks, the periods, durations, and deadlines of tasks, and sometimes their dependencies or exclusion relations.

– Synchronous data-flow (SDF) [LEE 87] and the derived formalisms. Like synchronous languages, these formalisms model systems with cyclic execution. The difference is that the synchronization between repetitions of various operations is not performed using logical time bases (clocks), but through lossless communication channels.

– The pair of formalisms SIMULINK/STATEFLOW [BOU 12, CHE 12] is the *de facto* standard for the modeling of control systems. These languages share with synchronous languages a great deal of their basic constructs: the use of logical and physical time bases, the synchrony hypothesis, a definition of causality and even a good part of the language instructions. However, the differences are also great: synchronous languages aim to give unique and deterministic semantics to every correct specification, and thus ensure the equivalence between analysis, simulation and execution of the implemented system. The objective of SIMULINK (as its name indicates) is to allow the simulation of control systems, whether they are specified in discrete and/or continuous time. The definition of causal dependencies is clear, but it depends on the chosen simulation mode, and the number of simulation options is such that it is sometimes difficult to determine which rules to be applied. To accelerate the simulations, there are options that explicitly allow for non-determinism. Finally, the determinism of the simulation is sometimes only acquired through the use of rules depending on the relative position of the graphical objects of a specification (in addition to the classical causality rules). By comparison, the semantics of a synchronous program only depends on the data dependencies between operations, which allows to preserve more concurrency and therefore give more freedom to the scheduling algorithms.

– The definition of a synchronized cyclic execution on physical or logical time bases is shared by formalisms such as STATECHARTS [HAR 87] or VHDL/VERILOG [IEE 05]. Like synchronous languages, these formalisms define a concept of execution time and allow a complex propagation of control within these instants. However, synchronous causality (and thus determinism) are not required.

4.3. Synchronous languages

4.3.1. SIGNAL

SIGNAL is a synchronous data-flow language [BEN 90, GUE 02]. We can write SIGNAL programs in a textual form according to the syntax and semantics given below or in a graphical form with the SME programming environment. POLYCHRONY, available under a free license, is the toolset comprised of the SIGNAL textual language compiler, the graphical programming environment SME and the formal verification tool SIGNAL.

To each input and output of the real-time control system modeled in SIGNAL is associated a SIGNALI, which is a potentially infinite sequence of valued *events*. There are four types of relations between events or signals:

1) *Precedence between two events* of a same signal. This is a total order relation denoted by $<$. The fact that the order is

total means that any two different events are strictly ordered. The events of a signal take their values in a set such as the set of real numbers, the set of integers, Booleans, etc., which we call the type of the signal. An example is provided in the timing diagram of Figure 4.3, where the events $e_1 < e_2 < e_3 \ldots$ take the values $11, 5, 3 \ldots \in \mathbb{N}$.

$$e1 < e2 < e3 < e4 < e5 < e6 < e7 < e8$$

Figure 4.3. *Precedence relation between events of a signal*

2) *Synchrony between two events* of different signals. Various constructs of the SIGNAL language, detailed below, can impose that two events of two different signals are synchronous, meaning that they happen at the same time. Formally, synchrony is an equivalence relation between events stating that all events of a given equivalence class must be executed as part of the same reaction of the system. Event synchrony must be compatible with the total orders on events of each signal, in the sense that two different events of the same signal may not be synchronous. Under this constraint, event synchrony can be combined with the total orders on events of each signal to define a partial order over all the equivalence classes of events.

The timing diagram of Figure 4.4 illustrates the partial ordering of equivalence classes of two signals. The synchrony between two events is represented by grouping them. To avoid overloading the figure, contrarily to Figure 4.3 above, the values are not represented. Note that some events are not synchronous with any other.

3) *Synchrony between two signals.* Two signals are called synchronous when all their events are two-by-two synchronous. Signal synchrony is an equivalence relation among signals. Equivalence classes of signals are logical clocks

of the SIGNAL program, as they define the logical time bases of the program. Obviously, the signals of an equivalence class have the same clock. The clock of a signal X is denoted by $P(X)$ for *presence of X.*

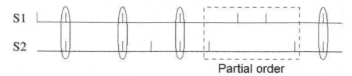

Figure 4.4. *Synchrony relations between events of two signals*

Clocks are partially ordered as follows: When all the events of a signal $S1$ are synchronous with some events of a signal $S2$, we say that the clock $P(S1)$ is smaller than the clock $P(S2)$, denoted by $P(S1) \leq P(S2)$.

In addition to the clocks of signals, the SIGNAL language allows the direct construction of clocks through manipulation using union and intersection operators. The intersection of two clocks $C1$ and $C2$, denoted by $C1.C2$ is a clock whose instants are the instants of $C1$ that are synchronous with instants of $C2$. The union of $C1$ and $C2$, denoted by $C1 + C2$, has as instants all the instants of both $C1$ and $C2$. The intersection and union relations on clocks, respectively, correspond to the greatest lower bound and least upper bound operators associated with the order relation on clocks. The introduction of explicit clock manipulations means that the set of clocks is a lattice, whose properties are used by the SIGNAL compiler during program analysis and code generation.

When a SIGNAL program contains a signal whose clock is greater than the clock of any other signal in the program, we call this clock the *base clock* or *global clock* of the program, and the program is called *single-clock*. The base clock defines the *unique time base* of the control system. When no base clock exists, then the program is called *multi-clock*. In this case, each of the maximal clocks associated to signals defines a time base of the system. This allows us to specify control systems with several time bases. These time bases can be periodic, sporadic or aperiodic.

Figure 4.5 shows a timing diagram illustrating signal synchrony. In this figure S1 and S2 have the same clock since they are synchronous. Some events of S1 and S2 are not synchronous with events of S3. The clock of the signals S1 and S2 is therefore smaller than the clock of S3.

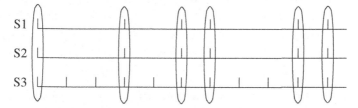

Figure 4.5. *Signal synchrony relation*

All these precedence and synchrony relations can be specified using the *four primitive instructions* of the SIGNAL language, which are also called *elementary processes*.[4] The instructions take signals as input and output arguments. A signal is either an input of the program, or is the output of exactly one instruction. Programs and sub-programs are called *processes*. Writing a process consists of composing, with the "|" character, elementary processes or sub-processes. SIGNAL being a declarative data-flow language, the instructions can be composed in any order. The *name identities* between the output signal names and the input signal names lead to dependencies between the instructions. The four primitive instructions are:

− *immediate function* $(O_1, \ldots, O_n) := F(I_1, \ldots, I_m)$

This instruction requires that the input signals I_k and output signals O_i have the same clock. At each cycle of this

---

4. Other instructions exist, but they can all be derived from the primitives.

clock, this instruction consumes one value (event) on each of the input signals and produces one value (event) on each of the output signals. The output values are obtained by applying function F to the input values. The input and output events are synchronous, meaning that the inputs are read and the outputs are produced during the same clock cycle (they are not delayed). However, function application is causal, in the sense that the outputs cannot be used before the inputs are read, and thus cannot depend transitively on themselves (as explained in section 4.1). A program is not causal if one signal, such as the output of an immediate function, depends on itself. We call such a cyclic dependency a *causality cycle*.

Figure 4.6 shows a timing diagram illustrating the immediate function. In this figure, the input signals S1 and S2 have the same clock as the output signal S3:= F(S1,S2) of the immediate function F.

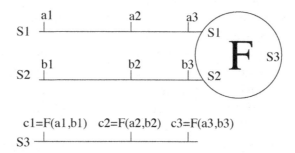

Figure 4.6. *Immediate function* S3:= F(S1,S2)

$-$ *sub-sampling*   X:= A when B

This instruction sub-samples signal A over the Boolean signal B. Whenever an event of A is synchronous with an event of B with value true, we create an event on X, synchronous with those of A and B, and having the same value of the A event. In more intuitive terms, an event is present on X whenever A and B are both present and B has value true.

The clock of the output signal is smaller than or equal to each of the two clocks of the input signals $P(X) \leq P(A)$ and $P(X) \leq P(B)$. We denote with when B the signal obtained from B by retaining only the events with value true. We denote with $T(B)$ the clock of when B (this can be defined for any Boolean signal). Then, we have $P(X) = P(A).T(B)$. Figure 4.7 shows a timing diagram illustrating the sub-sampling instruction. The value true is denoted here with T and the value false is denoted with F.

Data-flow instructions can be either composed using separate assignment instructions, or grouped into *expressions*. For instance, the following program fragment consisting of one sub-sampling and one immediate function:

```
X:= A when B | B:= E<0
```

can be replaced with the single instruction X:= A when E < 0. The second variant has the advantage of concision, avoiding the explicit definition of signal B.

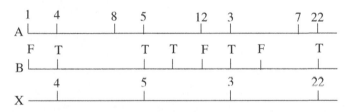

Figure 4.7. *The instruction* X:= A when B

– priority merge   Y:= X0 default X1

This instruction models a classical multiplexer. It merges onto the output signal Y the values (events) arriving on the input signals X0 and X1 in the order of their arrival. Whenever events arrive synchronously on both X0 and X1, the merge instruction gives priority to X0 by copying its value onto the output and throwing away the value arriving on X1. The priority rule ensures the determinism of the merge instruction, by opposition to multiplexers used in hardware design that are sometimes non-deterministic.

Formally, the clock of the output signal is the union of the clocks of the input signals $P(Y) = P(X0) + P(X1)$. In other terms, for any event of X0 and X1, there exists a synchronous event in Y. The value of this event is that of the synchronous event of either X0 or X1. When a synchronous event exists in both X0 and X1, the value of the X0 event is taken. Note that $P(Y) \geq P(X0)$ and $P(Y) \geq P(X1)$. Figure 4.8 shows a timing diagram illustrating the priority merge instruction.

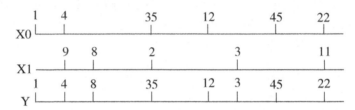

Figure 4.8. *The instruction* Y:= XO default X1

– delay   ZX:= X \$ 1 init v

This instruction has one input signal X, one output signal ZX, and one constant parameter v. Both signals and the parameter must have the same type. The instruction defines ZX as a signal having the same clock as X, but whose values are delayed by one clock cycle. More precisely, in the first cycle of $P(X)$ signal ZX will take the value v. In all subsequent cycles, ZX will take the value of X of the *previous* cycle. Thus, it allows the transmission of *state* information from one clock cycle to the next (it is the only instruction allowing this) and therefore also allows us to break the causality cycles whenever feedback is used in the description of complex automatic control systems. Figure 4.9 shows a timing diagram illustrating the delay instruction.

Figure 4.9. *The instruction* ZX:= X $ 1 init 0

Table 4.2 summarizes the syntax and the semantics of the four instructions of the SIGNAL language in terms of clock equations, input-output relations and signal value types.

Syntax	Clock equation	Input-output relation
Immediate function (Y1,.,Yn):= f(X1,.,Xm)	$P(Y1) = ...P(Yn)$ $= P(X1) = ...P(Xm)$	$(Y1,...,Yn) = f(X1,...,Xm)$ X and Y any type
Delay ZX:= X $ 1 init k	$P(ZX) = P(X)$	$ZX(t) = X(t-1)$ for $t \geq 1$ $ZX(0) = k$; ZX, X of same type
Sub-sampling Y:= X when B	$P(Y) = P(X).T(B)$	$Y = X$ if B **present and** true X any type and B boolean
Priority merge Y:= X0 default X1	$P(Y) = P(X0)+$ $P(X1)$	$Y = X0$ **if** $X0$ **present** $Y = X1$ **if** $X0$ **absent** $Y, X0, X1$ of same type

Table 4.2. *Primitive instructions of the Signal language*

When a signal is the output of instruction $S1$ and the input of instruction $S2$, then the execution of $s1$ must be performed before the execution of $S2$ inside each execution instant. For instance, in the following code fragment:

```
X:= A when B | B:= E<0
```

the computation of B must be realized before the sub-sampling. These dependencies define a partial order on the instructions executed inside each reaction of the program. The compiler of the SIGNAL language must enforce the respect of this partial order.

The compiler performs two types of verification in order to ensure that the SIGNAL program is correct:

– traditional compiler correctness checks:

- type verification, table indices, division by zero, etc.,

– logical time correctness checks (specific to the synchronous model):

- verify that all feedback loops contain delays, so that there are no causality cycles,

- verify whether the system of clock equations, formed by the set of clock equations associated with all the instructions, is correct. This amounts to being able to compute the clocks of the output signals in function of the input signals. If the system of equations cannot be solved, there are two possible cases, either the system of equations has too many constraints (no solution exists), or there are not enough constraints (the system is non-deterministic). In the latter case, the program can be further constrained through the (manual or automatic) addition of new signals and/or instructions.

The compiler generates a sequential program, for instance some FORTRAN or C, which allows, after compilation, to generate an executable which performs a *functional simulation* ensuring a correct ordering of events in logical time.

Using the SIGNAL language instead of say, directly the C language, has two advantages. First of all, the programming style of the language is closer to that used by control engineers, facilitating specification. The second advantage is related to the verification of timing correctness (in logical time), which is outside the scope of classical imperative languages such as C. Finding these logical errors very early in the development cycle avoids finding them at the moment of testing the embedded code. At that time it is very difficult to rewind, for instance from an erroneous bit observed on a signal analyzer, to the error committed at the functional specification level.

We give below an example of a SIGNAL program called cpt implementing a counter which is incremented by one each time that an event arrives on its first input signal TOP. The type of this signal is event, which means that we are only interested in the presence of the events, not in their values. Type event is seen as a subset of the boolean that only contains value true. The output N of the counter is reset when RAZ is present with value true. The reset value is 1 when TOP is also present, and 0 when TOP is not present.

```
process cpt = {}
( ? event TOP; boolean RAZ ! integer N )
(| ZN  := N $ 1 init 0         % P(ZN)=P(N)                    %
 | RAZT := RAZ when TOP         % P(RAZT)=T(RAZ).P(TOP)%
 | N1  := 1 when RAZT           % P(N1)=T(RAZT)                 %
 | RAZZ := 0 when RAZ           % P(RAZZ)=T(RAZ)                %
 | N2  := N1 default RAZZ       % P(N2)=P(N1)+P(RAZZ)           %
                                %       =T(RAZT)+T(RAZ) %
                                %       =T(RAZ)                 %
 | N3  := ZN+1                  % P(N3)=P(ZN)                   %
 | N   := N2 default N3         % P(N)=P(N2)+P(N3)              %
                                %       =T(RAZ)+P(ZN)           %
                                %       =T(RAZ)+P(N)            %
                                % =>  P(N)>=T(RAZ)              %
 | Q   := true when RAZ         % P(Q)=T(RAZ)                   %
 | N  ^= Q default TOP          % P(N)=P(TOP)+T(RAZ)            %
 |)
where integer ZN, N1, N2, N3, RAZT, RAZZ ; boolean Q
end
```

In the program above we have commented on each expression with its clock equation (comments are delimited by "%" characters). The first instruction is a delay, so the clocks of its input and output signals ZN and N are equal. Signal N1 is used to compute the value of the signal N when RAZ (with the value true) and TOP are present. Signal N2 uses N1 and RAZZ to compute the value of N when a reset occurs (when RAZ is present with the value true), hence its clock is equal to $T(RAZ)$. Signal N3 models the functioning of the counter in the absence of a reset. Finally, a priority merge is used to build N from N2 and N3. The last instruction of the program is an explicit *clock constraint* which states that the clock of N is equal to the union of the clocks $P(TOP)$ and $T(RAZ)$. Clock constraints can be derived from the primitives. In our case, this can be done by introducing three local signals Q, R, and S and then replacing the clock constraint with:

```
Q := true when RAZ | R := Q default TOP | S :=
                   sync(N,R)
```

where `sync` is a function that takes two values of type `event` and produces a value of type `event`.

Note how the local signals ZN, N1, N2, N3, RAZT, RAZZ are declared at the end of the program.

In order to verify that the program is correct, the compiler tries to determine that the system of clock constraints associated with program instructions has a unique solution. In our case, removing the explicit clock constraint instruction results in a program that may have multiple solutions. To see this, one can rewrite the clock constraints as detailed in the program comments and thus arrive at the single constraint $P(N) = T(RAZ) + P(N)$, which amounts to requiring that $P(N) \geq T(RAZ)$. Intuitively, this means that the counter must produce a value each time it is reset, but can produce values as fast as it wants between reset events. Clearly, the behavior of such a counter is non-deterministic, and the compiler rejects it. Adding the explicit clock constraint requires that values are produced exactly when TOP is present and/or when RAZ is present with value `true`. This makes the specification deterministic. The choice of clock constraints may be difficult. In our program, replacing the explicit clock constraint with the following one:

```
N ^= true when RAZ
```

is still correct, in the sense that the clock constraint system has a solution. However, doing so amounts to requiring that only a value is produced when reset (so that it will never increment its value like a counter does).

We explained earlier that SIGNAL instructions can be grouped into expressions to reduce the number of instructions and local signals. Applying this grouping to our program results in the following one, which is considerably more concise:

```
process cpt = {}
( ? event TOP; boolean RAZ ! integer N )
(| ZN := N $ 1 init 0
 | N := 1 when RAZ when TOP default 0 when RAZ default ZN +1
 | N ^= TOP default true when RAZ
 |)
where integer ZN
end
```

4.3.2. LUSTRE

LUSTRE [BER 85, HAL 93] is the oldest of the synchronous data-flow languages. There is a commercial version called SCADE. The LUSTRE language is textual, but the SCADE formalism also has a graphical version.

In contrast with the SIGNAL language, in which the input signals may not be synchronous and can therefore have different clocks, in the LUSTRE language every input signal of the program, called a *flow*, is synchronous. The unique clock of all the input flows, associated with every reaction of a LUSTRE program, is called *tick*. It defines the logical instants of the program. From the syntax point of view, a LUSTRE program or sub-program is called a *node*. As in the Signal language, it is the composition of instructions, expressions and nodes with the "*;*" character which, as in the Signal language, imposes a partial order of execution depending on the name identity of the input and output flow of the instructions, expressions and nodes. An output flow is connected to an input flow with the same name. As with

SIGNAL, we only present the core of the language. The instructions which are not part of the core are derived from the core instructions. The basic instructions of LUSTRE are called *operators*.

As in SIGNAL the functions can be extended to the flows with the same behaviour, in other words the valued events of the input flows have to be synchronous between each other and synchronous with those they allow to produce as output. When we write S3 = F(S1,S2) we obtain the same timing diagram as the one in Figure 4.6, corresponding to the immediate function of SIGNAL. These functions are called arithmetic nodes. Let us note that in LUSTRE we use "=" instead of ":=" to indicate a flow affectation.

The instruction Y = if C then A else B allows us to create an output flow Y in function of the values taken by the flow C taking its values in the Boolean set. If the value of C is true, Y takes the value of the flow A (then part) and if the value of C is false, Y takes the value of the flow B (else part). Every flow has the same unique base clock, tick. It is a direct extension of the if instruction usually employed in imperative languages such as C. Figure 4.10 shows a timing diagram illustrating this instruction in the case where the flows A and B are constant 0 and 1 flows.

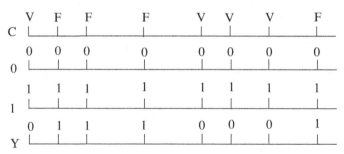

Figure 4.10. Y = if C then 0 else 1

This instruction sub-samples signal A over the Boolean signal B.

The instruction X = A when B sub-samples signal A over the Boolean signal B whose events take values in the Boolean set. The output flow X takes the values of the events of the input flow A when the events of the input flow B have the value true. The output flow X, when it takes its values in the Boolean set, can itself be used as a sub-clock of the tick base clock. Figure 4.11 shows a timing diagram illustrating this instruction, and it can be interesting to compare it with that of Figure 4.7. This latter one illustrates the when instruction of the SIGNAL language where we can see that the signals A and B are not necessarily synchronous themselves.

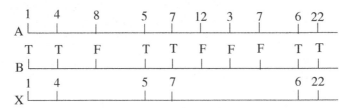

Figure 4.11. X = A when B

The instruction Y = current (X) allows to fill in the missing values of a flow obtained with a when instruction in order for the flow Y to have the base clock of the program (*tick*) or a sub-clock of this clock, obtained as explained above. Figure 4.12 shows a timing diagram illustrating this instruction applied to the flow X = A when B.

The instruction Y = merge C | N1 => A | N2 => B mixes two flows A and B which have been obtained by sub-sampling with the instruction when C in function of the flow C which can take one of the two enumerated values N1, N2. The simplest way to use the merge consists of taking a Boolean flow for C. We then only have two cases for C, true or false. And if we complete the flows A and B in order to give them the base clock, we obtain the behaviour of the instruction `Y = if C then A else B`.

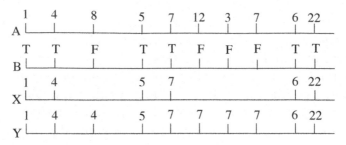

Figure 4.12. `Y = current (X)`

The `pre(x)` instruction produces, as the `$` instruction (delay) of SIGNAL, a flow delayed by a logical instant such that its first event takes the value `nil`. The `val ->` instruction allows to give the value `val` to this first event. Thus, the instruction `ZX = 0 -> pre(X)` corresponds to the timing diagram of Figure 4.9.

We give below an example of a LUSTRE program called `cpt`, which implements the same counter as the one seen for the SIGNAL language. It has to be noted that here `TOP` and `RAZ` have the same clock while they may be different in the case of the SIGNAL program.

```
node cpt (TOP, RAZ: bool) returns (N: int)
let
  ZN = 0 -> pre N;
  N =
      if TOP and RAZ then 1
      else if RAZ then 0
      else ZN + 1;
tel
```

The LUSTRE compiler verifies the causality and thus solves a system of clock equations in order to determine whether the program is correct. It also generates a sequential

C program allowing us to perform a *functional simulation* ensuring a correct ordering of events in *logical time*.

4.3.3. ESTEREL

ESTEREL [BER 83, HAL 93] is the oldest of the imperative synchronous languages. It has a textual form, described below, and a graphical form, known under the name of SYNCCHARTS or SAFE STATE MACHINES. There are several academic compilers. The SAFE STATE MACHINES formalism is one of the languages proposed by the commercial Scade Studio tool for the development of critical embedded systems.

The aim of ESTEREL is to describe complex control structures, such as those used in robotics, which was the initial application field of the language. We illustrate the constructions of the language by the following program, a variant of Berry's model of an "electronic sports coach".

```
module RUNNER:
constant NumberOfLaps, MaxHeartSpeed : integer;
input Morning, HSecond, Meter, Step, Lap, HeartBeat;
output Jump, Run;
relation HeartBeat => HSecond, Morning => HSecond,
        Meter => HSecond, Step => HSecond, Lap => HSecond;
every Morning do
  trap EndWorkout in
    signal HeartSpeed := 60 : integer in
      abort
        abort
          every Step do emit Jump end
        when 50 Step;
        sustain Run
      when 60000 HSecond;
      exit EndWorkout
    ||
      run HeartSpeed [signal HSecond/HS, HeartBeat/HB,
      HeartSpeed/HSpeed]
    ||
      every HeartSpeed do
        if ?HeartSpeed > MaxHeartSpeed then
          exit EndWorkout
end end end end end
end module
```

As in LUSTRE or SIGNAL, an ESTEREL program begins with a section of declarations introducing the types, the constants and the input and output signals of the program. The declarations are followed by the body of the program, which consists of a possibly hierarchical imperative instruction.

ESTEREL has a semantic model defining a single base clock, as does LUSTRE, which justifies its classification as a single-clock language. However, its programming style is based on the use of largely independent signals, like in SIGNAL, which would correspond to a multi-clock model in our classification. The link between these two apparently contradictory aspects, is made through a sampling the signals on the base clock of the program. Thus, we associate each signal of the program (input, output or internal signal) and each execution time with a *present* or *absent* value. For the input signals these values are obtained by sampling of the environment, whereas the presence or absence of an internal or output signal has to be computed by the program. The base clock of the ESTEREL program is assumed to be fast enough to ensure that there is no loss of information during sampling, for instance by losing significant values or events such as a button press.

Our program has six input signals and two output signals. The Morning input signal is true at the instants of the computation where we have detected the beginning of a new day. The Meter input signal is true in the cycles where we have detected that the runner has covered another meter. Each input signal corresponding to a physical measurement (time, meters) or purely logical defines its own logical time base, and the ESTEREL program allows us to synchronize the actions (computations, output values) with these logical time bases. We then refer to a *multiform time* programming approach.

The signals of an ESTEREL program can be linked with implication or exclusion relations. In our example, none of the input signals of the program can be present if the HSecond signal (one hundredth of a second) is not present. These relations are significant for the formal proof of properties and because they can facilitate the implementation. In our case, these relations mean that we can execute a program instance every hundredth of a second without loss of information.

The behaviour of the program is the following: every morning, the coach tells the athlete to exercise for 10 minutes (60000 HSeconds), starting with a succession of 50 jumps followed by running. In parallel to these sequences of operations, the coach computes the pulse of the athlete and asks him to stop if the pulse exceeds a certain critical limit.

4.4. Scheduling with synchronous languages

Synchronous languages have received much attention from academia and have been adopted by actors from several major critical systems industries. This explains the large amount of research on the implementation of real-time programs written in these languages. Due to space limitation, we cannot detail all these works. We only define some criteria allowing us to differentiate between the various approaches and provide references presenting the details of these implementation techniques. We will then give a detailed example of one of the possible approaches.

The most important classification criterion is the application of the synchrony hypothesis at the implementation level. There are two main approaches: in the first, the whole system globally satisfies the synchrony hypothesis and in the second the subsystems are synchronous, but the system itself is not. In the first approach, the specification is also synchronous, and the implementation techniques aim to satisfy the deterministic semantics of the specification [GRA 03, PAG 11, CAS 03]. However, it is difficult, or even undesirable, to satisfy the synchrony hypothesis at the level of the entire system. This is for instance the case in distributed avionics systems in which the on-board CPU clocks are not synchronized [CAS 01]. In this case, each CPU can be viewed as a synchronous system, but the phase shift of the clocks leads the computers to no longer being synchronous between each other. We refer in this case to *quasi-synchronous* systems. Defining and ensuring the global correctness of these systems has to be based on criteria coming from automatic control, like the relationships between the clock frequencies of the CPUs [CAS 01, TRI 08, CUR 05].

Following the type of the execution platform, there are two classification criteria: the number of processors in the system (uniprocessor vs. multi-processor) and the way the operations are triggered (event-driven vs. sampled/time-triggered). Some scheduling techniques have been defined (at least as a first step) for uniprocessor systems [PAG 11, CAS 03]. Taking into account the multi-processor architectures can be done on several levels of complexity: on symmetrical multi-cores [COR 11a], in which the computing resources are homogeneous and the communication costs are not taken into account, or on heterogeneous computing and communication resource systems, in which the communication and synchronization costs are taken into account [GRA 03, POT 09, TRI 08].

Some implementation techniques create a direct link between the clocks used in the specification and the physical time bases of the computer (timers). We then refer to *time-triggered* implementations. Such implementations are produced by several techniques where the synchrony hypothesis is satisfied at the system level [CAS 03, POT 09, COR 11a], but also in quasi-synchronous approaches, in which the link between synchronous clocks and physical timers is done at the level of each CPU separately [CAS 01, TRI 08]. Time-triggered systems are part of the larger class of systems in which the acquisition of the inputs is performed by sampling. In this class we can also find synthesized implementations, in the mono-period case by the SYNDEX language [GRA 03, CAR 13], and in the multi-period case by the approach proposed in [GIR 06]. In SYNDEX, the sampling of the environment is not performed by a timer given by the platform. The implementation on a uniprocessor can be seen here as a simple infinite loop, the sampling being performed at the beginning of each iteration of this loop. A global timer can also be synthesized automatically [POT 10] in the case of a multi-processor. Finally, an implementation may be *event-triggered*, at least partially. The implementation chain based on the PSYC language [CHA 05, LEM 10] allows us, for instance, to associate clocks with interrupts that do not come from timers [CHA 13].

Other classification criteria may be used, such as online approaches *vs.* offline approaches, preemptive approaches *vs.* non-preemptive approaches, etc. Furthermore, the schedulability analysis is only one of the issues which occur during real-time implementations that the synchronous languages allow to solve. Other issues include the analysis of the worst case execution time and the response time, the synthesis of the communication buffers, or the introduction of redundancies for fault tolerance purposes. We cannot present here in detail all these works. We will only detail one of the important choices which arises when we link logical clocks with physical timers.

Following the criteria defined above, we consider the case in which the synchrony hypothesis is globally satisfied, we use a uniprocessor platform and an *event-triggered* architecture. If we have a unique time base, meaning that every *operation* (instruction or external function of the synchronous language being considered) has the same base clock associated with this time base, it has to be ensured that the execution time of all these operations is smaller than the duration of the period of this time base. Therefore, a simple way to generate embedded code consists of implementing an infinite loop which performs the acquisition of data followed by the computations, and finally the update of the actuators. An idle operation is generally added in order to ensure the period of the base clock.

If some operations have clocks which are sub-samplings of the base clock, in other words that we are in the single-clock case;

Assuming we are in the single-clock case, in which operations have clocks that are sub-sampled from the base clock, there are two ways to solve the problem. In order to explain this, let us take the simple example in which we have two operations, one with a fast period of 10 ms and the other with a slower period of 40 ms, since its clock is sub-sampled by four from the fast period clock. Figure 4.13 illustrates this situation.

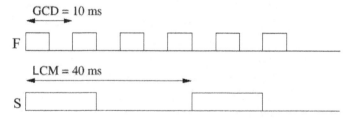

Figure 4.13. *Two operations – one with a fast period, the other with a slow period*

The first way consists of assuming that the base clock of the implementation has the GCD of the periods of the two operation, here equal to 10 ms. In this case, the operation with the slow period must finish its period after four instances of the operation with the fast period. The second way consists of assuming that the base clock of the implementation has a period equal to the LCM of the periods of the two operation, here equal to 40 ms. In this case, the operation with the fast period must execute four times inside the period of the operation with the slow period. In both cases, the operation with the fast period will not be preempted whereas for the operation with the slow period there are two possibilities. First, if it is possible to execute the operation with the slow period in one of the instances of the operation with the fast period, in this case the operation will not be preempted. If that is not possible the operation with the slow period will be preempted.

As soon as we have chosen the base clock, we may consider that we have a real-time characterization of every operation comprising a period, a relative deadline, often equal to the period (implicit deadline), and a WCET. Therefore, an operation becomes what is called in real-time scheduling theory a *real-time task*. At this moment, we have everything we need to perform real-time scheduling analysis and embedded code can be generated. A simple way to proceed consists of building a system of tasks with the same period equal to the GCD of the periods of the various operations and with implicit deadlines. Then, this system of tasks is scheduled online with a fixed-priority scheduling algorithm, such that the priorities of the tasks are the same. Thus, the tasks have the same release time and have to terminate before the next release time. The periods of the tasks being multiple of the GCD, it is sufficient to condition their execution according to this multiple, for them, to be executed the necessary number of times.

4.5. Synchronous languages extended to perform scheduling

4.5.1. LUSTRE

The LUSTRE language and its compiler have been extended with the instructions described below. These extensions, feasibility analysis techniques and the generation of code for distributed TTA architectures (Time-Triggered Architecture) are presented in the article [CAS 03].

(hyp) `basic period = p` declares a hypothesis such that the base clock has a period of p time units.

`periodic cl(k, p)` defines a base sub-clock which has a period k and an initial phase p. This instruction creates a Boolean flow which is `false` for the first p instants then becomes `true` every k instants. This operator can be derived from the core operators of the language. However, beyond the simplification of writing, it allows the compiler to identify the different sub-clocks of the base clock and therefore the periods of the nodes used in the program.

(hyp) `exec time(A) in [l,u]` declares a hypothesis such that the execution time of the node `A` or of an instruction, belongs to the time interval `[l,u]`.

(hyp) `Y=f(X) (location = P)` declares a hypothesis such that the node `f` has to be executed on the processor `P`.

The LUSTRE compiler verifies, as usual, whether the program is correct, but instead of generating sequential code, it exploits the additional information provided by the new instructions in order to perform, first of all, a feasibility analysis. This latter one uses the operators of the language as tasks, characterized by their period, deadline, WCET as well as the dependencies between tasks obtained by name identity of the output and input flows. By assuming that the tasks are non-preemptive, the compiler finds a solution to the multi-processor scheduling problem using the *partitioned approach*. This problem, equivalent to a "Bin Packing" problem, is known to be NP-hard. Its exact solution is obtained by using an optimal "Branch and bound"-type algorithm. Because of its complexity, we have to note that only simple instances of the problem can be solved with this algorithm. Finally, it is possible to generate distributed code on the different processors of a TTA architecture, which is a fault-tolerant synchronous distributed architecture [KOP 97].

4.5.2. PRELUDE

PRELUDE [FOR 09, FOR 10, PAG 11] is a synchronous data-flow language which is an extension of the LUSTRE language. It allows us to directly perform uniprocessor and multi-processor real-time scheduling. This extension allows us to specify, for each flow, each node or each external imported node in a program, hereafter generically referred to as node, a period and for each node a first release time, a relative deadline and a WCET. The latter is computed from the C-language program associated with each node. PRELUDE has an important feature that allows the programmer to specify *period transitions* in order to define precise and varied patterns of data transfer between the dependent nodes. This allows us to have data transfers between nodes of different periods, in the short period to long period direction, and/or in the long period to short period direction, by choosing precisely the exchanged data.

While the LUSTRE language is single-clock in the sense of the definitions given in section 4.2, the PRELUDE language allows the specification of affine clocks with constructions allowing to sub-sample, over-sample and shift the periods. The language also allows to link a clock to a "physical" time base which is unique throughout the program, used for giving the time unit. The affine relations between the clocks then allow us to associate a period and a shift at the origin with all the clocks of the program. PRELUDE thus manipulates the physical clocks, as defined in the introduction. A physical clock is associated with each flow and node of the program.

The node below denoted by `per` has an input flow `i` with a clock of period 10 and an output flow `o` with a clock of period 40 whose phases at the origin are equal to 0. The output flow `o` has a relative deadline of 35 with respect to the beginning of its period.

```
node per (i: int rate (10,0)) returns (o: int rate (40,0) due 35)
```

The `/^k` operator allows to sub-sample a flow by a factor k. The node below denoted by `sub-sam` has an input flow `i` with a clock of period 10 and an output flow `o` with a clock of period 40 obtained by sub-sampling the clock of its input `i`, by a factor 4.

```
node sub-sam (i: int rate (10,0)) returns (o: int rate (40,0))
  let
    o=i/^{}4;
  tel
```

Conversely, the `*^k` operator allows us to over-sample a flow by a factor k. The node below denoted by `over-sam` has an input flow `i` with a clock of period 40 and an output flow `o` with a clock of period 10 obtained by over-sampling the clock of its input `i`, by a factor 4.

```
node over-sam (i: int rate (40,0)) returns (o: int rate (10,0))
  let
    o=i*^{}4;
  tel
```

There are three operators for shifting a flow. These three operators together with the sub- and over-sampling operators allow to define with precision the way in which the nodes exchange data. As in LUSTRE, we can also use the when, merge, current, pre and -> operators.

A PRELUDE program is the composition of LUSTRE instructions and of extended instructions. Their goal is to define the clocks of flows and imported nodes, in particular the input and output flows of the program which correspond to the sensors and actuators. These imported nodes are the only ones which can be assigned a WCET.

The program denoted below by prog computes the output A from an imported node I with a WCET of 10, a sensor C with a WCET of 5 and an actuator A with a WCET of 5.

```
imported node I(i: int) returns (o:int) wcet 10;
sensor C wcet 5; actuator A wcet 5;
node prog (C: int rate (100,0) returns (A: int (100,0))
  let
    A=I(C);
  tel
```

In order to verify whether a program is correct, the compiler of PRELUDE solves the system of clock equations associated with the program after determining the clocks which are unknown. This allows us to determine the periods of the flows and of the nodes as well as the data transfer schemes between the nodes. From these schemes the compiler computes the release times and the deadlines of the nodes depending on the data they have to receive before being executed due to a dependency. Since it knows the WCET of all imported nodes, it can perform a uniprocessor schedulability analysis. The computation of the release times and the deadlines is performed according to the sub- and over-samplings as well as the shifts of the clocks, by using the principle given in [CHE 90]. Before the code can be generated, the compiler verifies whether the data transfers between tasks are consistent. This is achieved with a non-blocking protocol using memory buffers. This protocol, based on the *dependency words*, ensures that the inputs of a task remain available until its deadline. Finally, there is a prototype of uniprocessor embedded code generator which uses on the one hand the tasks written in C associated with the imported nodes, and on the other hand an operating system MARTE OS [RIV 02]. This latter one includes an EDF-type scheduler in order to take into account the re-computed deadlines, as indicated above. The schedulability analysis and the generation of code have been extended to the multi-core case. This multi-processor scheduling is performed according to the *global approach* in a programming and execution environment called SCHEDMCORE [COR 11b]. The multi-processor scheduler, which operates as a simulation under Linux, uses the gEDF (global Earliest Deadline First), gLLF (global Least Laxity First) and LLREF (Largest Local Remaining Execution First) algorithms.

4.5.3. SYNDEX

SYNDEX [LAV 91, GRA 99, SOR 05] is a synchronous data-flow language allowing us to directly perform real-time uniprocessor and multi-processor scheduling. As with PRELUDE, it is based on a language similar to LUSTRE, which is enriched in order to associate each *operation* (elementary process in SIGNAL, node in LUSTRE) with a period, a WCET and allocation constraints. This allows data transfers between dependent operations with different periods, in the short period to long period direction and/or in the long period to short period direction. A WCCT is associated with each data transfer between operations. SYNDEX therefore allows the specification of affine clocks. It also allows us to link a clock to a "physical" time base, unique in the program, which gives the time unit. It therefore manipulates physical clocks, such as they are defined in the introduction. A physical clock is associated to each operation of the program.

A SYNDEX program corresponds to a functional specification, called `Algorithm`, and to a non-functional specification, called `Architecture`. The latter describes the multi-processor platform and gives the real-time characterization of each operation with a period, an implicit deadline and a WCET. It also gives a real-time characterization of each data transfer (data dependency) between operations with a WCCT. Of course, only the WCETs and WCCTs depend, respectively, on the processors which can be of different types and of the inter-processor communication media which can also be of different types (bus or point-to-point link, and/or shared memory or message passing protocols). The operations, with their real-time characterizations, are similar to real-time tasks. In addition to the computing operations, equivalent to immediate functions of SIGNAL and to arithmetical operations of Lustre, the language contains instructions to specify a `delay` operation (equivalent to $ and `pre`), a conditioning operation allowing to perform the equivalent of LUSTRE's `merge` and finally a repetition operation allowing to perform the equivalent of SIGNAL's and LUSTRE's operations on tables. These latter ones have not been detailed before but can be expanded from elementary processes or kernel operations. SYNDEX aiming multi-processor scheduling, the *concurrence* aspect, even if it is significant in the previously seen languages, is even more so here. That is the reason why on the one hand, the programmer describes explicitly the data dependencies between the operations, defining thus a partial execution order (as in the data-flow languages SIGNAL and LUSTRE), and on the other hand he can indicate, in a repeated operation, whether it will be repeated in parallel or in sequence. The first way offers the maximum concurrence which will lead to exploiting the data-parallelism of the architecture, whereas the second way will lead to exploiting the pipeline parallelism of the architecture. Of course, the compiler will use this information to choose an allocation of the operations (tasks) to the processors and the data transfers (dependencies) to the communication media.

The SYNDEX compiler performs verifications on the causality and the clocks, equivalent to those performed by the LUSTRE compiler. Two kinds of multi-processor analyses are done following the partitioned approach, depending on whether the tasks are non-preemptive or preemptive. In both cases the periods of the operations are assumed to be equal or multiple in order to to ensure that there is no loss of data, either when the period of the producing operation is greater than the consuming operation, or in the opposite case. This leads to very simple data transfer schemes compared to those proposed by PRELUDE since here all the data is always transfered.

If the tasks are non-preemptive, the compiler performs a multi-processor feasibility analysis by using the feasibility test proposed in [KER 08] or a more complex one, proposed in [MAR 10]. This latter test strongly complicates the feasibility analysis which, as it has already been said, is basically NP-hard. For the allocation of the tasks to the processors and the data transfers to communication media, the feasibility analysis uses a greedy heuristic [KER 07] that ensures load balancing on the different processors. This heuristic uses a cost function which consists of minimizing the *makespan* which corresponds to the total execution time taking into account the inter-processor communication costs. This total execution time is also called the *input-output latency*. If the system is schedulable, the result of the schedulability analysis is an offline scheduling contained in a *scheduling table*. This table gives, for each operation, the processor where it is allocated, its starting execution time and its termination time. In the same way, it gives, for each data transfer, the communication medium where it is allocated, its starting execution time and its termination time. Finally, the compiler generates, from the scheduling table, a distributed embedded code for the platform described in the non-functional specification (architecture). It is assumed that each processor has a computing unit and one or several communication units. Those units operate in parallel or in pseudo-parallel. The compiler generates, using the scheduling table, for the computing unit of each processor an infinite loop (reaction) performing the sequence of tasks it has to execute (starting and termination times of each task) and for each communication unit of the processor an infinite loop performing the sequence of communications it has to execute (starting and termination times of each communication). Moreover, the compiler generates the set of semaphores necessary for the synchronization of the computing sequence and the communication sequences on each processor. The platform could have been specified with communication media of different types. For the communication media using the shared memory protocol, it also generates the set of semaphores necessary for the synchronization of the different processors operating in parallel. Likewise for the communication media using the message passing protocol, it generates the messages necessary for the synchronization of the different processors operating in parallel. For the two levels of intra- and inter-processor synchronizations, the aim is not to lose or duplicate any data and to ensure that the partial order described in the functional specification (algorithm) is compatible with the effective partial execution order of the real-time tasks. The generation of the code is detailed in [GRA 03].

If the tasks are preemptive, the compiler performs a multi-processor schedulability analysis by using a schedulability test which takes into account the *precise cost* of the preemption. This means that when a preemption occurs, we *have* to actually take into account its cost (saving and restoring the processor context), which can induce another preemption for which the cost has to be taken into account, and so on. This schedulability test is based on a fixed-priority

(RM, DM) or dynamic (EDF) scheduling algorithm. Dependent tasks can lead to priority inversions, due to data sharing, which are also taken into account by this schedulability analysis, detailed in [NDO 13]. As before, the task allocation is performed by a greedy algorithm using a cost function which consists of maximizing the scheduling margin of the tasks. If the system is schedulable, the result of the schedulability analysis is an offline scheduling contained in a scheduling table. The compiler generates the code from this scheduling table. It amounts to synthesizing an online scheduler. When the scheduler is executed, it finds the address of the task to execute in the scheduling table or, in short, whether the current task has been preempted. This online scheduler is called at the release and termination times of each task. In addition, it is also called at every reception of a piece of data that a task is waiting for. These instants are produced according to a *time-triggered* approach which requires a unique timer. By reading in this table, the scheduler satisfies the release times of the tasks. It knows when a task is preempted and therefore takes into account the cost of all the preemptions, even the ones involved in other preemptions. If a task terminates earlier than expected, no other task will be executed until the next task specified in the scheduling table. This guarantees the sustainability of the analysis. The cost of the scheduler can be precisely determined since it corresponds only to reading the table, which is a lot more simple than what a traditional scheduler has to do. This precise cost is taken into account in the WCET of the tasks without having to perform the usual approximation, as indicated explicitly by Liu and Layland [LIU 73] in their founding article. Note that, contrary to the tasks, the communications are not preemptive.

With a base clock associated to a time base of 1 millisecond, the program below first of all specifies a graph of operations (tasks) corresponding to an `algorithm` (section `algorithm` in the program) called `main`. This is composed of four operations: a sensor i of period 10 milliseconds referencing the definition of the input operation, an actuator o of period 20 milliseconds referencing the definition of the output operation, two computing operations comp1 of period 40 milliseconds and comp2 of period 60 milliseconds referencing respectively the definitions of the computation1 and computation1 operations. The inputs and outputs of these four references are connected with the characters "->" in such a way as to form a *diamond graph* of operations. In this graph the source vertex i is connected to comp1 and comp2 which are not connected to each other, but are connected to the same drain vertex o. Then, the program specifies an architecture (section architecture in the program) formed of three processors (operator) called u1, u2 of type uin and u3 of type uout. All three are connected to a bus of type SAMMP (medium). Finally, the program specifies the WCET of each operation depending on the processors which can execute it (section duration in the program) and the WCCT of each dependency depending on the communication medium which can execute it (section medium duration in the program). The compilation of this program performs the scheduling analysis and generates the corresponding distributed embedded code.

```
algorithm
{
actuator output () { int i1, int i2 }
sensor input() { int o }
function computation1 () { in: int[4] i; out: int o;}
function computation2 () { in: int[6] i; out: int o;}

function main () {
let i = input() [period = 10]; let o = output() [period = 20];
let comp1 = computation1 () [period = 40] ;
let comp1 = computation2 () [period = 60] ;
i.o -> comp1.i ;
i.o -> comp2.i ;
comp1.o -> o.i1;
comp2.o -> o.i2; } }

architecture {
operator type uin { gate x : med_sammp ;}
```

```
operator type uout { gate x : med_sammp ; }
operator u1 : uin { x -> bus ; }
operator u2 : uin { x -> bus ; }
operator u3 : uout { x -> bus ; }
medium type med_sammp : SAMMP
medium bus : med_sammp }

durations {
computation1 / uin = 2 computation2 / uin = 2
input /uin = 2   output / uin = 6
computation1 / uout = 2 computation2 / uout = 2
input / uout = 5 output / uout = 3 }

medium durations {
int / med_sammp = 2 }
```

The SIGNAL and SYNDEX languages are interfaced [YU 13], as are the SCICOS and SYNDEX languages [SOR 05]. This allows to compile a SIGNAL or SCICOS program and thus obtain a SYNDEX program containing the algorithm specification. After adding a non-functional specification inside this program, that is an architecture and the durations of the operations and dependencies, one can perform its compilation, which in turn performs the schedulability analysis and generates the distributed embedded code.

4.5.4. TAXYS

The aim of the TAXYS methodology [CLO 01] is to allow the analysis of the worst-case execution time and the schedulability analysis for applications specified in ESTEREL. In contrast to the traditional real-time approaches, the TAXYS methodology requires the modeling of the control system as well as of the controlled process, using extended ESTEREL programs. This allows us to represent and analyze periodic and aperiodic timing behaviours.

The TAXYS methodology extends the ESTEREL language in two directions. First, it introduces new instructions into the language allowing the modeling of the controlled process. This model can be non-deterministic in order to take into account the partial knowledge that we have of the process and the imprecision due to sampling (this model being in discrete time). Second, it defines a language with timing annotation inspired from timed automata [ALU 94] which allows, among others, to define worst case execution time, periodic and aperiodic release times, deadline and throughput. For the analysis, the two extended ESTEREL programs describing on the one hand the control system and on the other hand the process controlled, are both translated in a timed automaton. The composition of these two timed automata gives a global model whose analysis allows us to verify whether real-time timing constraints are met.

4.5.5. PSIC, *Embedded Code and Network Code*

A similar approach is used in the OASIS methodology [CHA 05, CHA 13] for the design of real-time embedded systems. The language supporting this methodology is PSIC [LEM 10]. There is a commercial tool dedicated to this methodology. A PSIC specification is structured in the form of a set of *agents* which communicate through shared memory and message passing mechanisms. The execution of each agent is paced by a single clock. The PSIC language allows the definition of several base clocks [CHA 13] from which other clocks may also be derived. The execution of the agents whose clocks are derived from the same base clock are synchronized by the latter.

The behaviour of each agent is defined by a *sequential* code which is a *subset of C*. This code can use all the control structures of the C language as well as use specific instructions. Among these specific instructions, we distinguish `before`, `after`, and `advance`, which allow the definition of *timing constraints* [LEM 10]. The following code snippet is the sequential code of an agent whose clock base is the `millisecond`.

```
while(1) {
  c = f() ;
  if(c) {
    g() ;
    advance (3) ;
  } else {
    h() ;
    advance (2) ;
  }
}
```

From a purely functional point of view, the execution of this code is performed as if the `advance` instructions did not exist. The only role of these instructions is to set the pace of the execution. The execution of the code begins at time 1 in the time base given by the `millisecond` clock. Then, each instruction `advance(k)` has to be traversed precisely at time $t + k$, where t is the date where the previous `advance` instruction has been traversed, or 1 if no `advance` instruction has been executed yet. This assumes two things: first, the code executed between time t and the execution of `advance(k)` has to have a shorter duration than k time units in the time base given by the `millisecond` clock. This property has to be assured by a worst-case execution time analysis. Second, if the execution of the code meets the `advance(k)` instruction before time $t + k$, then the execution of the code is delayed.

An interesting aspect of our example is that it represents an aperiodic behaviour: depending on the result of the computation of `f`, the execution of each cycle passes either by `advance(2)`, or by `advance(3)` according to the value of the condition `c`. Other languages allowing the expression of aperiodic behaviour are *"Embedded Code"* formalisms, used in the compilation of GIOTTO [HEN 07], and *"network code"* [FIS 06].

In order to allow scheduling analyses, the PSIC language also allows us to define the execution time of computing operations. The methodology found in PSIC is thus similar to the TAXYS methodology, with a lesser power of expression, but with simpler primitives which facilitate the analysis, and with an industrial quality tool chain.

4.6. Conclusion

It is probably obvious to the reader that we have merely scratched the surface of the "synchronous approaches and real-time scheduling" topic. We only wanted to provide theoretical foundations and links to the most important publications. We have also shown the close proximity of interest between the "synchronous languages" and "real-time scheduling" communities.

4.7. Bibliography

[ALU 94] ALUR R., DILL D.L., "A theory of timed automata", *Theoretical Computer Science*, vol. 126, pp. 183–235, 1994.

[BAR 03] BARUAH S., "Dynamic- and static-priority scheduling of recurring real-time tasks", *Real-Time Systems*, vol. 24, no. 1, pp. 93–128, 2003.

[BEN 90] BENVENISTE A., LE GUERNIC P., "Hybrid dynamical systems and the signal programming language", *IEEE Transactions on Automatic Control*, vol. 35, pp. 535–546, May 1990.

[BER 83] BERRY G., MOISAN S., RIGAULT J.-P., "Esterel: towards a synchronous and semantically sound high-level language for real-time applications", *Proceedings RTSS*, IEEE Catalog 83CH1941-4, Arlington, VA, 1983.

[BER 85] BERGERAND J., CASPI P., PILAUD D., *et al.*, "Outline of a real time data-flow language", *Proceedings RTSS*, San Diego, CA, December 1985.

[BOU 12] BOUISSOU O., CHAPOUTOT A., "An operational semantics for Simulink's simulation engine", *Proceedings LCTES*, pp. 129–138, 2012.

[BOU 13] BOURKE T., POUZET M., "Zelus: a synchronous language with ODEs", *16th International Conference on Hybrid Systems: Computation and Control (HSCC '13)*, Philadelphia, PA, pp. 113–118, March 2013.

[CAM 10] CAMPBELL S., CHANCELIER J.-P., NIKOUKHAH R., *Modeling and Simulation in Scilab / Scicos with ScicosLab 4.4*, 2nd ed., Springer, 2010.

[CAR 13] CARLE T., DJEMAL M., POTOP-BUTUCARU D., *et al.*, Off-line mapping of real-time applications onto massively parallel processor arrays, INRIA, Research report no. RR-8429, December 2013.

[CAS 01] CASPI P., MAZUET C., PALIGOT N.R., "About the design of distributed control systems: the quasi-synchronous approach", *Computer Safety, Reliability and Security*, Lecture Notes in Computer Science, Springer, vol. 2187, pp. 215–226, 2001.

[CAS 03] CASPI P., CURIC A., MAIGNAN A., *et al.*, "From Simulink to SCADE/Lustre to TTA: a layered approach for distributed embedded applications", *Languages, Compilers and Tools for Embedded Systems (LCTES 2003)*, ACM-SIGPLAN, San Diego, CA, June 2003.

[CHA 05] CHABROL D., DAVID V., AUSSAGUS C., *et al.*, "Deterministic distributed safety-critical real-time systems within the oasis approach", *Proceedings IASTED PDCS*, pp. 260–268, 2005.

[CHA 13] CHABROL D., ROUX D., DAVID V., *et al.*, "Time- and angle-triggered real-time kernel", *Proceedings DATE*, pp. 1060–1062, 2013.

[CHE 90] CHETTO H., SILLY M., BOUCHENTOUF T., "Dynamic scheduling of real-time tasks under precedence constraints", *Real-Time Systems*, vol. 2, no. 3, pp. 181–194, 1990.

[CHE 12] CHEN C., SUN J., LIU Y., *et al.*, "Formal modeling and validation of stateflow diagrams", *STTT*, vol. 14, no. 6, pp. 653–671, 2012.

[CLO 01] CLOSSE E., POIZE M., PULOU J., *et al.*, "TAXYS: a tool for the development and verification of real-time embedded systems", *Proceedings CAV*, pp. 391–395, 2001.

[COR 11a] CORDOVILLA M., BONIOL F., FORGET J., *et al.*, "Developing critical embedded systems on multicore architectures: the Prelude-SchedMCore toolset", *Proceedings RTNS*, pp. 107–116, 2011.

[COR 11b] CORDOVILLA M., BONIOL F., FORGET J., *et al.*, "Developing critical embedded systems on multicore architectures: the Prelude-SchedMCore toolset", *19th International Conference on Real-Time and Network Systems*, Nantes, France, September 2011.

[CUR 05] CURIC A., Implementing lustre programs on distributed platforms with real-time constraints., PhD Thesis, University Joseph Fourier, Grenoble, 2005.

[DOY 90] DOYLE J., FRANCIS B., TANNENBAUM A., *Feedback Control Theory*, Macmillan Publishing Co., 1990.

[FIS 06] FISCHMEISTER S., SOKOLSKY O., LEE I., "Network-code machine: programmable real-time communication schedules", *Proceedings RTAS*, pp. 311–324, 2006.

[FOR 09] FORGET J., A synchronous language for critical embedded systems with multiple real-time constraints., PhD Thesis, University of Toulouse, Toulouse, France, 2009.

[FOR 10] FORGET J., BONIOL F., LESENS D., *et al.*, "A real-time architecture design language for multi-rate embedded control systems", *Proceedings of the 2010 ACM Symposium on Applied Computing*, Sierre, Suisse, pp. 527–534, 2010.

[GIR 06] GIRAULT A., NICOLLIN X., POUZET M., "Automatic rate desynchronization of embedded reactive programs", *ACM Transactions on Embedded Computer Systems*, vol. 5, no. 3, pp. 687–717, August 2006.

[GRA 99] GRANDPIERRE T., LAVARENNE C., SOREL Y., "Optimized rapid prototyping for real-time embedded heterogeneous multiprocessors", *Proceedings of 7th International Workshop on Hardware/Software Co-Design, CODES '99*, Rome, Italy, May 1999.

[GRA 03] GRANDPIERRE T., SOREL Y., "From algorithm and architecture specification to automatic generation of distributed real-time executives: a seamless flow of graphs transformations", *Proceedings of 1st ACM and IEEE International Conference on Formal Methods and Models for Codesign, MEMOCODE '03*, Mont Saint-Michel, France, June 2003.

[GUE 02] GUERNIC P.L., PIERRE TALPIN J., CHRISTOPHE LE LANN J., "Polychrony for system design", *Journal for Circuits, Systems and Computers*, vol. 12, pp. 261–304, 2002.

[HAL 93] HALBWACHS N., *Synchronous Programming of Reactive Systems*, Kluwer, 1993.

[HAL 06] HALBWACHS N., MANDEL L., "Simulation and verification of asynchronous systems by means of a synchronous model", *Proceedings ACSD*, pp. 3–14, 2006.

[HAR 85] HAREL D., PNUELI A., "On the development of reactive systems", in APT K.R. (ed.), *Logics and Models of Concurrent Systems*, Springer-Verlag, New York, pp. 477–498, 1985.

[HAR 87] HAREL D., "Statecharts: a visual formalism for complex systems", *Science of Computer Programming*, vol. 8, no. 3, pp. 231–274, June 1987.

[HEN 03] HENZINGER T., HOROWITZ B., KIRSCH C., "Giotto: a time-triggered language for embedded programming", *Proceedings of the IEEE*, vol. 91, pp. 84–99, 2003.

[HEN 07] HENZINGER T.A., KIRSCH C.M., "The embedded machine: predictable, portable real-time code", *ACM Transactions on Programming Langyages and Systems*, vol. 29, no. 6, pp. 33.1–33.29, 2007.

[IEE 05] IEEE, IEEE Standard 1364-2005 for Verilog Hardware Description Language, 2005.

[KER 07] KERMIA O., SOREL Y., "A rapid heuristic for scheduling non-preemptive dependent periodic tasks onto multiprocessor", *Proceedings of ISCA 20th International Conference on Parallel and Distributed Computing Systems (PDCS '07)*, Las Vegas, NV, September 2007.

[KER 08] KERMIA O., SOREL Y., "Schedulability analysis for non-preemptive tasks under strict periodicity constraints", *Proceedings of 14th International Conference on Real-Time Computing Systems and Applications (RTCSA '08)*, Kaohsiung, Taiwan, August 2008.

[KOP 97] KOPETZ H., *Real-Time Systems: Design Principles for Distributed Embedded Applications*, 1st edition, Kluwer Academic Publishers, Norwell, MA, 1997.

[LAV 91] LAVARENNE C., SEGHROUCHNI O., SOREL Y., *et al.*, "The SynDEx software environment for real-time distributed systems, design and implementation", *Proceedings of European Control Conference (ECC '91)*, Grenoble, France, July 1991.

[LEE 87] LEE E., MESSERSCHMITT D., "Synchronous data-flow", *Proceedings of the IEEE*, vol. 75, no. 9, pp. 1235–1245, September 1987.

[LEG 87] LE GUERNIC P., BENVENISTE A., Real-time, synchronous, data-flow programming: the language SIGNAL and its mathematical semantics, INRIA, Research report no. RR-620, 1987.

[LEM 10] LEMERRE M., DAVID V., AUSSAGUS C., *et al.*, "An introduction to time-constrained automata", *Proceedings ICE*, pp. 83–98, 2010.

[LIU 73] LIU C., LAYLAND J., "Scheduling algorithms for multiprogramming in a hard real-time environment", *Journal of ACM*, vol. 14, no. 2, pp. 46–61, January 1973.

[MAR 10] MAROUF M., SOREL Y., "Schedulability conditions for non-preemptive hard real-time tasks with strict period", *Proceedings of 18th International Conference on Real-Time and Network Systems (RTNS '10)*, Toulouse, France, November 2010.

[NDO 13] NDOYE F., SOREL Y., "Monoprocessor real-time scheduling of data dependent tasks with exact preemption cost for embedded systems", *Proceedings of 16th IEEE International Conference on Computational Science and Engieering (ICSE '13)*, Sydney, Australia, December 2013.

[PAG 11] PAGETTI C., FORGET J., BONIOL F., *et al.*, "Multi-task implementation of multi-periodic synchronous programs", *Discrete Event Dynamic Systems*, vol. 21, no. 3, pp. 307–338, 2011.

[POT 09] POTOP-BUTUCARU D., DE SIMONE R., SOREL Y., *et al.*, "Clock-driven distributed real-time implementation of endochronous synchronous programs", *Proceedings EMSOFT*, pp. 147–156, 2009.

[POT 10] POTOP-BUTUCARU D., AZIM A., FISCHMEISTER S., "Semantics-preserving implementation of synchronous specifications over dynamic TDMA distributed architectures", *Proceedings EMSOFT*, pp. 199–208, 2010.

[RIV 02] RIVAS M.A., HARBOUR. M.G., "POSIX-compatible application-defined scheduling in MaRTE OS", *Proceedings of 14th Euromicro Conference on Real-Time Systems (ECRTS '02)*, Washington, WA, 2002.

[SOR 05] SOREL Y., "From modeling/simulation with Scilab/Scicos to optimized distributed embedded real-time implementation with SynDEx", *Proceedings of the International Workshop on Scilab and Open Source Software Engineering (SOSSE '05)*, Wuhan, China, October 2005.

[TRI 08] TRIPAKIS S., PINELLO C., BENVENISTE A., *et al.*, "Implementing synchronous models on loosely time triggered architectures", *IEEE Transactions on Computers*, vol. 57, no. 10, pp. 1300–1314, October 2008.

[YU 13] YU H., MA Y., GAUTIER T., *et al.*, "Exploring system architectures in AADL via Polychrony and SynDEx", *Frontiers of Computer Science Journal*, vol. 7, no. 5, pp. 627–649, 2013.

5

Inductive Approaches for Packet Scheduling in Communication Networks

5.1. Introduction

The deployment of real-time traffic on a communication network requires compliance with several variable constraints, including sufficient availability of the bandwidth and above all a guarantee of response time. In fact, the emergence of new types of applications such as multimedia applications (voice over Internet protocol (VoIP), videoconferencing, etc.), and those whose requirements cannot be met by a basic *best-effort* type service (which is what has, for a long time, been delivered by the Internet), means that a wider bandwidth is now required to meet the real-time constraints and quality of service (QoS) is needed for these applications. Meeting the varying constraints of traffic thus implies the Priority Queuing the varying applications with differentiated QoS levels which are suited to their needs. There are many tools for implementing QoS in a network, and these have been previously discussed in many studies. In this chapter, we will focus on the mechanisms inherent to scheduling packets and managing

Chapter written by Malika BOURENANE and Abdelhamid MELLOUK.

queuing which work toward ensuring allocation of resources between the flows [KLE 75].

Several scheduling techniques have been applied so as to achieve service differentiation and, thus, guarantee QoS to applications in line with their constraints. In general, the main aim of the scheduler is to ensure a certain level of equity in the distribution of critical resources to different flows. What is required is the maximization of the network capacity, while also paying heed to time constraints and application QoS. Over the last few years, a range of scheduling techniques has been suggested in the literature for different purposes. The First In-First Out (FIFO) scheduler is the most basic of these. It has been designated for networks such as the Internet, which work on the principle of basic service (*best-effort*), and where there is no requirement for a guaranteed QoS level. This algorithm has a very simple design and implementation, and the only data required by the scheduling decision are the arrival time of the packets. The packets are served according to the order in which they arrive, and are treated in the same way, without taking any of their characteristics into consideration. Although this system works well for elastic data transfer applications such as e-mail, chat groups, file transfer, etc., the FIFO scheduler is not quite sufficient when it comes to multimedia applications, which have real-time constraints that are difficult to meet with best-effort service. Since the emergence of these applications with heavy time constraints alongside best-effort traffic, new approaches have been developed which stipulate the necessary QoS level for each type of traffic. One of the first approaches attempted was to construct scheduling algorithms that allocated resources with a view to guaranteeing QoS levels for individual flows. In order to handle the problem of scaling, the flows were bundled according to the service they required, forming flow aggregates or service classes. Algorithms of proportional differentiation were then designed, based upon the principle of allocating resources per service class. In general, scheduling techniques may be divided into three main categories: techniques driven by priority, techniques driven by sharing the bandwidth (*share-driven scheduling algorithms*) and techniques driven by deadline (*deadline-driven scheduling algorithms*).

The priority-driven approach: this is the simplest form of service differentiation. Following this approach, the high priority traffic always obtains optimal QoS. Scheduling based on this principle is generally used for a traffic of the type *"hard real-time"*, which requires a high level of resource availability. It guarantees low response times for high-priority (real-time) applications. However, it may lead to starvation for low priority traffic. If this occurs, the priority scheduler uses a supplementary mechanism to control the allocation of the available bandwidth and avoid the monopolization of the resources by the priority classes. However, it is still difficult for best-effort traffic and real-time traffic to coexist in the same network and ensure resources are shared fairly [CHI 89]. Also, using this scheduling method in a wireless environment partially prevents efficient use of the air interface resources.

The shared bandwidth driven approach (SD): for this approach, the scheduler is based on the general processor Sharing (GPS) paradigm [TOU 98], which provides differentiated sharing of the bandwidth with a guaranteed minimum for each queue. The GPS principle involves visiting each non-empty queue in turn and serving an infinitesimal quantity of weighted data as a function of the QoS parameters for each of these queues. A queue may temporarily benefit from a higher bit-rate when the packets from one or several other queues are not waiting to be transmitted. In this case, the surplus capacity is equitably shared between the queues present, depending on their weight. Well-known scheduling mechanisms based on sharing bandwidth include *Weighted Fair Queuing (WFQ)*

[DEM 89, PAR 94], also known as *packet-by-packet generalized processor sharing (PGPS)* and its variants [WAN 02], and also *Virtual Clock (VC)* [ZHA 90]. These techniques are generally used in multimedia networks to provide support to the IntServ [BRA 94] or DiffServ [BLA 98] architecture. The basic idea is to guarantee the bandwidth required for each data flow while also guaranteeing a maximum response time [ZOR 10]. However, the response time which results from the use of these techniques depends both on the burst size of the traffic and on the bandwidth reserved. In fact, for highly dynamic traffic (also known as peak traffic rate), end-to-end delays increase linearly with the increase in the peak size. These delays handicap applications sensitive to delays, and especially those sensitive to packet delay variation. The complexity of schedulers is often in the order of $O(log(n))$, where n is the number of flows. This means that they cannot really be deployed on a large scale within the IntServ approach. However, this complexity can be accepted in a DiffServ-type approach, because n is reduced to the number of service classes.

The deadline-driven approach: for networks providing real-time service, such as multimedia applications, *Earliest Due Date* (EDD), suggested in [JAC 55] and [LIU 73], also known as *Earliest Deadline First (EDF)*, is one of the most satisfactory scheduling algorithms. It is based on deadlines where packets are served following the principle of earliest delivery depending on their QoS parameters. EDD was originally designed to serve individual flows, but it can also be applied to differentiated service classes. Its main drawback is that, since there is no fixed service deadline, best-effort traffic may be disadvantaged in the attribution of resources. However, some versions of this approach allow a more flexible use of packet deadline tolerance, favoring low-priority traffic whenever the high-priority traffic is not at risk of passing its deadline. This approach leads to more efficient use of air interface resources in wireless networks, when combined with opportunistic algorithms.

The inductive approach: static scheduling algorithms are heavily based on parameterization, which in turn is based on an offline estimation of the traffic loads supplied to the different classes and their required QoS level. The major disadvantage of this approach is that once the parameters have been set, they can no longer be modified, even if the profile of the traffic undergoes significant change. In fact, in practice, the loads of different classes may vary widely over a very short timeframe due to traffic peaks. They may also vary over a longer timescale as a result of traffic evolution. If resources are attributed statically, the scheduling algorithm will not be able to adapt to the dynamic loading conditions. In a worst-case scenario, this might lead to a situation where a higher-quality class receives a service level which is low in comparison to its requirements. Thus, it is necessary to consider adaptive scheduling policies, which can dynamically adjust the resources allocated to different traffic classes, while taking the state of the network and its instantaneous loading fluctuations into consideration. This is referred to as a scheduling algorithm based on state-dependent QoS level.

To achieve optimal scheduling, allowing the taking over of the environment dynamics (also known as variability), a network node needs to have complete knowledge of the state of the network and a precise prediction of its evolution. At this level, scheduling involves giving the node the ability to establish a decision on the change in configuration of the network, on the basis of policies and information collected. Another possibility is to allow nodes to interact with their neighborhood so that they may accomplish a given management task. This communication can also be useful for simply collecting information on how the network is operating.

In this chapter, we will present a detailed description of the current state of the art on real-time scheduling algorithms and we will also describe our work, which involves using the concepts of reinforcement learning (RL) in the design of an adaptive scheduling algorithm for packets in wired networks. We will concentrate on the development of an algorithm of this type, called *Phero-Q multi-learning*, based on a cooperative multi-agent approach and a bio-inspired approach built on a theory of collective intelligence. The concept of scheduling will be developed in sections 5.2 and 5.3 will contain a presentation of the set of adaptive strategies. Following this, we will outline our research based on RL in this field. Finally, we will make some concluding comments and outline possible future developments made possible by our work.

5.2. Scheduling problem

The evolution of packet commutation networks and the use of new real-time multimedia services such as VoIP and real-time video have led to an increased need to support quality service demands and to be able to adapt to different service levels. According to the recommendations of the UIT-TE.800 [ITU 94], QoS is defined as the collective performance efficiency of a service which determines the satisfaction level of the end user of a given service. To provide QoS in IP networks, the *Internet Engineering Task Force (IETF)* has developed various QoS mechanisms, such as DiffServ (differentiated services) [BLA 98] and IntServ (integrated services) [BRA 94]. The IntServ model defines an architecture which can handle the QoS without impacting the IP protocol. To achieve this, it uses a particular signaling protocol called *Resource ReSerVation Protocol (RSVP)* [BRA 97]. However, the main difficulty with this model is its scalability when the number of flows is high. In fact, each router must maintain state information for each flow that passes through it, and then allocate a queue for each flow.

When the number of flows increases, the number of states becomes large, and the traffic is even more saturated because there is significant updating between routers which generates too much traffic signaling (also known as *overhead*). Moreover, there is the complexity of the scheduler, which must manage all the queues. In order to compensate for these difficulties, DiffServ model introduces the concept of aggregation of flows in classes so as to simplify classification, marking and scheduling requirements.

Real-time adaptability to variable parameters which have an impact on communication networks leads to new requirements for the scheduling algorithm. The desirable properties in the development of adaptive scheduling algorithms are:

1) Efficiency: the basic function of a scheduling algorithm is to establish a transmission order for packets placed in a queue within a network, on the basis of the availability of the shared resource, so as to satisfy all of the QoS requirements of each flow. A scheduling algorithm is said to be more efficient than another if it can deliver the same QoS guarantees under higher traffic load.

2) Robustness: the adaptive algorithm must operate correctly whatever the traffic and network conditions. As a result, the algorithm should not rely on predefined parameters, but rather should use real-time measurement information over different timescales, so that it is truly adaptive.

3) Isolation of the flows: whenever there is a high-speed flow, lower-speed flows must not be penalized. This is particularly important on networks which are not protected by an admission control.

4) Flexibility: a packet-scheduling algorithm should be able to support flows with different QoS requirements.

5) Equity: the scheduling mechanism should aim to equitably share resources between flows as a function of their requirements.

6) Implantation complexity: a packet-scheduling algorithm should have low calculation complexity. Owing to the rapid increase in bandwidth and speed in today's communication networks, the speed with which the packets are treated is becoming increasingly important.

5.3. Approaches for real-time scheduling

Many packet scheduling algorithms for wired and wireless communication networks have been successfully presented. In most of them, the main goal of the packed scheduling algorithms is to maximize the system capacity while satisfying the QoS of users and achieving a certain level of fairness. Scheduling in a wired environment is relatively easy because the capacity of the resources is constant. Consequently, these algorithms aim to distribute these fixed resources equitably between the different traffic flows, often by taking into account the different QoS levels agreed at the time of admission of the flows. Each of the network's routers uses a certain scheduling policy to determine the transmission order for the packets from different flows which share the same output line. In this section, we will examine a few representative algorithms, outlining their strengths and weaknesses.

5.3.1. *The strict priority*

This is the primitive form of service differentiation. It makes it possible to attribute strict priority to a queue. In this approach, the traffic classified as priority will always receive the best possible QoS [HUI 00, NAG 87, SAN 02]. The strict priority algorithm is useful for managing critical traffic, but its disadvantage lies in the strong penalty for obtaining resources for low-priority traffic if there is a high volume of high-priority traffic on the network.

5.3.2. *The Generalized processor sharing paradigm*

The ideal aim for bandwidth sharing algorithms is to provide an equitable weighted sharing for different flows or classes of traffic [WAN 01]. The GPS paradigm [PAR 92] is a theoretical reference which responds to this aim, where the flows are treated like fluids (i.e. they have no granularity). This policy is not praticable in practice, but gives an ideal model to approach as closely as possible. For each flow i there is an associated weight ϕ_i which corresponds to its available share of bandwidth, such that:

$$\Sigma_{i \in [1,N]} \phi_i = 1 \qquad [5.1]$$

where N is the number of the flows.

If $S_i(\tau_1, \tau_2)$ denotes the quantity of service that the flow i received in the temporal interval $[\tau_1, \tau_2]$, then for any flow i waiting to be served in the interval, the GPS server guarantees that:

$$\frac{S_i(\tau_1, \tau_2)}{S_j(\tau_1, \tau_2)} \geq \frac{\phi_i}{\phi_j} \; ; i, j \in [1, N] \qquad [5.2]$$

By combining the equations [5.1] and [5.2], a server of throughput C allocates a service share of $g_i = \phi_i C$ to the flow i. In addition, for each subset $B(\tau_1, \tau_2) \subset \{1, 2, ..., N\}$ of queuing flows, the remaining capacity is distributed proportionally to the weight of each active flow, which leads to an increase in its service share:

$$g_i^{inc} = \frac{\phi_i}{\Sigma_{j \in B} \phi_j} r; i \in B \qquad [5.3]$$

Thus, the aim of this model is to guarantee a minimum bandwidth, i.e. a minimum throughput, for each flow. Packets scheduling techniques, such as packet-by-packet GPS (PGPS) suggested in [PAR 93], also known as WFQ, is a good approximation of the GPS model.

5.3.3. *The packet-by-packet generalized processor sharing (PGPS) scheduler*

PGPS is a scheduling mechanism which provides an excellent approximation of the ideal GPS properties, and is also quite practically applicable in packet-switching networks. The notion of PGPS was initially suggested in [DEM 89] under the name of WFQ; however, a good generalization and a thorough analysis were performed by Parekh and Gallager in [PAR 93] and [PAR 94]. The basic concept of WFQ is to simulate the GPS transmission order. More specifically, WFQ uses a temporal calculation process and attaches to each packet the time at which it has been served by the GPS. The packets are transmitted to the output queue on the basis of increasing order of their start time in the GPS.

5.3.4. *Earliest deadline first*

Following this policy, a deadline is assigned to each flow; a packet j of a flow i which arrives at the time a_{ij} is thus allocated a deadline of $a_{ij} + d_i$. The packets are then served according to urgency, where the level of urgency is measured by proximity to their deadline. This means that a packet may only be served if all the packets with shorter deadlines have been served or are not yet active. In comparison with strict priority, EDF may be considered as a scheduling policy which provides a priority depending on time [CHA 97] to each active packet. This priority becomes higher as the absolute deadline approaches. As a result, it is possible to guarantee QoS, as long as each flow obeys certain specific characteristic constraints. EDF is an algorithm with a complexity in $O(N)$ where N is the number of active packets. Thus, for traffic with deadline constraints, we may say that EDF is an optimal scheduling algorithm. However, it does not provide protection (isolation) for different flows, an aspect which is often compensated for through the use of a traffic-shaping mechanism. Several versions of EDF have been suggested, for example in [PIN 04, ZAI 01], which make it possible to isolate flows from each other, leaving network resources free to distribute themselves as is most efficient.

5.3.5. *Adaptive scheduling*

Static scheduling techniques base their scheduling decisions on parameters assigned in a fixed manner to the different flows before they are activated. These scheduling techniques have oriented operation as their basis and do not take certain strict conditions into account. For example, in WFQ, for each flux served, the bandwidth, set by its sharing coefficient and an upper limit for response time, needs to be guaranteed. This delay is closely linked to the allocated quantity of bandwidth. However, for some applications, flows may require more stringent delay guarantees but reserve only a low bandwidth. New techniques which are oriented toward dynamic adaptation of the scheduling parameters and give better overall performance have been developed. Some studies have had as their focus the improvement of WFQ, bearing in mind both the dynamic aspect and the heterogeneity of the traffic. The adaptive approach developed in [HOR 01] is a variant of the equitable fair queuing (FQ) algorithm and dynamic priority scheduling. [CRA 01] suggest a new more rapid algorithm for scheduling packets, called *Dynamic Weighted Fair Queuing* (DWFQ). A new adaptive WFQ approach using the concept of revenue to adapt weights is presented in [SAY 03]. Later, this approach was extended on the basis of a comparison and an analysis of several adaptive scheduling algorithms [SAY 06] such as: *Revenue Adaptive-WFQ* (RA-WFQ), *Revenue Adaptive-Weighted Round Robin* (RA-WRR) and *Revenue Adaptive-Deficit Round Robin* (RA-RRC). Although all of these techniques, and indeed some others, have contributed to a solution, they, nonetheless, remain ineffective insofar as they are not able to challenge the initial choices to adapt these depending on what is really happening in the environment. Dynamic or adaptive approaches allow us to face different forms of uncertainty. However, some of these approaches generally require a high quantity of online calculation, which means they cannot be used for very high-speed links. They often work on the basis of a monocriterion optimization and attempt to respond to a single QoS parameter. Among adaptive methods, we can mention:

Genetic algorithms – these algorithms may be used to resolve search and optimization issues.

Algorithms based on fuzzy logic – the concept of fuzzy logic was developed to model imprecise and uncertain data and represent knowledge in an operational form. Fuzzy control is based on the relatively simple idea of a fuzzy subset, which is a generalization of an ordinary set that allows a degree of belonging. This degree of belonging is obtained by using sets of inference rules [MUN 94, GOM 98] and is a real number in the interval [0, 1]. Fuzzy control is useful within the design of a packet scheduler, mainly for the following reasons:

1) fuzzy control enables decision-making in situations where the available information is incomplete or imprecise;

2) several variables of the problem do not have clearly defined limits, such as the use of resources (bandwidth/buffer) in the router, which may be labeled as very high, high, medium and low;

3) scheduling decisions may be described by heuristic rules;

4) The rules may consider several QoS parameters;

5) fuzzy control rules are usually simpler and easier, they often require only a few rules, and thus offer both efficiency and robustness.

However, the main drawback of mechanisms based only on fuzzy control is that they cannot learn.

Algorithms based on learning – adaptive learning [OBA 98] is one of the main fields of artificial intelligence. It allows the design of intelligent optimization methods [BAT 08]. Learning automaton [OBA 98, PAP 94] is one of the most powerful tools in this area. It is defined as a finite state machine that interacts with a stochastic environment, trying to learn the optimal action given by the environment via a learning process. Most of the available work relates to the behavior of a learning automaton in stationary environments. The problem of behavior in non-stationary environments appears difficult. However, the learning automaton approaches can track the optimal action for non-stationary environments as long as the statistic characteristics of the environment do not change very rapidly.

To provide a solution to the problem of static approaches in packet scheduling, several adaptive approaches have been proposed for assigning weights to each traffic class [ANK 01, HAL 98]. In particular, Hall and Mars have suggested an adaptive approach based on a stochastic learning automaton [HAL 98]. In this study, they showed that their automaton was able to exceed the FIFO, EDF and (PQ) policies. In fact, they noticed that the scheduling policy learned by the stochastic automaton was sufficient to satisfy the delay constraints for two classes of traffic without disadvantaging a third class which required a *best-effort* basic service.

However, a limitation of this approach is that the scheduling policy does not take into account the current state of the system when selecting an action. As an alternative approach, many works have turned toward the concept of RL [SUT 88, SUT 98]. This is an automatic learning approach that enables the development of systems which can improve on the basis of interactions with their environment.

Research into genetic algorithms, initiated by John Holland [HOL 75, HOL 86], played an influential role in research into RL, and also in the theory of learning automata [NAR 74]. Later, Chris Watkins [WAT 89], Paul Werbos [WER 87] and several others reinvigorated theoretical research into RL by linking it to optimal control and dynamic programming theory. One essential advantage of this type of learning over other approaches lies in the fact that it does not require information on the environment apart from the reinforcement signal [SUT 88].

RL is usually defined as the problem faced by a learner of how to determine correct behavior through trial-and-error interactions with a dynamic environment in order to achieve a goal. In the standard RL model, the learner and decision maker is called an agent and is connected to its environment via perception or sensing, and action, as shown in Figure 5.1.

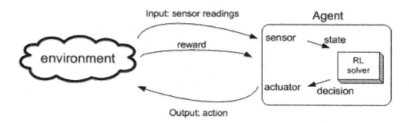

Figure 5.1. *Abstract view of an agent in its environment in RL*

More specifically, the agent learns from the interaction with the environment at each of a sequence of discrete time steps t. At each step of the interaction, the agent senses some information about its environment (input), determines the world state and then, on that basis selects and takes an action (output). The action changes the state of the environment and the agent. One time step later, the value of the state transition following that action is given to the agent by the environment as a scalar called reward. The agent should behave so as to maximize the received rewards, or more particularly, a long-term sum of rewards.

In its learning, the autonomous agent must compromise between the diversification of experience so as to improve (exploration) and the attainment of a maximum number of rewards by using its current knowledge (exploitation). Each decision it takes influences subsequent decisions and, therefore, RL may be viewed as an adaptive method which resolves problems of sequential decision in absence of certainty. These problems have been the subject of many formalizations and resolution methods. Markov decision processes (MDPs) are one of the approaches which define the formal framework for RL. They generalize shortest path research methods in a stochastic and stationary environment.

5.4. Basic concepts

5.4.1. *Monoagent learning*

Markov decision process

An MDP is a controlled stochastic process which satisfies the Markov property [PUT 94]. It allows us to show the evolution of the environment in which an agent evolves as a function of the actions carried out by this agent. It is described by a tuple $\langle S, A, P, R \rangle$ where:

– S is the state space;

– A is the action space;

– P: S × A × S → [0, 1] is the transition function. It defines the transition probability for an agent from state s ∈ S to s'∈ S after performing action a ∈ A;

– R: S × A × S → [0, 1] is the reward function.

In the given definition, P and R are stationary (invariable in time). In addition, the MDP is in general finite, i.e. the sets S and A are finite.

Thus, at each timestep, the agent observes the current state s ∈ S, executes an action a ∈ A, receives a reward R(s, a) and observes a new state s'∈ S, which depends on the function P. The agent's goal is to maximize the cumulative gain in time. To take the time horizon into account, it is sufficient to consider the sum of rewards that it will receive in the future:

$$R_t = r_{t+1} + \gamma . r_{t+2} + \gamma^2 . r_{t+3} + \cdots = \sum_{k=0}^{\infty} \gamma^k . r_{t+k+1} \qquad [5.4]$$

Where γ is a weighting factor, $\gamma \in$ [0, 1[. This factor is functionally interesting: it favors the maximization of rewards while reducing the time to obtain them. The influence of time is more significant when γ is close to 1. If γ equals 0, the goal of the agent is to maximize immediate reward without being concerned with those that follow.

An MDP verifies the Markov property, in the sense where the transition function of the environment only depends on the previous state of the agent, and on the action that the agent has just carried out, and does not depend on states and actions before this. Thus, the agent's decision is based solely on the current state:

$$\forall s' \in S \; P(s_{t+1} = s'|s_t, a_t) =$$
$$P(s_{t+1} = s'|s_t, a_t, s_{t-1}, a_{t-1}, \dots, s_1, a_1) \qquad [5.5]$$

The resolution of an MDP consists of finding the optimal policy π of the agent such that π: S $\rightarrow$ A determines the best action a $\in$ A which can be carried out at each state s $\in$ S with the aim of optimizing the expectation of reward. If the model of the MDP, i.e. the functions P and R, is known, then are there algorithms from dynamic programming which allow us to resolve the MDP [BEL 57].

In our case, the agent does not know the dynamics of its environment. Therefore, we decided to study RL techniques which would allow us to find the solution for an MDP by trial and error.

Q-learning

Q-Learning is a model-free iterative RL algorithm for MDP suggested by Watkins [WAT 89]. It is an algorithm developed from the theory of dynamic programming for delayed RL that does not need a model of the environment and can be used online. In Q-learning, the policies and the value function are represented by a two-dimensional lookup table indexed by state-action pairs. Formally, for each state s and action a, we define the Q value under policy π to be:

$$Q(s, a) = r(s, a) + \gamma \sum_{s' \in S} P(s, a, s') \max_{a \in A} Q(a, s') \qquad [5.6]$$

Its update equation is as follows:

$$Q(s, a) \leftarrow Q(s, a) + \alpha[r + \gamma \max_{a'} Q(s', a') - Q(s, a)] \qquad [5.7]$$

Where $\alpha = 1/n$ is the rate of learning inversely proportional to the number of times that the state s has been visited. It determines the size of the correction that needs to be made to the value Q(s, a). The parameter γ is a discount factor which determines the present value of future rewards, $\gamma \in [0, 1[$.

The principle of Q-learning is based on a coevaluation of a policy and an associated table of Q-values. The policy π is deduced from the Q-values by considering the best course of action which will maximize Q(s, a). The algorithm is based on each new experiment associated with the policy π for updating the evaluation of Q. Once the Q-function has been learned, the agent can deduce from it the optimal policy π^*, maximizing Q:

$$\pi * (s) = \text{argmax}_a \big(Q * (s, a) \big) \qquad [5.8]$$

In the Q-learning process, a learned action value function Q directly approximates Q* through value iteration. There are different action selection strategies to take when learning. Two of them are shown below:

1) ε-greedy (where $\varepsilon \in [0, 1]$): this strategy consists of choosing, with a probability ε the greediest action a = argmax$_{a \in A}$Q(s, a) (exploitation), and choosing an action at random in A with a probability $1 - \varepsilon$ (exploration).

2) Boltzmann: this is a probabilistic approach, in which the probability of choosing an action is proportional to the estimation of the Q value. This probability is assigned following the Boltzmann distribution function:

$$Pr(s|a) = \frac{e^{\frac{Q(s,a)}{T}}}{\sum_{a \in A} e^{\frac{Q(s,a)}{T}}} \qquad [5.9]$$

where factor T represents temperature. It allows us to control exploration in relation to the exploitation of estimations of Q. If T is high, the effect of the upper values of Q will be lessened. A null temperature leads to exploitation. So, to promote visiting of all the state-action pairs at the beginning of learning, it is better to vary the temperature, beginning with a high temperature to make sure that the actions explore the space, and then progressively decreasing it toward zero at each iteration to ensure that what has already been learnt is exploited.

In the random strategy, the agent chooses an action randomly among the possible actions. This exploration policy is very easy to implement and makes it possible to visit all state-action pairs infinitely often for an infinite number of iterations. However, this method may require extensive exploration time since the agent must find its goal randomly during each episode of learning. Another method consists of taking into account the estimated Q obtained during learning for selecting in a state an action maximizing Q(s, a). So, the agent learns from the closest optimal path in the random case. This consequently reduces the time needed to find a goal in each episode. A limitation of this technique is that if the agent chooses the action maximizing the Q-value every time, it has not visited all possible state-action pairs and continually performs the same suboptimal paths. One solution is to use a probabilistic approach in which the probability of choosing an action is proportional to its estimated Q-value. However, it is necessary that all actions have a non-zero probability of being selected. This is a compromise between exploitation of known estimates of Q and exploration pairs non-visited state-action.

Algorithm: the principle of Q-learning is to iteratively update the Q-value function based on observation of the instantaneous transitions and their associated rewards. The convergence of Q-values to optimal Q-values, and consequently toward optimal policy, has been shown in [WAT 92] following this hypothesis:

– finite S and A;

– each state-action pair is visited infinite number of times;

– $\sum_n \alpha_n(s, a) = \infty$ and $\sum_n \alpha_n^2(s, a) < \infty$;

– $\gamma < 1$ or if $\gamma = 1$.

Q-learning algorithm
Initialize Q(s, a)
Initialize s,
Repeat infinitely
a ← ChoiceAction(s)
carry out the action a; observe r, s'
$Q(s, a) \leftarrow Q(s, a) + \alpha[r + \gamma \max_{a'} Q(s', a') - Q(s, a)]$
s ← s'

Limitations

Most of the RL algorithms [SUT 98] represent the value function in the form of a consultation table with an entry for each state-action pair. Although this approach has a solid theoretical basis, [DAY 92, JAK 93] and is efficient in many applications, it becomes a severe limitation when it is applied to problems which have large state and action spaces or when it is applied in continuous domains, due to the phenomenon known as the curse of dimensionality [SUT 98]. In these cases, it leads to slow convergence. Several approaches have been attempted to remedy this, by applying the approximation of functions with a view to approximating the value function with a small number of parameters. As a result, the agent can experience a limited subset of the state space, then, by generalization, it can produce a good approximation of a larger part of the state space.

The problem of constructing an approximation function on the basis of an input-output interaction mapping has mostly been studied by a supervised-type learning [MIT 97]. However the approximation function and generalization in the RL are more difficult to apply in supervised learning: the learning data are not communicated in advance, but determined in parts by the output of the learned function. As the learning must take place online, in interaction with the environment, the approximation function methods used in supervised learning are not all well suited for use in RL. The aggregation of states is a function approximator that has been much studied. In this case, the subsets of original states are aggregated, and the size of the state space is reduced. Several algorithms use several overlapping partitions of state space, and so, the value function is approximated by a linear combination of the values in each partition. Many learning algorithms [AND 94] are based on a multigrid approach which uses partitions with different resolutions to speedup the learning process. Another possible solution is to introduce soft-state aggregations [SIN 95], in which the states are soft-clustered. Most approaches to state aggregation have two drawbacks. The first drawback has to do with partitioning the state space into small regions, which results in a reduction of the advantages of aggregation. In addition, the criterion used to partition the state space is essential for obtaining an efficient approximation of the value function across the entire state space. However, when there are no indications as to the way in which the state space should be divided, uniform partition is widely used. As a result of this, there may be a large set of input characteristics. For many real applications, the agent has to choose the actions with precision within the state space. Most of the suggested solutions adapt techniques used for state spaces to action spaces.

5.4.2. Multi-agent reinforcement learning

Multi-agent learning refers to systems where several agents act conjointly in a common environment. In the case of scheduling and, thus, in the case of the management of resources, the resources may be centrally controlled, but the management of each resource by its own agent may make a useful contribution, distributed to the system. The agents may act together (cooperation) or may have individual aims (competition). As all the agents share a common environment, this environment becomes non-stationary for each of them. The reward received by each agent is influenced by the actions of other agents. The Multi-agent Markov Decision Processes (MMDPs) [BOU 99] form a formal framework which corresponds to a generalization of the MDP to cooperative multi-agent systems. To resolve an MMDP, it is necessary to consider either a centralized control or a communication between agents.

In a cooperative centralized system, optimal management of resources can be obtained by a global MDP built upon a single vision from a central agent [BOU 99]. This solution cannot be implemented in practice because agents are often distributed within the space and none of them possesses sufficient information to carry out centralized control. In addition, the need to take all the joint actions into account considerably increases the complexity of learning because the size of the space of joint actions grows exponentially as a function of the number of agents. In decentralized control, the agents need to communicate with each other to exchange information on their states in order to determine the global state of the system. In this context, MMDP policy may be calculated in a completely decentralized manner. Each agent individually calculates the optimal joint policy. The agents then coordinate their choice of the optimal policy to be followed so that optimal overall performance is guaranteed. However, this coordination is guaranteed using information which may possibly be insufficient for making a correct decision. When the agents can share their observations completely at each state, the issue resembles that of an MMDP [BOU 99], and may be reduced to an MDP, which is of polynomial complexity. Here, we will further study the model where interaction between the agents takes place through the reward function [BEC 03].

Formal definitions of the model

DEFINITION 5.1.– *an MMDP is defined by a tuple ⟨S, A, P, R⟩ where*:

$-$ S = $S_1 \times S_2 \times ....\times S_n$ is a finite set of states where S_i is the state space discreet from the agent i.

$-$ A = $A_1 \times A_2 \times....\times A_n$ is a finite set of actions. A_i is the set of actions of the agent i. The joint action a $\in$ A is the vector of all the individual actions.

$-$ P: S $\times$ A $\rightarrow\Delta$ (S) is the probability of transition obtained by

$$P^a_{ss'} = \prod_{i=1}^{n} P(s_i, a_i, s'_i)$$ [5.10]

$-$ R: S $\times$ A $\times$ S $\rightarrow$R is the reward function such that $R = \sum_{i=1}^{n} r_i(s_i, a_i, s'_i)$

where r_i is the reward obtained by the agent when it carries out action a_i in the state s_i and transits on the state s_i'.

In an MDP, the objective of the agent is to find a policy π which maximizes total reward. It has been proven that an optimal policy π^* exists such that for any $s \in$ S, the Bellman equation [BEL 57] is written:

$$V(s, \pi *) = \max_a\{r(s, a) + \gamma \sum_{s'} P(s, a, s')V(s', \pi *)\}$$ [5.11]

When the transition function is unknown, the Q-learning [WAT 89] is one of the most used algorithms for finding the optimal policy. This algorithm builds the values Q(s, a) by using the following update rule:

$$Q(s, a) \leftarrow (1 - \alpha)Q(s, a) + \alpha[r(s, a) + \gamma \max_{a'} Q(s', a')]$$ [5.12]

where α is a rate of learning and γ a discount factor which enables regulation of the importance allocated to future rewards compared to immediate rewards. It has been proven in [WAT 92] that this equation converges toward the optimum Q*(s, a) in the case of an MDP and that the optimal policy π^* can be derived as follows:

$$\pi * (s) = arg \max_a Q^*(s, a) \qquad [5.13]$$

The extension of Q-learning to the multi-agents context takes the influence of actions by other agents into account. This influence is shown by joint Q-values for each agent i. We formally define a Q-value as follows:

$$Q_i\left(s, a_{1,...,}a_n\right) =$$
$$r_i(s, a_1, ..., a_n) +$$
$$\gamma \sum_{s' \in S} P(s, a_1, ..., a_n, s') \Gamma_{\pi_1,...,\pi_n} \left[V_{i\pi_1,...,\pi_n}(s')\right] \qquad [5.14]$$

In this equation, $\Gamma_{\pi_1,...,\pi_n}$ is a generic operator which defines the joint policy. This operator describes the required optimality criterion. In Q-learning, $\Gamma_\pi = \max_{a \in A}$

The update rule for the Q-values is:

$$Q_i\left(s, a_{1,...,}a_n\right) \leftarrow (1 - \alpha)Q_i(s, a_1, .., a_n) + \alpha\left[r_i(s, a_1, ..., a_n) + \gamma \sum_{s' \in S} P(s, a_1, ..., a_n, s') \Gamma_{\pi_1,...,\pi_n}\left[V_{i\pi_1,...,\pi_n}(s')\right]\right] \qquad [5.15]$$

From a particular agent's point of view, multi-agent systems differ from single-agent systems most significantly in that the environment dynamics can be influenced by other agents. In addition to the uncertainty (i.e. stochasticity) that may be inherent in the environment, other agents can affect the environment in unpredictable ways due to their actions. However, the full power and advantage of a multi-agent system (MAS) can be realized when the ability for agents to communicate with one another is added, enabling learning to be accelerated, more information to be gathered about the world state, and experiences of other agents to be shared.

One of the important aspects of multi-agent systems is that they consider that intelligent agents are able to reach objectives in a complex environment. These multi-agent systems specifically handle the behavior of the agent in relation to changes in its environment [BOU 99]. Here, we are concerned with systems whose control is decentralized and where communication is performed through mobile agents, like in a colony of ants. These agents operate within a special information infrastructure based on the aggregation, evaporation and diffusion of artificial pheromones and can emulate the behavior of the system several times before decision-making, through moving around, collecting and transmitting the information available within the multi-agent system. The information provided by the mobile agents is dependent upon a belief factor which in turn depends upon the level of concentration of the synthetic pheromone. This belief factor reflects the level of confidence which the agent will attribute to the information provided by other agents from the same group, and will be used to update policies. The belief factor may well be useful in situations where the information is not reliable, due to changes in the environment. Its formula [MON 04] is:

$$B(s,a) = \frac{\sum_{s \in Na} \Phi(s)}{\sum_{\sigma \in Na} \Phi_{max}(\sigma)} \qquad [5.16]$$

where $\Phi(s)$ stands for a synthetic pheromone, a scalar value which integrates the dynamic basic nature of the pheromone, i.e. the aggregation, evaporation and diffusion.

5.5. Proposed model

We define an MMDP with decentralized control with a 4-tuple $\langle S, A_i, P_i, r_i \rangle$, where S is the state space, A_i is the set of the agent's actions i, P_i: S × $A_i \rightarrow \Delta(S)$ is the probability of transition and r_i: S × A_i × S $\rightarrow$R, is the reward function such that r_i(s, a_i, s') is the reward obtained by the agent i when it executes the action a_i in the state s and transits toward s' [BOU 09a].

The local policy π_i for each agent is:

$$\pi_i: S \rightarrow A_i \qquad [5.17]$$

The value function anticipated by the agent i is:

$$V_i(s, \pi_i) = E(\pi_i)[r_i / s_0 = s]$$
$$= E(\pi_i)\left[\sum_{t=0} \gamma^t r_i^{t+1} / s_0 = s\right] \tag{5.18}$$

Where r_i^t is the immediate reward at the time t of the agent i and γ is a counting factor.

The local Q-function is given by:

$$Q_i \pi_i(s, a_i, s') = E(\pi_i)[r_i \,|\, s_0 = s, a_i, s'] = r_i(s, a_i, s') + \gamma \sum P(s' \,|\, s, a_i) V_i(s', \pi_i) \tag{5.19}$$

The update equation which is suited to the local decision process as a function of the global state space is modified with the belief factor and is given by the following formula [BOU 09a]:

$$Q_i(s, a_i) \leftarrow Q_i(s, a_i) + \alpha\{R + \gamma \max_{a'_i}[Q_i(s', a'_i) + \xi B(s', a'_i)] - Q_i(s, a_i)\} \tag{5.20}$$

Where the parameter ξ is a sigmoid function of periods of time such that $\xi \geq 0$. The value of the parameter ξ increases with the number of agents which successfully accomplish the task in progress. The problem is non-stationary; we will chose a rate of learning α, which is constant, $\alpha \in [0, 1]$. Usually $\gamma \in [10,1]$ and if:

– $\gamma = 0$ then future rewards are ignored in favor of immediate rewards;

– $\gamma = 1$ then future rewards are as important as immediate rewards (ant agent).

The optimal policy for each agent i may be obtained by using the following formula:

$$V_i(s_1, \ldots, s_n, \pi_i^*) = \max_{a_i} Q_i^* (s_1, \ldots, s_n, a_n) \tag{5.21}$$

Learning in a multi-agent system must take interaction between the agents into consideration. Individual actions cannot be considered independent from actions by other agents, because their consequences are interdependent. When only one agent uses RL, it can converge to an optimal policy when faced with stationary agents. However, when faced with non-stationarity, which has been induced by other agents, monoagent RL does not allow us to take the presence of other agents into account. To achieve this, we calculate the optimal Q function Q* of the multi-agent system as the combination of the optimal Q-functions Q_i* learnt by each agent of an MMDP with decentralized control. Each agent may have a different estimation of these values, depending on its level of belief in the policy of the other agents. In order to take the presence of other agents into account, we adapt these values by an estimation factor $\omega_i(s, a_i)$ calculated by using the following formula:

$$\omega_i(s, a_i) = \frac{exp(h_i(s,a_i)/\eta)}{\sum_{j=1}^{n} exp(h_j(s,a_i)/\eta)} \qquad [5.22]$$

Where exp is the exponential function, $h_i(s, a_i)$ is the number of updates of the estimations carried out by the agent i executing the action a_i on the state $(s_1, ..., s_n)$ and η is an adjustable parameter. Thus, the optimal Q-value is given by the following formula:

$$Q^*(s_1, ..., s_n, a_1, ..., a_n) = \sum_{i=1}^{n} \omega_i(s, a_i)Q_i^*(s_1, ..., s_n, a_i) \qquad [5.23]$$

At the end of learning, an optimal policy may be derived in the following way:

$$\pi^*(s_1, ..., s_n) = argmax_{(a_1,...,a_n)} Q^*(s_1, ..., s_n, a_1, ..., a_n) \qquad [5.24]$$

Learning algorithm:

We suggest an algorithm which extends monoagent Q-learning to a multi-agent context. This extension takes the influence of the actions of other agents into account through the definition of conjoint Q-values $Q_i(s, a_1,..., a_n)$ for each agent i. In monoagent learning, the Q-learning converges toward the optimal policy, which consists of choosing the optimal action to be carried out, independent of the action selection strategy. In the multi-agent context, this selection strategy determines convergence.

In phase 1 of the algorithm, the agent determines the action that it should carry out as a function of the state s it is currently in. Even though the strategy ε-greedy is very popular in RL, or at least in the exploration phase where an action selected at random may not be good, this method cannot lead to good results in cases where carrying out such an action can have very negative consequences. To improve exploration and prioritize it at the start of learning, we have chosen to use a selection strategy based on Boltzmann distribution [KAP 02]. Thus, the probability of choosing this action is written as:

$$\pi_i(s, a_i) = \frac{exp\left(Q_i(s,a_i)/T\right)}{\Sigma_{a_i' \in A_i} exp\left(Q_i(s,a_i')/T\right)} \qquad [5.24]$$

where T is the distribution temperature. The value of this parameter determines the possibility for an agent to find an equilibrium between exploration and exploitation. When T is high, distribution is almost uniform, when $T \to 0$ the policy becomes greedy. In practice, we decrease temperature, which allows us to modulate exploration and exploitation without making an explicit distinction between these two phases. We consider the factor T, defined as a function of iterations, given by:

$$T(x) = (e^{-sx} * T_{max}) + 1$$

where x is the iteration number, s is the rate of reduction and T_{max} is the initial value of T.

Below is our optimal action learning algorithm for multi-agent systems.

Phero-Q multi-learning algorithm

Repeat
Initialize s = (s$_1$,...,s$_n$)
   Repeat
      For each agent i
      Choose a$_i$ using Boltzmann formula
      Execute action a$_i$, observe reward r$_i$ and state s'

$$Q_i(s, a_i) \leftarrow Q_i(s, a_i) + \alpha\{R + \gamma \max_{a'_i}[Q_i(s', a'_i) + \xi B(s', a'_i)] - Q_i(s, a_i)\}$$

      s←s'
   Until s is terminal
Until algorithm converges

In a multi-agent system, the Markov property is no longer verified because the learning agent cannot totally observe the state of the environment. In order to gather information on the states of other agents, we use mobile agents (ants) which allow us to provide information to an agent on the value of the state of other agents in the system. A belief factor will be attached to this value and will allow us to measure the credibility of the information for use in decision-making.

5.6. Q-learning with approximation

Q-learning is quite simple in principle and in application. However, one of the main problems encountered is that of visiting all the state-action pairs. This becomes quite difficult if there is a combinatory explosion of state spaces and actions when the number of agents increases. The Q function table becomes large and the Q-learning algorithm, therefore, requires a relatively long learning time to update all Q-values. This fact makes the implementation of the algorithm in real-time control architecture difficult. To overcome this problem it is appropriate to interpolate the value of the Q function by replacing the Q-table with a Multilayer perceptron (MLP). The MLP is a multilayer artificial neural network used to approximate the Q function. The advantage of this approximation is that it makes it possible to obtain a continuous estimation of the function. In terms of storage needs, the approach requires fewer storage memories for saving the neuron network weights. Its input variables are the state spaces of the queues and the actions, which have n and m dimensions, respectively. The output from the network corresponds to the Q-value for current states and actions. The number of hidden layers depends on the complexity of the function Q. Figure 5.2 shows the schema of such a network. The technique used to learn the Q function is the back-propagation algorithm [HAY 99]. This algorithm uses the error between the output neuron and the desired response to adjust the weights of the network.

Thus, the NQ-learning algorithm combines two learning processes. It is important to note that these two learning processes run simultaneously, interacting directly with each other. In the first process, the execution of the Q-learning algorithm leads to the update of the Q-values in order to converge to the optimal Q function. In the second process, the neural network algorithm updates its weights to approximate the Q-values. When optimality is not reached, both processes update the weights of the network to achieve the learning objectives. This duality in learning could affect the stability and convergence of the NQ-learning algorithm [BOU 07, BOU 09b].

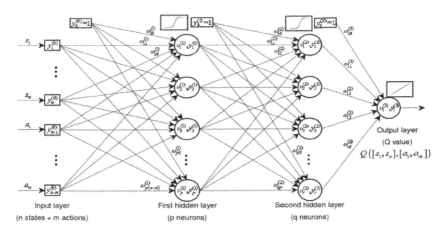

Figure 5.2. *Approximation of the Q-function. The input layer is made up of states and actions. The output layer has a single neuron which contains the Q-value for current entry values*

Each node in each layer calculates its activation as the weighted sum of its inputs as a function of:

$$\mu_j = \sum_i x_j w_{ij} \qquad [5.26]$$

where x_j is the ith input to the node j and w_{ij} is the weight of the synapses which link the node i to the node j from a higher level. A common activation function for the MLP is the sigmoid function, applied to the hidden layer:

$$\sigma(y) = (1 + e^{-y})^{-1} \qquad [5.27]$$

The technique used for learning the Q-function is the back-propagation algorithm [VAM 05], which uses the error between the output neuron and the required response to adapt the synaptic weights W of the network. The update of the weights may be expressed by a descent in the gradient, where the weights are adjusted, at each iteration, by the value of:

$$\Delta w = -\eta \frac{\partial E}{\partial w} \qquad [5.27]$$

Where η is the rate of learning. To calculate the desired response of the neuron network, we use the equation:

$$Q(s,a) = R + \gamma \max_{a'_i}[Q_i(s',a'_i) + \xi B(s',a'_i)] \qquad [5.29]$$

The network error is propagated backward through the network of neurons, from the output to the input of the space, where, at each node, we aim to make the output y_k correspond as much as possible to the desired output t_k. The error δ_k, for the output nodes k, may be calculated as follows:

$$\delta_k \leftarrow y_k(1 - y_k)(t_k - y_k) \qquad [5.30]$$

For the hidden nodes h, δ_h may be calculated as follows:

$$\partial_h \leftarrow y_h(1 - y_h)\sum_{k \, \epsilon \, outputs} w_{kh}\delta_k \qquad [5.31]$$

The back-propagation algorithm of the gradient propagates the mean quadratic error of the pair <actual, desired> backward through the network, by updating the weighting coefficients so as to reduce the mean quadratic error and, thus, to make the real network output (y_k) correspond to the desired output (t_k) as far as possible.

$$E(w) = \frac{1}{2}\sum_{k \, \epsilon \, outputs}(t_k - y_k)^2 \qquad [5.32]$$

Initially, the network weighting values are random. Subsequently a set of pairs ⟨inputs, outputs⟩ is used to build the weightings of the network. During this process, the weightings are adjusted as a function of the weighting updates carried out in line with the gradient descent, up to convergence of the mean quadratic error.

Evaluation

We adopt a multi-agent view of the communication network, where each router is represented by an agent. In the routers, the queues are classified according to priority, where the highest-priority queue is that which contains the flows with strict temporal constraint. The goal of an adaptive optimal scheduling is to serve a queue depending on its priority level, as a function of the variable conditions of the network and such that we ensure that the flows proceed, while guaranteeing their QoS constraints.

Our evaluation was carried out in two phases. The first phase consists of scheduling queues at the level of a router. At this level, the problem can be solved using an MDP which converges toward the optimal solution. The second phase allows us to solve the global problem concerning the optimization of the end to end delay through an optimization of all the delays in the queues.

Case of a sole agent

Let Q_1, Q_2,..., Q_n be queues, each of which is accorded a priority which links to the QoS criterion required by the type of flow it contains. Q_n denotes the best-effort traffic queue. Let R_1,..., R_{n-1} be the delay constraints of the queues Q_1,..., Q_{n-1} and M_1,..., M_{n-1} their measured delays. The goal is to learn a scheduling policy for these queues that ensures that $M_i \leq R_i$, for $i = 1$,..., n-1.

Action space:

$A = \{a_1,..., a_n\}$ where a_i is the action of serving the first packet in the queue i, for $1 \leq i \leq n$

State space:

$$S = \{s_1,..., s_{n-1}\} \text{ where } s_i = \begin{cases} 0, M_i \leq R_i \\ 1, M_i > R_i \end{cases}$$

Reward function:

$$r_i = (M_i - R_i)^+ = \begin{cases} 0 & \text{if} \quad M_i \leq R_i \\ M_i - R_i \text{ if} \quad M_i > R_i \end{cases}$$

The total reward is defined by the weighted sum of the reward for each queue:

$$r_{del} = \sum_{i=1}^{n} \omega_i r_i$$

where ω_i, $0 < \omega \leq 1$ for $1 \leq i \leq n\text{-}1$

The weightings allow the scheduler to handle the queues in situations where there is insufficient return. To guarantee QoS, the mean delay measured must be equal or as close as possible to the constraint of the mean delay. The scheduling policy consists of serving the priority queue (choosing that which has a strict delay constraint), while taking the variable network conditions into account. This involves maximizing gain and, as a result, minimizing delay. The reward on the delay constraint would then be: $(-r_{del})$. We also define a positive reward when the available bandwidth is allocated to delay-sensitive traffic. We denote this reward by r_{bw}. Let $r_{bw,i}$ be the reward for each queue i such that:

$$r_{bw,i} = \begin{cases} K & \text{if } R_i \leq \min R_j \forall\ j=1,n\text{-}1 \text{ and } i \neq j \\ 0 & \text{if not} \end{cases}$$

$$r_{bw} = \sum_{i=1}^{n-1} \psi_i r_{bw,i}$$

Where $0 < \psi_i \leq 1\ \forall\ i = 1, n - 1$ and K is a constant. The total reward is:

$$r = -r_{del} \times r_{bw}$$

the maximum reward value is zero. It is produced when the mean delay constraints for all traffic classes are satisfied.

Learning algorithm:

The following algorithm gives the learning of the optimal policy for an agent. The function ChoiceAction(s, T) selects, according to the Boltzmann distribution of temperature T, an action from the set of possible actions in the state s.

Monoagent algorithm:

Initialize Q(s, a) = 0 for any s and a
Repeat the following steps until goal satisfaction
a ← choiceAction (s, T) // *s is the current state and T is the temperature*
s' ← execute (a)
Consider the next state s' and assign reward r
Update Q values according to the following rule

$$Q(s,a) \leftarrow Q(s,a) + \alpha \left[r(s,a) + \gamma \max_{a'} Q(s',a') - Q(s,a) \right]$$

s←s'
Until s is terminal

In the simulation phase, we consider two scenarios according to the available quantity of bandwidth and use a three-queue system Q_1, Q_2 and best-effort. In the first scenario, we assume that there is a sufficient quantity of bandwidth for all three queues. In this case, the algorithm equitably distributes the bandwidth depending on the needs of each queue (see Figure 5.3). The second scenario refers to the case where there is insufficient bandwidth (Figure 5.4). The bandwidth is then allocated first, as a priority, to the delay-sensitive traffic (Q_1). Tables 5.1 and 5.2 summarize the simulation parameters for the two scenarios; Table 5.1 for the first scenario, and Table 5.2 for the second scenario.

Queue	Arrival rate packets/time slot)	Mean delay constraints	EBi Kbps
Q_1	0.30	8	64
Q_2	0.20	2	128
Best-effort	0.40	Best-effort	Best-effort

Table 5.1. *Simulation parameters (scenario 1)*

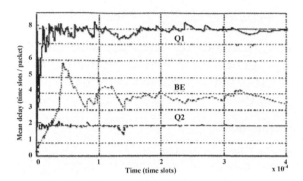

Figure 5.3. *Mean delay for two classes of traffic*

Queue	Arrival rate packets/time slot)	Mean delay constraints	EBi Kbps
Q_1	0.30	4	128
Q_2	0.20	6	256
Best-effort	0.40	Best-effort	Best- effort

Table 5.2. *Simulation parameters (scenario 2)*

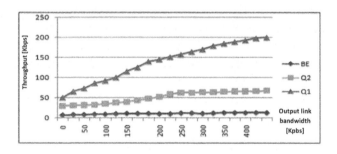

Figure 5.4. *Mean flow rate for two classes of traffic*

Multi-agents case

We evaluate our approach (Phero-Q multi-agent algorithm) by considering, for this second phase, a multi-agent system (network with four routers), which aims to achieve an optimal scheduling strategy allowing it to serve priority queues and optimize the delay of a source to a destination. The problem is modeled by an MMDP with decentralized control, where mobile agents (ant colony) provide additional necessary information on the global state. These agents collect and distribute the information which is necessary for updating knowledge on the environment. Figures 5.5 and 5.6 show that, these mobile agents allow us to improve the incomplete observation by agents about the environment.

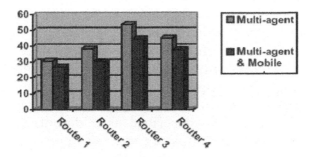

Figure 5.5. *Mean delay through the network (scenario 1)*

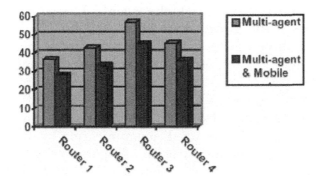

Figure 5.6. *Mean delay through the network (scenario 2)*

5.7. Conclusion

We have suggested a theoretical decision-making framework for modeling the problem of scheduling packets in a dynamic environment, represented by a multi-agent system. We have placed our emphasis on cooperative systems, in which the agents share the same aim of maximizing the total forecast reward. More particularly, we have used a local MDP to describe the state space of each agent and the actions of the space. In order to take the cooperative nature of the system into account, a global reward function is used to describe the relationship and the dependency on states of the agent. In our model, we assume that each agent knows its current state, in other words, the local state of the agent is immediately (entirely) observable. The issue here is finding the set of local policies (a policy for each agent) which produces the maximal forecast global reward. This defines a multi-agent decision process which may be described as a decentralized MDP, shown to be a NEXP-complete complexity problem [BER 00]. One limitation of a decentralized MDP lies in the fact that it does not take on the agent's communication. Our model is close to the MMDP framework suggested by Boutilier [BOU 99], which considers that the agents have, at all times, knowledge of the global state of the system. The advantage of this principle means that the system can be modeled by a classical MDP. However, it does not reflect the "multi-agent" nature of the system in which an agent cannot directly observe the local state of the other agents. In this case, it must use communication so that information on this state can be shared. We have used communication by mobile agent as our communication system. A potentially interesting direction for future study might be the study of a formal basis for coordination in a multi-agent system, so that an optimal global decision can be reached.

5.8. Acknowledgment

We extend our special thanks to Nasreddine Yousfi (LSV – ENS – Cachan) for all of his suggestions.

5.9. Bibliography

[AND 94] ANDERSON C., CRAWFORD-HINES S., Multigrid Q-learning, Technical report CS-94-121, Colorado State University, Fort Collins, CO, 1994.

[ANK 01] ANKER T., COHEN R., DOLEV D., *et al.*, "Probabilistic fair queuing", *IEEE 2001 Workshop on High Performance Switching and Routing*, pp. 397–401, 2001.

[BAT 08] BATTITI R., BRUNATO M., MASCIA F., *Reactive Search and Intelligent Optimization*, Operations Research/Computer Science Interfaces, Springer Verlag, vol. 45, p. 1, 3, 7, 2008.

[BEL 57] BELLMAN R.E., *Dynamic Programming*, Princeton University Press, Princeton, NJ, 1957.

[BER 00] BERNSTEIN D., ZILBERSTEIN S., "The complexity of decentralized control of mdps", UAI, pp. 819–840, 2000.

[BLA 98] BLAKE S., BLACK D., CARLSON M., *et al.*, An architecture for differentiated services, Technical report RFC 2475, IETF, December 1998.

[BEC 03] BECKER R., ZILBERSTEIN S., LESSER V., *et al.*, "Transition-independent decentralized Markov decision processes", *Proceedings of the 2nd International Joint Conference on Autonomous Agents and Multi Agent Systems*, ACM Press, Melbourne, Australia, pp. 41–48, July 2003.

[BOU 99] BOUTILIER G., "Sequential optimality and coordination in multiagent systems", *Proceedings of the 16th International Joint Conference on Artificial Intelligence (IJCAI '99)*, pp. 478–485, 1999.

[BOU 07] BOURENANE M., MELLOUK A., BENHAMAMOUCH D., "A QoS-based scheduling by neurodynamic learning", *System and Information Sciences Journal*, vol. 2, no. 2, pp. 138–142, July 2007.

[BOU 09a] BOURENANE M., MELLOUK A., BENHAMAMOUCH D., "State-dependent packet scheduling for QoS routing in a dynamically changing environment", *Telecommunication Systems Journal*, vol. 42, pp. 249–261, 2009.

[BOU 09b] BOURENANE M., MELLOUK A., BENHAMAMOUCH D., "A neurodynamic approach for a packet scheduling in IP-routers", *International Transactions on Systems Science and Applications (ITSSA)*, vol. 5, no. 4, pp. 149–155, December 2009.

[BRA 94] BRADEN R., CLARK D., SHENKER S., Integrated services in the Internet architecture: an overview, Technical report RFC 1633, IETF, June 1994.

[BRA 97] BRADEN B., Resource reservation protocol (RSVP) – version 1 functional specification, Technical report RFC 2205, IETF, September 1997.

[CHA 97] CHAUDHRY S., CHOUDHARY A., "Tune dependent priority scheduling for guaranteed QoS Systems", *Proceedings of the 6th International Conference on Computer Communications and Networks*, pp. 236–241, September 1997.

[CHI 89] CHIPALKATTI R., KUROSE J.F., TOWSLEY D., "Scheduling policies for real-time and non-real-time traffic in a statistical multiplexer", *Proceedings of IEEE Infocom '89*, Ottawa, pp. 774–783, 1989.

[DAY 92] DAYAN P., "The convergence of td(λ) for general λ", *Machine Learning*, vol. 8, no. 3–4, pp. 341–362, 1992.

[DEM 89] DEMERS A., KESHAVT S., SHENKER S., "Analysis and simulation of fair queuing algorithm", *Proceedings of ACM SIGCOMM Symposium on Communication Architectures and Protocols*, pp. 3–12, September 1989.

[GOM 98] GOMIDE F., PEDRYCZ W., *An Introduction to Fuzzy Sets – Analysis and Design*, MIT Press, Cambridge, 1998.

[HAL 98] HALL J., MARS P., "Satisfying QoS with a learning based scheduling algorithm", *6th International Workshop on Quality of Service (IWQoS)*, Nappa, pp. 171–176, 1998.

[HAY 99] HAYKIN S., *Neural Networks, A Comprehensive Foundation*, Prentice Hall, 2nd ed., 1999.

[HOL 75] HOLLAND J.H., *Adaptation in Natural and Artificial Systems*, University of Michigan Press, Ann Arbor, MI, 1975.

[HUI 00] HUITEMA C., *Routing in the Internet*, 2nd ed., Prentice Hall PTR, Upper Saddle River, NJ, 2000.

[ITU 94] ITU, "ITU-T recommendation E.800: terms and definitions related to quality of service and network performance including reliability", ITU-T recommendation E.800, August 1994.

[JAC 55] JACKSON J., Scheduling a production line to minimize maximum tardiness, Research report no. 43, Management Science Research Project, University of California, Los Angeles, CA, 1955.

[JAK 93] JAKKOLA T., JORDAN M., SINGH S., "On the convergence of stochastic iterative dynamic programming", *Neural Computation*, vol. 6, pp. 1185–1201, 1993.

[KAP 02] KAPETANAKIS S., KUDENKO D., "Reinforcement learning of coordination in cooperative multi-agent systems, *Proceedings of the 19th National Conference on AAAI*, pp. 326–331, 2002.

[KLE 79] KLEINROCK L., *Queueing Systems, Volume 1: Theory*, John Wiley & Sons, Hoboken, NJ, 1979.

[LIU 73] LIU C.L., LAYLAND J.W., "Scheduling algorithms for multiprogramming in a hard-real-time environment", *Journal of the ACM*, vol. 20, no. 1, pp. 46–61, January 1973.

[MIT 97] MITCHELL T., *Machine Learning*, McGraw-Hill, New York, 1997.

[MON 04] MONEKOSSO N., REMAGNINO P., "The analysis and performance evaluation of the pheromone Q-learning algorithm", *Expert Systems*, vol. 21. no. 2, pp. 80–91, 2004.

[MUN 94] MUNAKATA T., JANI Y., "Fuzzy systems: an overview", *Communications of the ACM*, vol. 37, no. 3, p. 6976, March 1994.

[NAG 87] NAGLE J., "On packet switches with infinite storage", *Communications, IEEE Transactions on [legacy, pre – 1988]*, vol. 35, no. 4, pp. 435–438, 1987.

[NAJ 94] NAJIM K., POZNYAK A.S., *Learning Automata: Theory and Applications*, Pergamon Press, 1994.

[NAR 74] NARENDRA K.S., THATHCHAR M.A.L., "Learning automata – a survey", *IEEE Transactions on Systems, Man and Cybernetics*, vol. SMC-4, no.8, pp. 323–334, July 1974.

[OBA 98] OBAIDAT M.S., "Artificial neural networks: characteristics, structures, and applications", *IEEE Transactions on Systems, Man and Cybernetics*, Part B: cybernetics, vol. 28, no. 4, pp. 489–495, August 1998.

[PAP 94] PAPADIMITRIOU G.I., "A new approach to the design of reinforcement schemes for learning automata: stochastic estimator learning algorithms", *IEEE Transactions on Knowledge and Data Engineering*, vol. 6, no. 4, pp. 649–654, August 1994.

[PAR 93] PAREKH A., GALLAGER R.G., "A generalized processor sharing approach to flow control in integrated services networks: the single-node case", *IEEE/ACM Transactions On Networking*, vol. 1, pp. 1234–1256, June 1993.

[PAR 94] PAREKH A., GALLAGER R., "A generalized processor sharing approach to flow control in integrated services networks: the multiple node case", *IEEE/ACM Transactions on Networking*, vol. 2, pp. 137–150, April 1994.

[PIN 04] PINEY J.R., SALLENT S., "Performance evaluation of a normalized EDF service discipline," *Proceedings of the IEEE Melecon 2004*, Dubrovnik, Croatia, May 2004.

[PUT 94] PUTERMAN M.L., *Markov Decision Processes*, John Wiley & Sons, New York, 1994.

[SAN 02] SANJAY K., HASSAN M., *Engineering Internet Qos*, Artech House, Inc., Norwood, MA, 2002.

[SIN 95] SINGH S.P., JAAKKOLA T., JORDAN M.I., "Reinforcement learning with soft state aggregation", in TESAURO G., TOURETZKY D., LEEN T. (eds.), *Advances in Neural Information Processing Systems*, Denver, CO, pp. 361–368, 1995.

[SUT 88] SUTTON R.S., "Learning to predict by the methods of temporal differences", *Machine Learning*, vol. 3, pp. 9–44, 1988.

[SUT 98] SUTTON R.S., BARTO A.G., *Reinforcement Learning: An Introduction*, MIT Press, Cambridge, MA, 1998.

[TOU 98] TOUTAIN F., "Ordonnancement de paquets équitable par les disciplines GPS et DGPS", *Annals of Telecommunications*, vol. 53, no. 9–10, pp. 126–145, 1998.

[VAM 05] VAMPLEW P., OLLINGTON R., "Global versus local constructive function approximation for on-line reinforcement learning", *The Australian Joint Conference on Artificial Intelligence*, Sydney, Australia, pp. 5–8, December 2005.

[WAN 01] WANG Z., *Internet QoS: Architecture and Mechanisms for Quality of Service*, Morgan Kaufmann Publishers, 2001.

[WAN 02] WANG S., WANG Y., LIN K., "Integrating priority with share in the priority-based weighted fair queuing scheduler for real-time networks", *Journal of Real-Time Systems*, pp. 119–149, January 2002.

[WAT 89] WATKINS C.J.C.H., "Learning with delayed rewards", PhD dissertation, Psychology Department, Cambridge University, 1989.

[WAT 92] WATKINS C.J.C.H., DAYAN P., "Q-learning", *Machine Learning*, vol. 8, no. 3, pp. 279–292, 1992.

[ZAI 01] ZAI K., ZHANG Y., VINIOTIS Y., "Achieving end-to-end delay bounds by EDF scheduling without traffic shaping," *Proceedings of Infocom'01*, 2001.

[ZHA 90] ZHANG L., "Virtual clock: a new traffic control algorithm for packet switching networks", *Proceedings of Sigcomm '90*, pp. 19–29, 1990.

[ZOR 10] ZORIC S., BOLIC M., "Fairness of scheduling algorithms for real-time traffic in DiffServ based networks," *Proceedings of 15th IEEE Mediterranean Electrotechnical Conference (MELECON 2010)*, pp. 1591–1596, 2010.

6

Scheduling in Networks

6.1. Introduction

Real-time systems distributed around a network can be found in many current applications such as embedded electronic systems (in vehicles around a controller area network (CAN) network and in airplanes around an avionics full duplex switched Ethernet (AFDX) network), automated production systems in which the sensors, actuators and controllers are interconnected through fieldbuses or industrial Ethernet, interactive and multimedia applications on the Internet, etc. The validation of the temporal correctness of these distributed real-time systems requires not only to study the problem of the scheduling of tasks on CPUs, but also the scheduling of messages in the network. For instance, the end-to-end transmission of a message, generated by a task and consumed by another distant one, is often subject to a deadline constraint. The underlying network then has to provide a Quality-of- Service guarantee (for example, that the response time of the network has to be bounded) in order to adequately schedule the transmission of the messages.

Chapter written by Ye-Qiong SONG.

Message scheduling in networks is not new and can be retraced to the 1960s with the development of packet data transmission networks and the pioneering works of L. Kleinrock on Advanced Research Projects Agency Network (ARPANET). Aside from the natural scheduling of packets in first-in-first-out (FIFO), various scheduling policies have been studied, mainly under the angle of queueing theory [KLE 75] to evaluate stochastic performances. Since the 1990s, the Internet has become an indispensable support for increasingly diversified distributed applications. The issue of managing data flows with different priorities was then raised, and many scheduling algorithms have been developed, mainly the generalized processor sharing (GPS) [PAR 93] and weighted fair queuing (WFQ) algorithms [STI 98] that allow us to guarantee an upper bound on the response time of the packets if the input data flow is bounded by a "leaky-bucket" (we also refer to a (σ, ρ)-bounded input flow). Moreover, the network calculus approach that was founded by Rene Cruz [CRU 91a], [CRU 91b] provides a mathematical tool for evaluating the guaranteed performances. With respect to the real-time scheduling approach, as we will show in this chapter, this network calculus approach offers an alternative to the temporal validation of the messages through the calculation of an upper bound on the response times that is often higher than the worst-case response time. It has been, for instance, applied to the evaluation of the response times of messages traversing an AFDX (switched Ethernet avionics) network 7.

Parallel to the development of local computer networks (Ethernet, Token Ring, FDDI, etc.), the 1980s saw the appearance of a large number of works related to industrial networks, also called fieldbuses. The aim of these networks (often in bus topology), which are found at the field level of an automated production system for process control and automation, is to allow the exchange of data between the industrial sensors, actuators and controllers [THO 05]. Since they essentially have to transmit samples and control loop commands, supervision and alert data, aside from the physical robustness aspect of the network in order to operate in a hostile environment, the problem of real-time data transmission was raised for the first time. These networks are also qualified as "real-time networks". They often use a bus as a transmission medium shared by the set of stations. The scheduling of the messages is performed through the design of specific medium access control (MAC) protocols. In contrast with the MAC protocols found in local computer networks, the MAC protocols of fieldbuses manage messages of small size (sensor data and commands), of the mainly periodic traffic (related to the sampling periods of control loops) whose transmission is subject to real-time constraints (for instance, a sample has to be transmitted with a relative deadline that is typically smaller than or equal to the sampling period). Figure 6.1 shows an example of application of an Factory Instrumentation Protocol (FIP) fieldbus [THO 05]. Three sensors, two actuators and two controllers are interconnected by the FIP fieldbus.

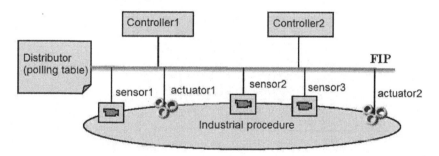

Figure 6.1. *Example of application of an FIP fieldbus*

In order to schedule the set of messages that to be exchanged through the bus, FIP assumes that the application is known in terms of the process state variables and commands. The sensors are variables that periodically produce data (values of the variables), the controllers are at the same time consumers of the sensors' data and producers of data (commands) for the actuators and the actuators are command data consumers. The scheduling of the periodic traffic is performed by a central station called a "distributor" or "bus arbitrator" through a polling table that can be easily configured offline. For instance, let us denote by $M_i(C_i, T_i)$ a variable with a transmission delay of C_i and period of T_i, let us consider a simple application composed of the following three variables: $A(1, 2)$, $B(1, 4)$ and $C(1, 8)$. We define an elementary cycle $CE = GCD(T_i)$ and a macro cycle $MC = LCM(T_i)$. The three variables can then be scheduled as shown in Figure 6.2.

The scheduling of real-time traffic can be achieved with the non-preemptive and offline scheduling of periodic tasks. The approach proposed by FIP assumes that the application is known *a priori* and does not evolve once it is configured. It is, therefore, not suited for cases where the application (or applications) is (are) partially known or evolves dynamically.

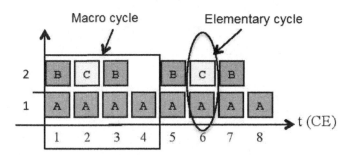

Figure 6.2. *FIP polling table of the example with the periodic variables A, B and C*

Today, in the field of industrial networking, there is a growing willingness to integrate a large number of services that share the same network and a need to dynamically adapt to the evolution of the traffic. It is for this reason that the industries are highly interested in the use of switched Ethernet that offers a greater bandwidth and a possibility to schedule real-time traffic. Chapter 7 gives an example of scheduling periodic message flows in this type of networks.

Embedded networks share certain characteristics common to industrial real-time networks. The two most widespread networks are CAN for vehicles and AFDX for avionics. This chapter shows how certain results of real-time task scheduling, introduced in the previous chapters, can be applied to the problem of scheduling real-time messages in networks. It also underlines certain specificities to consider, mainly the necessity to properly characterize network protocols and the fact that the transmission of a message in the form of a packet is in general not preemptable. This requires certain modifications in the existing method of analysis. Furthermore, as an alternative, we also introduce the calculation of the response times of the fixed-priority messages through the network calculus approach.

In what follows, we present the methods that can be used to validate fixed-priority scheduling of CAN messages, thus through an embedded automotive application case study.

6.2. The CAN protocol

CAN is a serial communication bus designed by Robert Bosch GmbH in 1983 to replace the point-to-point links between electronic control units (ECUs), which are increasingly numerous in vehicles. CAN was then standardized in 1993 by ISO under the number ISO 11898-1.

The CAN bus is a transmission medium shared by all the nodes it connects. From this fact, a specific MAC protocol is designed to separate competing accesses to the bus, with the concept of priority.

Each message on CAN is identified by a unique identifier (encoded on 11 bits for CAN2.0A standard CAN, and on 29 bits for CAN2.0B extended CAN). Here, the concept of message is analogous with the concept of variable in a fieldbus, and its contents are the same as the value of the variable. Due to the unique identifier, all the messages have different properties. Thus, CAN is called a "prioritized bus". Table 6.1 gives the format of a CAN frame.

Length (bit)	1	11/29	1	2	4	0-64	16	2	7
field	SOF	Identifier	RTR	Reserved	DLC	Data	CRC	ACK	EOF

Table 6.1. *Format of a CAN frame*

Where:

– Start of frame (SOF): bit at the beginning of the frame (dominating bit);

– Identifier: identifier of the message in 11/29 bits (CAN2.0A/2.0B);

– Remote transmission request (RTR): type of frame (data or request);

– Reserved: 2 bits reserved for future extension of the protocol. "00" in CAN 2.0;

– Data length code (DLC): length of the data field (in bytes);

– Data: between 0 and 8 data bytes;

– Cyclic redundancy code (CRC): polynomial checksum in 15 bits + 1 delimiting bit;

– Acknowledgment (ACK): 1 bit overwritten by the other nodes + 1 delimiting bit;

– End of frame (EOF): 7 bits ending the frame followed by a 3 bit-time interframe space.

Furthermore, the physical layer adopts the non-return to zero (NRZ) code with high voltage as a "logical 1" and zero voltage as a "logical 0". If two nodes transmit, each a different bit, at the same time, the result on the bus is zero voltage (logical 0). By this fact, we say that the nodes are wired on the bus by the "logic and wiring" principle from a logical point of view, which means that in case of a simultaneous emission of frames from two nodes, the value 0 overrides the value 1. We say that the logical state 0 is the "dominating" state, while the logical state 1 is the "recessive" state.

The MAC protocol of CAN follows the same principle of carrier sense multiple access (CSMA). In other words, each node listens if the medium is free before transmission. It continues to listen during the transmission in order to detect an eventual collision by comparing what it has heard on the medium with what it has sent. In contrast to Ethernet's CSMA/CD, collisions can be resolved due to an "identifier" field. In fact, CSMA is applied on a bit-level in CAN (instead of a frame-level as in Ethernet), thus allowing each emitting node to know whether it is in collision when it detects a difference between what it has sent and what it has heard on the medium (due to a logical AND of NRZ). Consequently, the unique identifier allows the smallest identifier (and therefore, the highest priority one) to gain access in case of simultaneous transmissions. Figure 6.3 gives an example of bit-by-bit arbitration in the case of the simultaneous transmission of two CAN messages.

It has to be noted that this bit-by-bit arbitration technique enforces keeping the bit-time duration long enough for each node of the network to be listening to the same bit for some amount of time. From this fact, it seriously reduces the possibility of increasing the throughput for a cable of given length, since this bit-time has to cover the entire length with at least two propagation times. From a conceptual point of view, determining the minimum duration of the bit-time is analogous to determining the minimum Ethernet frame size (64 bytes to be sure that the sender can detect a collision before the end of the transmission of the frame).

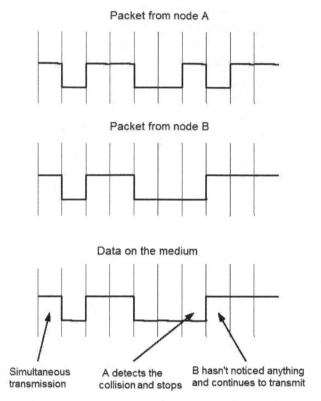

Figure 6.3. *Arbitration of CAN medium access*

Another consequence of using an NRZ is the risk of losing the synchronization between the sender and the receiver during the transmission of a large number of identical consecutive bits. Indeed, since the clocks are not synchronized, a receiver needs to regularly detect bit changes (transitions from 0 to 1 or from 1 to 0) in order to be synchronized with the rhythm of the sender. If that does not cause any problems with a biphase code (for instance, the Manchester code in which there is a transition at every bit), we have to be able to artificially create transitions from time to time in CAN. The CAN protocol uses the bit stuffing method. After five identical consecutive bits, the sender automatically inserts a different bit. This bit is removed when the data are received, as we can see in Figure 6.4.

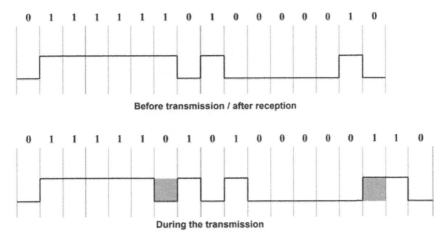

Figure 6.4. *The bit stuffing method*

It has to be noted that the "bit stuffing" principle is applied to the CAN frame from the beginning (SOF) until the CRC fields (excluding the CRC delimiter bit). Since the stuffing bit is itself also subject to the same principle of "counting until 5, then inserting a reverse bit", the worst case is inserting a stuffing bit after every four bits. It is clear that the stuffing bits increase the size of a frame, and therefore its transmission delays on the network.

Equation 6.1 gives the maximum transmission delay of a CAN frame of s_i bytes of data ($s_i = DLC$) in the case of a standard CAN whose identification is coded on 11 bits. The 3-bit interframe spacing is also included in it.

$$C_i = (\left\lfloor \frac{34 + 8 \times s_i}{4} \right\rfloor + 47 + 8 \times s_i)\tau_{bit} \qquad [6.1]$$

where τ_{bit} is the duration of a bit and $\lfloor \frac{a}{b} \rfloor$ is the integer part of the division a/b.

6.3. Example of an automotive embedded application distributed around a CAN network

The chosen intersystem network example comes from a case study proposed by PSA Peugeot–Citroën [SIM 06]. It implements a material architecture (ECUs connected on a CAN network with a throughput of 250 Kbit/s). The abstraction we have of this system is limited to the network and to the messages exchanged between the ECUs under hypotheses of message transmission by the tasks situated on each ECU. In the context of embedded automotive electronics, this part of the system is called a messaging system. The ECUs connected on the CAN are the following:

– CM: supports the tasks implementing engine control functions;

– ABS/CDS: the tasks related to ABS (antiblocking system) and ESP (stability control) are executed on this ECU;

– BSI: the dashboard gateway of the embedded system ; it serves as a gateway between various networks present in the architecture and transmits certain orders of the driver to the functions executing on other ECUs;

– SUS: the tasks implanted on this ECU are in charge of the control of the dynamic suspension;

– BVA: the tasks implanted on this ECU are related to the management of the automatic gearbox;

– SAS/HA: measure of the steering angle (steering angle sensor) and headlamp adjustment compose the two functionalities supported by this ECU.

Figure 6.5 gives a partial example of this system that shows the tasks in the CM and BVA nodes, as well as their generated and consumed messages.

We will limit ourselves to the analysis of the scheduling of the set of messages generated by this application. The specification of the messaging system, in other words the set of messages that passes through the CAN network is given in Table 6.2. This messaging system is entirely defined under hypotheses of periodicity of the transmission requests of the messages by the tasks situated on the ECUs mentioned above. The messages are classified by descending priorities (M_i has higher priority than M_j if $i < j$) ; for each message, we give its transmission source, ECU_i, which supports the task transmitting this message, s_i is the size in bytes of the useful data it contains (let us recall that, during the transmission of application information, additional fields are added to this information in order to create a "frame"; in the case of CAN networks, the real size of the frame is upper bounded by $\lfloor \frac{34+8 \times s_i}{4} \rfloor + 47 + 8 \times s_i$ bits), T_i is the period, in milliseconds, of the transmission of the message.

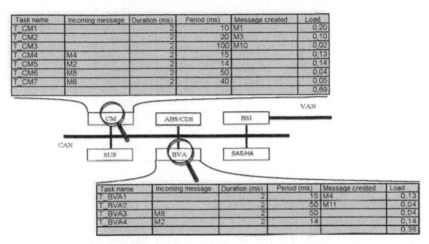

Task name	Incoming message	Duration (ms)	Period (ms)	Message created	Load
T_CM1		2	10	M1	0,20
T_CM2		2	20	M3	0,10
T_CM3		2	100	M10	0,02
T_CM4	M4	2	15		0,13
T_CM5	M2	2	14		0,14
T_CM6	M8	2	50		0,04
T_CM7	M6	2	40		0,05
					0,69

Task name	Incoming message	Duration (ms)	Period (ms)	Message created	Load
T_BVA1		2	15	M4	0,13
T_BVA2		2	50	M11	0,04
T_BVA3	M8	2	50		0,04
T_BVA4	M2	2	14		0,14
					0,36

Figure 6.5. *Example of a PSA application*

The second to last column in Table 6.2 gives C_i the transmission delay according to equation 6.1, in milliseconds, of the frame containing message M_i, with τ_{bit}, the transmission delay of one bit (in other words, $\tau_{bit} = \frac{1}{250}ms$ for a network throughput of 250 Kbits/s). Finally, in the last column, D_i represents the deadline imposed on the response time of each instance of the message M_i. We consider that the temporal property to verify is expressed by a constraint on the response time of each message: the duration between the transmission time of each instance of message M_i and the end of its transmission on the network has to be smaller than D_i. Let us note that with respect to the real application of PSA, this deadline is much lower than the period. It has been added in order to better illustrate the principle of the approach developed in the following section. Knowing that taking $D_i = T_i$ would not change anything in the method of analysis itself.

Message	ECU_i	s_i	T_i	C_i	D_i
M_1	CM	8	10	0.54	2
M_2	SAS/HA	3	14	0.34	2
M_3	CM	3	20	0.34	2
M_4	BVA	2	15	0.30	2.5
M_5	ABS/CDS	5	20	0.42	2.5
M_6	ABS/CDS	5	40	0.42	10
M_7	ABS/CDS	4	15	0.38	10
M_8	BSI	5	50	0.42	10
M_9	SUS	4	20	0.38	10
M_{10}	CM	7	100	0.50	10
M_{11}	BVA	5	50	0.42	10
M_{12}	ABS/CDS	1	100	0.2	100

Table 6.2. *Specification of the messaging system*

6.4. Response time analysis of CAN messages

The aim of a response time analysis of the messaging system above is to allow us to verify, by comparing with the deadlines of the messages, whether the set is schedulable or not. In this section, we present two approaches: the analysis of the worst-case response time, which arises from the real-time scheduling community, and the calculation of the bounds of the response times through the network calculus approach [CRU 91a], [CRU 91b], which arises from the networking community.

6.4.1. *Worst-case response time analysis method*

The first works applying the results of non-preemptive fixed-priority task scheduling to CAN were introduced by Tindell and Burns [TIN 94]. Since then, there have been numerous works extending this result, mainly by including transmission error handling into the calculation of the response time [NAV 00], [BRO 02]. The last result presented in [DAV 07] corrects an error in the initial formula introduced by Tindell and Burns [TIN 94] that did not take into account the fact that during a busy period of priority i, every instance of M_i has to be examined. The first instance is not always the one that incurs the most amount of delay, mainly due to the non-preemption. We present in the following the method introduced by Davis *et al.* [DAV 07].

Let us consider a set of N messages M_i with priorities $i(i = 1, 2, ..., N)$, with transmission delays C_i, periods T_i and jitters J_i, the calculation of the worst-case response time of the message M_i, denoted by R_i, is performed as follows.

We define t_i as the busy period of level i. Its evaluation is given by recurrence relation 6.2.

$$t_i^{n+1} = B_i + \sum_{j=1}^{i} \left\lceil \frac{t_i^n + J_j}{T_j} \right\rceil C_j \qquad [6.2]$$

where $\left\lceil \frac{a}{b} \right\rceil$ is the integer immediately greater than or equal to $\frac{a}{b}$. $B_i = \max_{i+1 \leq j \leq N}(C_j)$ is the blocking factor corresponding to the maximum time duration due to the wait for a frame with lower priority than i (let us note that this term does not exist in for calculating the lowest priority busy period N). This recurrence relation converges when the utilization rate (or the load), caused by the messages with higher or equal priority than i, does not exceed 1 (in other words, $\sum_{j \le i} \frac{C_j}{T_j} \le 1$). The calculation begins with $t_i^0 = C_i$ and stops at the convergence point when $t_i^{n+1} = t_i^n$.

Once the level-i busy period t_i is calculated, the method continues with the evaluation of Q_i, the number of messages with priority i arriving during the busy period.

$$Q_i = \left\lceil \frac{t_i + J_i}{T_i} \right\rceil \tag{6.3}$$

The next step consists of evaluating $w_i(q)$, the waiting delay of each message q ($q = 0, 1, ..., Q_i - 1$). The longest delay starting from the beginning of the busy period until the time when the qth message starts its transmission with success is given by equation 6.4.

$$w_i^{n+1}(q) = B_i + qC_i + \sum_{j=1}^{i-1} \left\lceil \frac{w_i^n(q) + J_j + \tau_{bit}}{T_j} \right\rceil C_j \tag{6.4}$$

This recurrence relation begins with the value $w_i^0(q) = B_i + qC_i$ and stops when $w_i^{n+1}(q) = w_i^n(q)$. Moreover, for values of $q > 0$, a more efficient starting point could be $w_i^0(q) = w_i(q - 1) + C_i$.

Finally, the response time of every message q is calculated by equation 6.5.

$$R_i(q) = J_i + w_i(q) - qT_i + C_i \tag{6.5}$$

The worst-case response time is then the maximum delay incurred by one of the q messages of the level-i busy period given by equation 6.6.

$$R_i = \max_{0 \le q \le Q_i - 1} (R_i(q)) \tag{6.6}$$

Let us note that equations 6.2–6.6 are general for calculating the worst-case response time, whether it be shorter or longer than the deadline. In our case, which imposes a deadline on each message, we can stop the calculations earlier when $J_i + w_i^{n+1}(q) - qT_i + C_i > D_i$, since in this case we know that the message is already unschedulable.

In [DAV 07], Davis *et al.* have also presented a simple numerical example that we reproduced here for pedagogical purposes (see Table 6.3).

Message	C_i	T_i	D_i
M_1	1	2.5	2.5
M_2	1	3.5	3.25
M_3	1	3.5	3.25

Table 6.3. *Numerical example of the CAN messaging system*

We illustrate the method on the worst-case response time of M_3. Since there are no lesser priority messages, $B_3 = 0$. Starting from $t_3^0 = C_3 = 1$, equation 6.2 gives the following iterations: $t_3^1 = 3$, $t_3^2 = 4$, $t_3^3 = 6$, $t_3^4 = 7$, $t_3^5 = 7 = t_3^4 = t_3$. The duration of the busy period is, therefore, equal to $7ms$. The number of instances of this message to be examined is given by equation 6.3: $Q_3 = \left\lceil \frac{7}{3,5} \right\rceil = 2$. The evaluation of the delay for the first instance of the message is first of all obtained by applying equation 6.4, and then equation 6.5. This gives: $w_3^0(0) = 0$, $w_3^1(0) = 2$, $w_3^2(0) = w_3^1(0) = 2 = w_3(0)$. And we obtain, $R_3(0) = 3$. For the second instance, we have: $w_3^0(1) = w_3(0) + C_3 = 3$, $w_3^1(1) = 4$, $w_3^2(1) = 5$, $w_3^3(1) = 6$, $w_3^4(1) = w_3^3(1) = 6 = w_3(1)$. Thus, we have $R_3(1) = 3, 5ms$. This finally gives the worst-case response time $R_3 = 3, 5ms$. Let us note that this response time exceeds the deadline that is fixed at $3, 25ms$ for M_3.

6.4.2. *Method of computing the response time bounds*

Instead of looking at the trajectory of the worst-case input streams (in other words, for periodic message streams, we seek to study the combination of the phase shifts of these streams that creates the longest response time), network calculus looks at replacing a periodic stream (arrival step function) by a linear curve that is an upper bound on the real arrival stream function. Hence, the approach based on network calculus results in a small overestimation of the response time (upper bound). Insofar as the network not being very loaded, this approach can provide a faster solution than the previously presented worst-case response time approach, even if it is less precise.

In order to provide Quality- of- Service in the networks, we use traffic limiters in input; it is under these hypotheses that a traffic model, referred to as (σ, ρ)-bounded, was proposed. This model is widely used in the Internet community for controlling the Quality-of-Service [LEB 01], since it is easy to implement in admission control mechanisms in order to estimate online the response times. This approach views the system as a set of N sources having cumulative arrival functions corresponding, for each source M_i, to a request of a quantity of resources (or a work request) $F_i(t)$ characterized by:

$$F_i(t) - F_i(s) \le \sigma_i + \rho_i(t - s); \ \forall 0 \le s \le t \qquad [6.7]$$

where σ_i represents the size of the maximum burst and ρ_i is the long-term average throughput of the ith source. The quantity of work brought by a packet generated by the source M_i, in other words, the number of bits to transmit on the network, is defined by W_i bits. We consider that a network has a throughput c (in bit/s).

Let us now consider a set of N (σ_i, ρ_i)-bounded sources $(i = 1, 2, ..., N)$ sharing a non-preemptive transmission medium with a transmission capacity of c bit/s, and the packets are served according to a fixed-priority policy. Let us recall that a packet of the source M_i has higher priority than a packet of M_j if and only if $i < j$. The bound of the response time $\hat{R}_i$ of a packet from the ith source (in other words, the one with priority equal to i) is obtained using the network calculus technique [LEB 01] and is defined by:

$$\hat{R}_i = \frac{\sum_{j=1}^{i} \sigma_j + \max_{i+1 \leq j \leq N}(W_j)}{c - \sum_{j=1}^{i-1} \rho_j} \qquad [6.8]$$

In order for $\hat{R}_i$ to be bounded, we need $c \geq \sum_{j=1}^{i} \rho_j$.

In order to apply this technique to a set of periodic messages, it is necessary, beforehand, to translate the periodic stream model $M_i = (C_i, T_i)$ to a traffic model $(\sigma, \rho) - bounded$), or in other words:

$-$ ρ_i, value of the long-term average throughput for a source M_i

$$\rho_i = \frac{W_i}{T_i} \qquad [6.9]$$

Let us note that, in order to evaluate W_i, it is sufficient to point out that the processing time C_i induced by each instance of M_i is due to a charge W_i for a network with a throughput of c ($C_i = W_i/c$). In other words, W_i is the size of the frame of M_i in our CAN example.

$-$ σ_i, the maximum size of the burst ; this is defined as the smallest value of σ_i that satisfies constraint 6.7. In general, the burst exists when the periodic traffic is disturbed by a variation of the jitter. The size of the burst then strongly depends on the values of the jitter. By considering the worst case, which corresponds to an arrival effectively generated J_i time units before the expected activation time, it has been shown in [KOU 04] that the optimal size of the burst (minimum σ_i that is an upper bound on the arrival curve) is given by:

$$\sigma_i = \frac{W_i}{T_i}(T_i + J_i) \qquad\qquad [6.10]$$

6.4.3. *Application to CAN messaging*

The two methods presented above are applied to the messaging in Table 6.2. We now add two columns corresponding to R_i (assuming zero jitter) and $\hat{R}_i$, as shown in Table 6.4.

We may note that each of the two techniques applied above allows us to obtain a bound on the response time and thus verify, in a deterministic way, whether a response time constraint is met or not. The worst-case response time analysis provides bounds that are smaller than or equal to those provided by the network calculus approach, and thus the results obtained by the latter are more pessimistic. Indeed, in the example presented here, it is not possible to obtain a deterministic guarantee on the response time of the message M_5 by applying the network calculus technique, while it is possible to guarantee it by the worst-case response time analysis approach. However, it has to be noted that the network calculus technique may take into account a more general traffic model (with an upper bound), including the periodic/sporadic traffic and be used to integrate online verifications (for instance, in admission control mechanisms in Quality-of-Service architectures), mainly due to its very low computational complexity.

Message	ECU_i	s_i	T_i	C_i	D_i	R_i	$\hat{R}_i$
M_1	CM	8	10	0.54	2	1.04	1.04
M_2	SAS/HA	3	14	0.34	2	1.38	1.46
M_3	CM	3	20	0.34	2	1.72	1.87
M_4	BVA	2	15	0.30	2,5	2.02	2.23
M_5	ABS/CDS	5	20	0.42	2,5	2.44	2.76
M_6	ABS/CDS	5	40	0.42	10	2.86	3.31
M_7	ABS/CDS	4	15	0.38	10	3.24	3.80
M_8	BSI	5	50	0.42	10	3.66	4.42
M_9	SUS	4	20	0.38	10	4.04	4.93
M_{10}	CM	7	100	0.50	10	4.46	5.57
M_{11}	BVA	5	50	0.42	10	4.72	5.93
M_{12}	ABS/CDS	1	100	0.2	100	4.72	6.00

Table 6.4. *Specification of the messaging system*

6.5. Conclusion and discussion

The scheduling of messages in networks can benefit from some of the results in monoprocessor task scheduling, but with the particularity of non-preemption. In this chapter, through an example of message scheduling in a CAN network, we have illustrated how the existing results in the calculation of the worst-case response time are extended in order to be applied to our case study. Furthermore, the approach of calculating the response time bounds using network calculus theory is also applied to the same case study. We may conclude that, depending on the needs, one or the other technique might be interesting when evaluating the response time of a set of streams of periodic messages.

What we have not discussed in this case study is the evaluation of the end-to-end delay. In other words, the beginning of a message-transmitting task and the end of execution of a message-receiving task. A so-called holistic approach exists. The same method presented in section 6.4.1 is applied in order to compute the worst-case response time of the task and of the message at the same time, since the two are linked together by the jitter. This method can lead to an overestimation of the delay, since the sequence of worst cases (transmitting task – message – receiving task) may never occur. A so-called "trajectory" method [MAR 04] can be used in this case, allowing to produce the real end-to-end delay for the worst-case trajectory. The idea is to consider the worst case of a stream on its entire path (if it is known), and not node by node. However, this approach presents an important complexity of analysis that makes it difficult to apply to large systems. Moreover, the identification of the worst-case trajectory constitutes an additional difficulty. In the same vein, the network calculus approach can be used to evaluate the end-to-end delay bound when a message has to traverse several network nodes (this is the case of switches or routers in a multi-hop network).

In this case, the same problem of overestimation is also raised when we chain the local end-to-end delay bounds of each node to obtain the global delay, even though applying the "Pay Multiplexing Only Once" principle that allows to mitigate the overestimation. In conclusion to this discussion on the evaluation of the end-to-end delay, there are indeed interesting techniques today, which, however, have to be used in a restrained manner with real industrial-size problems due to their large complexity. Chapter 7 presents an example of evaluating the response times of message traversing several AFDX switches.

Today, for satisfying the increasing needs in mobility and flexibility, industrial networks integrate more and more wireless technologies (industrial wireless networks, wireless sensor networks, etc.). The scheduling of messages in a wireless network raises new issues, mainly linked to the specificity of the protocols and to unreliable radio transmission nature. For instance, in order to save energy, a wireless sensor network adopts the principle of functioning by a cycle of activity/sleep (duty-cycle). One of the new functionalities of the MAC layer is to ensure the synchronization of the active period of a transmitting node with that of the receiving node (or relay node). Scheduling these active periods in a large-scale multihop network while providing a delay guarantee still remains a challenge [MAH 10]. When we consider a multihop "mesh" sensor network, the problem of scheduling the messages in the routers is another interesting point to study [NEF 12]. Indeed, how to locally schedule the messages waiting in a router in order to satisfy a global end-to-end response time still remains an open issue. In the framework of wired multihop networks, elements of an answer can be found in Chapter 5.

6.6. Bibliography

[BRO 02] BROSTER I., BURNS A., RODRIGUEZ-NAVAS G., "Probabilistic analysis of CAN with faults", *23rd IEEE Real-Time Systems Symposium (RTSS'02)*, pp. 269–278, 2002.

[CRU 91a] CRUZ R.L., "A calculus for network delay, part I: network elements in isolation", *IEEE Transactions on Information Theory*, vol. 37, no. 1, pp. 114–131, January 1991.

[CRU 91b] CRUZ R.L., "A calculus for network delay, part II: network analysis", *IEEE Transactions on Information Theory*, vol. 37, no. 1, pp. 132–141, January 1991.

[DAV 07] DAVIS R.I., BURNS A., BRIL R.J., *et al.*, "Controller area network (CAN) schedulability analysis: refuted, revisited and revised", *Real-Time Systems*, vol. 35, pp. 239–272, 2007.

[KLE 75] KLEINROCK L., *Queueing Systems. Volume 1: Theory*, vol. 1, John Wiley, 1975.

[KOU 04] KOUBÂ A.A., SONG Y.Q., "Evaluation and improvement of response time bounds for real-time applications under non pre-emptive fixed priority scheduling", *International Journal of Production Research*, vol. 42, no. 14, pp. 2899–2913, July 2004.

[LEB 01] LE BOUTEC J.Y., THIRAN P., *Network Calculus: A Theory of Deterministic Queuing Systems for the Internet*, Springer-Verlag, Lecture Notes in Computer Science edition, 2050, 2001.

[MAH 10] MAHFOUDH S., MINET P., AMDOUNI I., "Energy efficient routing and node activity scheduling in the OCARI wireless sensor network", *Future Internet*, vol. 2, no. 3, pp. 308–340, 2010.

[MAR 04] MARTIN S., Maîtrise de la dimenion temporelle de la qualité de service dans les réseaux., PhD thesis, Université Paris XII, 2004.

[NAV 00] NAVET N., SONG Y.Q., SIMONOT F., "Worst-case deadline failure probability in real-time applications distributed over CAN (controller area network)", *Journal of Systems Architecture – the EUROMICRO Journal*, vol. 46, pp. 607–617, 2000.

[NEF 12] NEFZI B., SONG Y.Q., "QoS for wireless sensor networks: enabling service differentiation at the MAC sub-layer using CoSenS", *Ad Hoc Networks*, vol. 10, no. 4, pp. 680–695, June 2012.

[PAR 93] PAREKH A.K., GALLAGER R.G., "A generalized processor sharing approach to flow control in integrated services networks: the single-node case", *IEEE/ACM Transactions on Networking*, vol. 1, no. 3, pp. 334–357, June 1993.

[SIM 06] SIMONOT-LION F., SONG Y.Q., BERTHOMIEU B., *et al.*, "*Encyclopédie de l'informatique et des systèmes d'information*", Chapter Vérification des applications temps réel, pp. 761–773, Vuibert, 2006.

[STI 98] STILIADIS D., VARMA A., "Latency-rate servers: a general model for analysis of traffic scheduling algorithms", *IEEE/ACM Transactions on Networking*, vol. 6, no. 5, pp. 611–624, October 1998.

[THO 05] THOMESSE J.P., "Fieldbus technology in industrial automation", *Proceedings of the IEEE*, vol. 93, no. 6, pp. 1073–1101, 2005.

[TIN 94] TINDELL K.W., BURNS A., "Guaranteeing message latencies on controller area network (CAN)", *1st International CAN Conference*, pp. 1–11, 1994.

7

Focus on Avionics Networks

Avionics full duplex switched Ethernet (AFDX) has become the standard for data exchange between avionic functions. It is a switched Ethernet network adapted to the constraints of civil avionics. It has replaced mono-transmitter buses, in particular since it allows us to considerably reduce the wiring and offers a much higher throughput. The flows share the communication links and can therefore be delayed at the output ports. The certification requires the guarantee that these delays can be bounded.

This chapter will summarize first the context of civil avionics and the main characteristics of AFDX. It will then detail the components of the delay incurred by a flow transmitted on an AFDX network. It will finally show the various approaches, which allow us to bound this delay.

7.1. Introduction

Avionics denotes the set of electronic control and command systems embedded on board an aircraft. This includes in particular the CPUs and their software, the sensors, the actuators and the interconnection between these elements.

Chapter written by Jean-Luc SCHARBARG and Christian FRABOUL.

Today, this interconnection is implemented by the AFDX network.

AFDX [ARI 05] is a full duplex switched Ethernet network, in other words a set of switches with Ethernet links supporting simultaneous transmissions from each end. This is not sufficient to guarantee that every frame will traverse the network in a bounded time. Indeed, each switch output port is shared by a set of flows. These flow convergences can lead to waiting delays at the output ports of the switches.

The certification of an avionics network is mandatory in a civil context. In particular, this requires knowing the worst-case end-to-end delay of every frame transmitted on the AFDX network. Such a worst case can be obtained in particular because the traffic generated by each flow is bounded.

The first solution to obtain this worst case consists of exploring every possible scenario. This exhaustive search has been, up to now, impossible for a realistic configuration including around a thousand flows, since the number of scenarios is huge. Research has shown that a small part of these scenarios present characteristics that can lead to the longest delay for a flow [ADN 11]. It is then possible to analyze a significant part of a realistic configuration (about two thirds of flows). The search space remains too large for a third of the remaining flows.

The second solution consists of determining an upper bound for this worst case. The principle is to define a model that includes all possible scenarios. Two approaches have been proposed to obtain this bound. The first approach is based on network calculus [LEB 01, BAU 10]. It has allowed the certification of the AFDX network embedded on board an A380. The second approach is based on the concept of trajectory followed by a flow [MAR 06, BAU 10].

Section 7.2 summarizes the historical evolution of avionic networks and presents the main characteristics of AFDX. Section 7.3 explains the components of the delay of a flow transmitted in an AFDX network. Section 7.4 illustrates the characteristics of a candidate worst-case scenario using an example. Section 7.5 shows how the network calculus and trajectory approaches take into account the set of scenarios candidate to the worst case. Section 7.6 summarizes the results of an analysis of a realistic configuration of type A380. Section 7.7 gives an assessment and shows some paths for the evolution of avionics networks and their analysis.

7.2. Avionics network architectures

Avionics denotes the set of electronic control and command systems embedded on board an aircraft. This includes, in particular, the CPUs and their software, the sensors, the actuators and the interconnection between these elements. Today, this interconnection is implemented by a switched Ethernet network, i.e. AFDX [ARI 05]. Section 7.2.1 summarizes the evolution of avionics network architectures up until the introduction of AFDX. The main features of the AFDX technology are then presented.

7.2.1. *Historical evolution*

In the 1950s, avionics was implemented by very simple systems that could be executed on a single CPU. Modern avionics appeared in the 1960s with the replacement of analogue components by their digital counterparts. This phenomenon continued to increase, with further, regular addition of new functions. These functions correspond to new needs or provide better solutions to existing problems. This increase in volume of avionics systems can be illustrated by the numbers corresponding to the A310 (1983) and A340 (1993). The number of embedded avionics systems has increased by around 50% – from 77 to 115 – and the computing power has been multiplied by 4 – from 60 to 250 Mips. This development of the avionics functions has led to an increase in communication needs.

These communication needs were first covered by ARINC 429 [ARI 01], which has been used for most Airbus and Boeing aircraft. It is a mono-transmitter bus allowing the transmission of frames containing four bytes of data with a throughput between 12.5 and 100 Kbps. An ARINC 429 link being point-to-multipoint and unidirectional, the avionics systems includes an ARINC 429 bus for every data to transmit. Furthermore, an ARINC 429 transmitter can transmit to up to 20 recipients. The considerable increase in the number of communication links therefore makes the use of the single ARINC 429 technology unacceptable in terms of weight and wiring complexity.

In the early 1990s, the concept of integrated modular avionics (IMA) [ARI 91, ARI 97] has introduced the sharing of execution and communication resources. Each subsystem is assigned one or more temporal windows on a shared execution unit. These subsystems exchange messages through communication ports that can be of two types: ports in *sampling* mode, in which only the last value of the data is stored and ports in *queuing* mode in which all the values are stored. We then define logical channels, which are multicast links (1 to n) between these communication ports. These logical channels are independent of the underlying communication technology. IMA was used for the first time by Boeing for the 777, coupled with the ARINC 629 communication technology. Airbus also introduced IMA for the A380, coupled with the ARINC 664 technology, or AFDX. ARINC 629 [ARI 99] is a multi-transmitter data bus whose implementation turned out to be too costly in the avionics context. AFDX [ARI 05] has therefore become the reference communication technology in the context of civil avionics, allowing the multiplexing of communication streams in a full duplex switched Ethernet network. We briefly present AFDX in the following section.

7.2.2. *The AFDX network*

AFDX [ARI 05] is a switched Ethernet network that takes into account the constraints of the avionics context. Figure 7.1 shows a small example of an AFDX configuration.

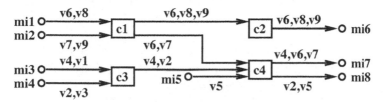

Figure 7.1. *A small AFDX network*

There are four switches $c1 \ldots c4$. A *first come first serve* queue is associated to each output port. The end systems ($mi1 \ldots mi8$ in Figure 7.1) compose the inputs and outputs of the network. Each end system is connected to exactly one port of the switch and each port of a switch is connected to at most one end system. All links are full duplex.

The traffic on the network is characterized by *virtual links* (VLs) that allow the static definition of flows entering the network. A VL defines a unidirectional logical connection between a source end system (mono-transmitter flow) and one or more destination end systems. In Figure 7.1, $v4$ is a unicast VL (path $mi3 - c3 - c4 - mi7$), while $v6$ is a multicast VL (paths $mi1 - c1 - c2 - mi6$ and $mi1 - c1 - c4 - mi7$). The routing of each VL is defined statically. Moreover, a VL v is defined by a *bandwidth allocation gap* ($BAG(v)$), a minimum frame length ($s_{min}(v)$) and a maximum frame length ($s_{max}(v)$). The BAG is the minimum delay between two consecutive frames of the associated VL. A VL therefore defines a sporadic flow.

7.3. Temporal analysis of an AFDX network

The embedded avionics network on board a civil aircraft has to be certified in order for the commercial exploitation of the plane to be authorized. It is particularly indispensable, first to bound the delay of every data transmission on this network, and second to guarantee that the output port queues of the switches never overflow.

Let us consider a path p_x of a VL v and a frame f of v transmitted on this path p_x. The end-to-end delay of f on p_x is denoted by $D(f, p_x)$. It is defined by:

$$D(f, p_x) = DL(f, p_x) + DC(f, p_x) + DP(f, p_x) \qquad [7.1]$$

$DL(F_v, p_x)$ is the transmission delay on the full duplex links (without collision). The transmission delay on a link is therefore $t_{byte} \times s_f$, t_{byte} being the transmission time of a byte and s_f the length in bytes of the frame f. If all the links of the network have the same throughput (100 Mbps in the case of AFDX), we therefore have, for a path p_x containing nbl_{p_x} links,

$$DL(f, p_x) = nbl_{p_x} \times (t_{byte} \times s_f) \qquad [7.2]$$

$DC(f, p_x)$ is the switching time between the input and output ports of the switches. In the context of AFDX, we consider in general that this delay takes a constant value dt (typically 16 μs). Therefore, we have, for a path p_x containing nbs_{p_x} switches,

$$DC(f, p_x) = nbs_{p_x} \times dt \qquad [7.3]$$

$DP(f, p_x)$ represents the time spent by the frame in the queues of the switches and the end systems. This time depends on the load of each output port at the time when the frame f reaches this port. We have

$$DP(f, p_x) = DP(f, p_x, mi_v) + \sum_{c_k \in \Psi_{p_x}} DP(f, p_x, c_k) \qquad [7.4]$$

where mi_v is the source end system of the VL v, Ψ_{p_x} is the set of switches contained in p_x, $DP(f, p_x, xx)$ is the delay in the queue of the output port of the component xx.

The end-to-end delay $D(f, p_x)$ therefore contains a fixed part $DL(f, p_x) + DC(f, p_x)$ that can be calculated statically and a variable part $DP(f, p_x)$. This variable part is a function of dynamic data:

– The sequence of frames generated by each VL (length of each frame, transmission instants).

– The phase between the various VLs, in other words the transmission instant of the first frame of each VL.

A set of these dynamic data defines a scenario.

To determine the largest possible delay for a frame of a given VL v transmitted on a given path p_x of v, it is necessary to take into account all the possible scenarios. This number of scenarios is enormous. However, most of them do not have the required priorities to lead to worst-case delays.

In section 7.4, we show the characteristics that have to be verified by a scenario in order to have a chance of leading to the worst case.

7.4. Properties of a worst-case scenario

In a worst-case scenario, the frame being studied f is delayed as much as possible all along its path. The properties of such a scenario have been established in [ADN 11]. They concern, first the end system that generates the frame, and second the output port of the switches traversed by the frame.

On the level of its source end system, the frame f has to be generated at the same time as a frame of all the other VLs emanating from the same end system. This maximizes the impact of these competing VLS on f. Indeed, if the frame of a competing VL is generated after the frame f, it will not delay f at any moment in the network, given the *first come first serve* discipline implemented by the end system and the output ports of the switches traversed by f. If the frame of a competing VL is generated before f, this could possibly move the transmission instant of this frame forward on the level of the end system or the output ports of the switches, which could then reduce the delay that this frame creates for f. On the other hand, this can never delay this transmission instant.

As an example, let us consider the AFDX configuration in Figure 7.2.

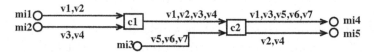

Figure 7.2. *Example of an AFDX configuration*

It includes seven unicast VLs $v1 \ldots v7$ whose features are detailed in Table 7.1.

We study the end-to-end delay of a frame of VL $v1$. Figure 7.3 shows such a scenario. To simplify the figure, the frame of VL v_i is denoted by i and the switching delay dt is assumed zero. For this scenario, the end-to-end delay of the frame of v_1 is 170 μs.

To maximize the delay at the source end system, the generation of the frame of v_2 is delayed until the generation time of the frame of v_1. The end-to-end delay of the latter then becomes 200 μs, as is illustrated by Figure 7.4.

	$BAG(v_i)$	$s_{min}(v_i)$	$s_{max}(v_i)$	Tx
v_1	4 ms	625 bytes	625 bytes	50 μs
v_2	4 ms	625 bytes	625 bytes	50 μs
v_3	4 ms	750 bytes	750 bytes	60 μs
v_4	4 ms	500 bytes	500 bytes	40 μs
v_5	4 ms	625 bytes	625 bytes	50 μs
v_6	4 ms	500 bytes	500 bytes	40 μs
v_7	4 ms	625 bytes	625 bytes	50 μs

Table 7.1. *Characteristics of VLs*

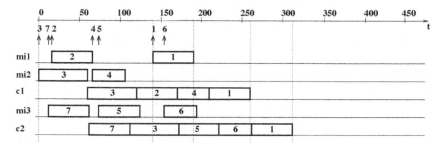

Figure 7.3. *Frame transmission scenario*

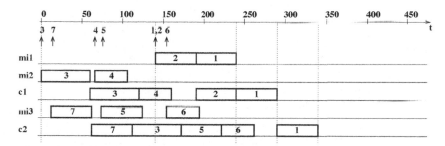

Figure 7.4. *Scenario maximizing the delay of v_1 over mi1*

At the output ports of the traversed switches, the studied frame f is joined by the frames of VLs coming from other end systems, via other input links of these switches. The waiting delay of f in an output port is maximized when the frames of these new competing VLs arrive at the latest possible, but not after f (for similar reasons to those described for the end systems). A sequence of contiguous frames is therefore created for every input link other than the one through which f arrives. The last frame of each of these sequences arrives at the output port at the same time as f and it is transmitted before f.

This property of a worst-case scenario is not respected by the scenario in Figure 7.4. Indeed, the frames of v_7, v_5 and v_6 coming from $mi3$ do not constitute a continuous sequence. Moreover, this sequence does not end with the arrival of the frame of v_1. This is the same for the frames of v_3 and v_4 output from $mi2$.

Figure 7.5 presents a scenario in which the frame generation times are modified in order to respect the properties of a worst-case scenario at the output ports of the switches. The frames of the VLs v_3 and v_4 coming from the end system $mi2$ are transmitted in this order by $mi2$ and the frame of v_4 arrives at the output of the switch $c1$ at the same time as the frame of v_1. The same principle is applied to the frames of v_5, v_6 and v_7 between $mi3$ and $c2$. The end-to-end delay of the frame of v_1 is 410 μs.

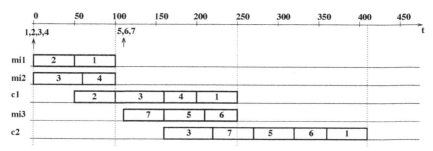

Figure 7.5. *Candidate worst-case scenario*

There are other scenarios that respect the properties of a worst-case scenario, for instance the scenario in Figure 7.6. For this last scenario, the end-to-end delay of the frame of v_1

is 400 μs. As a matter of fact, each candidate worst-case scenario is defined by the order of the frames in the sequences and the order of transmission for the frames arriving at the same time in an output port of a switch. Thus, the scenario of Figure 7.5 is characterized by the order of the frames coming from $mi2$ (v_4 followed by v_3) and from $mi3$ (v_7, followed by v_5, and v_6). Moreover, the frame of v_3 is transmitted before the frame of v_7 coming from $c2$. In the scenario in Figure 7.6, the frames of v_3 and of v_4 are swapped at the output of $mi2$. The scenario of Figure 7.5 leads to a greater delay for v_1 than that of Figure 7.6.

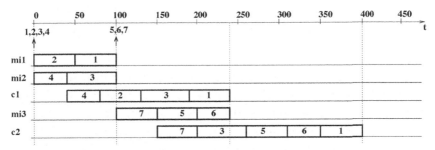

Figure 7.6. *Another candidate worst-case scenario*

We can thus envision the possibility of more accurately characterizing the sequences of frames that can lead to the worst case.

The impact of a frame f' on the frame f being studied depends on two factors:

– The transmission delay of f', which is a function of the number of bytes to transmit.

– The number of output ports shared by f and f'.

On the example in Figure 7.2, a frame of v_3 is longer than a frame of v_4 and shares more output ports with v_1 (2 versus 1). The scenarios in Figures 7.5 and 7.6 make different choices for the order of transmission of the frames of v_3 and v_4.

– In Figure 7.5, the longest frame (v_3) is transmitted first. The delays for the frame of v_1 in the buffers of c_1 and c_2 are, respectively, 100 μs and 110 μs.

– In Figure 7.6, the shortest frame (v_4) is transmitted first. The delays for the frame of v_1 in the buffers of c_1 and c_2 are, respectively, 90 μs and 110 μs.

The order therefore has an impact on the output of $c1$. This is related to the arrival time of the first frame in the output port of c_1 (the frame of v_2 at time $t = 50$ μs in Figure 7.5, the frame of v_4 at time $t = 40$ μs in Figure 7.6). The amount of data to be transmitted being the same in both cases, the frame of v_1 incurs an additional delay of 10 μs in the scenario in Figure 7.5.

In this specific case, the order does not have an impact on the delay in the output port of $c2$. Nevertheless, the VL v_4 leaving v_1 in the switch c_2, a hole will appear in the sequence coming from c_1. Figures 7.7 and 7.8 show that such a hole can have an impact on the delay incurred by the frame of v_1 in $c2$. These two figures show two candidate worst-case scenarios for the configuration in Figure 7.2 without v_7. In both scenarios, the frame of v_3 is the first frame that can delay the frame of v_1 to arrive in the output port of $c2$. When it is transmitted by $mi2$ before the frame of v_4 (scenario of Figure 7.7), it arrives earlier in $c2$ than when it is transmitted after the frame of v_4. It is therefore transmitted earlier by $c2$ and delays the frame of $v1$ less. The cumulated delay of v_1 is therefore equal to 160 μs (100 μs in $c1$, 60 μs in $c2$) for the scenario of Figure 7.7 and is equal to 190 μs (90 μs in $c1$, 100 μs in $c2$) for the scenario of Figure 7.8.

In summary, sorting the frames in the sequences by decreasing length leads to the longest delay for the frame studied in the first output port, but this can create holes in the following output ports. These holes can decrease the delay of the frame studied in these output ports. Depending on the configurations, the worst case will thus be obtained when sorting the frames in the sequences by applying one of the following strategies:

– By decreasing length.

– By increasing number of shared output ports with the frame being studied (to limit the holes in the sequences).

– By mixing the two previous criteria.

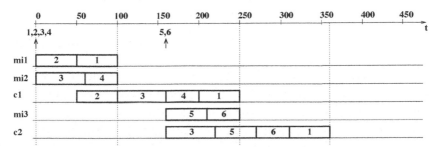

Figure 7.7. *Scenario without hole in the sequence c1 – c2*

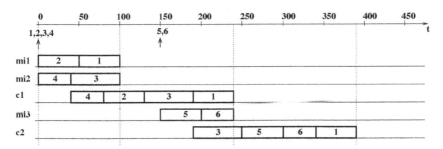

Figure 7.8. *Scenario with a hole in the sequence c1 – c2*

It is therefore necessary to examine the set of scenarios built by applying one of these strategies to determine the worst-case delay of a VL. This exhaustive examination remains impossible for around a third of VLs of realistic configuration (of type A380), as we will see in section 7.6. Section 7.5 shows how it is possible to overcome this problem.

7.5. Calculating an upper bound of the delay

The alternative is to define a scenario model that, for the studied VL, is at least as unfavorable as each of the candidate worst-case scenarios. This scenario model allows us to calculate an upper bound for the end-to-end delay of this VL.

Two approaches have been proposed for calculating this bound. These are presented in sections 7.5.1 and 7.5.2.

7.5.1. *An upper bound on the delay by network calculus*

Network calculus [LEB 01] allows the computation of deterministic upper bounds on the delay and the jitter of a flow transmitted on a network. Its application to avionic flows has allowed the certification of the AFDX network of the A380.

In the general case, a flow is modelized by an envelope α, which overestimates the number of bits generated by the flow over any time interval.

In the context of AFDX, the traffic generated by a VL v is a step curve, as illustrated in Figure 7.9. The height of each step corresponds to the maximum length $s_{max}(v)$ of a frame of v, whereas the length of a step corresponds to the minimum duration $BAG(v)$ between two consecutive frames of the VL. This curve, being unpractical in network calculus, is overestimated by the envelope:

$$F(t) = \frac{s_{max}(v)}{BAG(v)} \times t + s_{max}(v)$$

as is illustrated in Figure 7.9.

Each element of a network is modeled by a service curve. In the context of AFDX, every output port of every switch offers a service curve of the form:

$$B_{R,T} = R\,[t - T]^+ \quad avec \quad [x]^+ = max(0, x) \tag{7.5}$$

where R is the throughput of the output link (100 Mbps in our case) and T is the maximum technological latency (16 μs in our case).

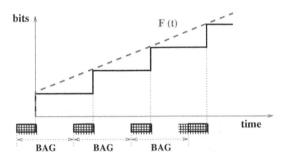

Figure 7.9. *Traffic envelope of a VL*

The calculation of the upper bounds is based on the traffic envelope and the service curves. The delay incurred by a VL v constraint by an arrival curve F traversing a node, which offers a service curve B, is bounded by the maximum horizontal difference between the curves F and B. This difference, illustrated in Figure 7.10, is defined by:

$$h(F, B) = \sup_{s \geq 0} \left(\inf \{\tau \geq 0 \mid F(s) \leq B(s + \tau)\} \right) \tag{7.6}$$

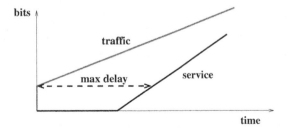

Figure 7.10. *Maximum delay* $h(F, B)$

Every output port of the AFDX network is shared by several VLs. The bound on the delay in a given output port is obtained by summing the envelopes of the various flows sharing this port, taking into account the fact that the VLs come from the same input link and that their frames cannot arrive at the same time. This amounts to consider that a sequence of contiguous frames arrives at each input link and that the ends of sequences are simultaneous. This corresponds to the properties of a worst-case scenario.

To calculate the end-to-end delay of a VL crossing several switches, it is necessary to determine the output envelope of the VL for each of the ports it crosses. Each of these output envelopes becomes the envelope of the following input port on the path of the VL. This propagation is simple insofar as there are no circular dependencies in the industrial AFDX configurations.

The output envelope of a flow for a given output port is:

$$F' = F \oslash \delta_{jitter} \qquad\qquad [7.7]$$

where $\oslash$ is the deconvolution operator. F is the arrival envelope of the flow in the port, *jitter* is the maximum jitter incurred by the flow in the port and δ_{jitter} is a guaranteed delay service curve. We have:

$$\delta_d(t) = 0 \; if \; t \leq d \qquad\qquad [7.8]$$

$$\infty \; otherwise$$

Graphically, this means shifting the arrival envelope F toward the left, of the value of the maximum jitter. The maximum jitter in an output port corresponds to the difference between the minimum delay and the maximum delay in this same port. We have shown in section 7.3 that the minimum delay corresponds to the scenarios in which the frame does not wait in the queue associated with the output port. The maximum jitter in an output port corresponds to the maximum waiting time in the queue associated with this port.

The calculation method is illustrated on the VL v_1 of the example in Figure 7.2. The envelopes of the various VLs are the following:

$$F_1 = F_2 = F_5 = F_7 = 1.25 \times t + 5000$$
$$F_3 = 1.5 \times t + 6000$$
$$F_4 = F_6 = t + 4000$$

For instance, for v_3, the burst is 6000 bits (the maximum frame length $s_{max}(3) = 750$ bytes). The long-term throughput is 1.5 ($\frac{s_{max}(v_3)}{BAG(v_3)} = \frac{6000}{4000}$).

The envelope of each VL at its source end system integrates the maximum delay incurred by this VL at this stage. Each VL can be delayed by a frame of the other VLs with which it shares the end system. Thus, v_1 can be delayed by a frame of v_2, by 50 μs. The envelope of v_1 at $mi1$ is therefore its starting envelope shifted by 50 μs toward the left with removal of the negative time part. This curve is shown in black in Figure 7.11. The envelopes of the VLs at their source end systems are therefore as follows:

$$1.25 \times t + 5062.5 \; for \; v_1 \; and \; v_2$$
$$1.5 \times t + 6060 \; for \; v_3$$
$$t + 4060 \; for \; v_4$$
$$1.25 \times t + 5112.5 \; for \; v_5 \; and \; v_7$$
$$t + 4100 \; for \; v_6$$

The global traffic envelope of the only output port of the switch $c1$ is obtained by summing the envelopes of the sequences of every input link of $c1$ ($mi1 - c1$ and $mi2 - c1$).

The input link envelope $mi1 - c1$ is obtained by considering that the largest frame, for instance a frame of $v2$, arrives (burst), followed by the second frame (of $v1$) which arrives at the speed of the link (100 Mbps). This envelope is shown in Figure 7.12. The envelope of the input link $mi2 - c1$ is obtained in the same manner ($v3$ constitutes the burst, then $v4$ arrives with the speed of the link). The horizontal distance between the global envelope at $c1$ and the service curve of the output port is equal to 167.825 μs. This distance contains the switching delay (16 μs), the transmission delay of the frame of $v1$ (50 μs) and the time spent by it in the queue (101.825 μs).

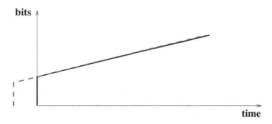

Figure 7.11. *Curve of $v1$ output from $mi1$*

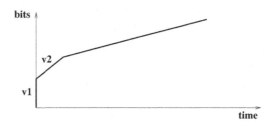

Figure 7.12. *Envelope of the link $m1 - c1$*

The output curve of v_1 at $c1$ is therefore:

$$1.25 \times t + 5189.78125$$

The curves of v_2, v_3 and v_4 are obtained in the same way.

The same process is applied to the switch $c2$. For v_1, it leads to a time of 115.142375 μs spent in the queue of c_2.

In total, the bound on the end-to-end delay of v_1 is equal to 448.967375 μs. It is composed of the transmission delays of the frame of v_1 on the links (three links, therefore 150 μs), the switching delays (two switches, therefore 32 μs) and the time spent in the queues ($50 + 101.825 + 115.142375 = 266.967375$ μs). This bound is slightly pessimistic. Indeed, a worst-case scenario, such as the scenario shown in Figure 7.14, leads to a delay of 442 μs.

7.5.2. *An upper bound on the delay by the trajectory method*

The trajectory approach was initially developed to calculate guaranteed upper bounds on the response time of sporadic streams in distributed systems [MAR 06]. The distributed system considered is composed of a set of computing nodes interconnected by links. Each stream follows an ordered sequence of nodes defined statically. It is executed for a bounded time in each of the computing nodes it traverses. The scheduling algorithms of the streams in the nodes is *first come first serve*. The transmission delay of a stream from a node to another is within a known interval.

The trajectory approach was adapted and optimized for calculating upper bounds on the end-to-end delays of VLs transmitted on an AFDX network [BAU 10]. As shown in Figure 7.13, a computing node is an output port of a switch or an end system with the corresponding output link. Indeed, the transmission delay of a frame of a VL corresponds to the execution time of a stream on a node and the output ports schedule the frame following the *first come first serve* algorithm. A link between two nodes is a switch (switching logic between an input port and an output port). Indeed, the switching delay of an AFDX switch is bounded.

As presented in section 7.3, the end-to-end delay of a VL is composed of several parts. The basic idea of the trajectory approach is to calculate an upper bound on each of these parts. We illustrate this calculation on the example in Figure 7.14. It is the worst-case scenario for the VL v_1 of the configuration in Figure 7.2, with a switching delay of 16 μs. The trajectory approach considers two parts in the delay:

– The switching delays or technological latencies of the switches.

– The time spent by the frame in the output port buffers and the transmission delays of the frame on the successive links.

The algorithm is detailed in [BAU 10]. We summarize the calculation here.

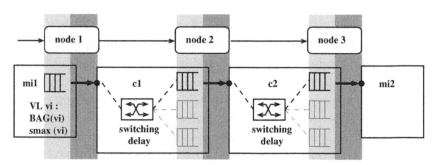

Figure 7.13. *The trajectories for AFDX*

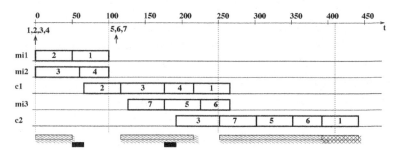

Figure 7.14. *A worst-case scenario*

Let us consider a VL v_i following a path $\mathcal{P}_i = first_i, \ldots, last_i$. $first_i$ is the end system generating the

VL and $last_i$ is the output port of the last switch traversed by v_i. An upper bound $R_{i,t}$ on the end-to-end delay of a frame of the VL v_i generated at time t is obtained by the following formula.

$$R_{i,t} = \left(1 + \left\lfloor \frac{t}{T_i} \right\rfloor \right) \cdot C_i \qquad\qquad [7.9]$$

$$+ \sum_{\substack{j \in [1,n] \\ j \neq i \\ \mathcal{P}_j \cap \mathcal{P}_i \neq \emptyset}} \left(1 + \left\lfloor \frac{t + A_{i,j}}{T_j} \right\rfloor \right) \cdot C_j \qquad\qquad [7.10]$$

$$+ \sum_{\substack{h \in \mathcal{P}_i \\ h \neq last_i}} \left(\max_{\substack{j \in [1,n] \\ h \in \mathcal{P}_j}} \{ C_j \} \right) \qquad\qquad [7.11]$$

$$+ (| \, \mathcal{P}_i \, | - 1) \cdot L_{max} \qquad\qquad [7.12]$$

$$- \sum_{\substack{N_h \in \mathcal{P}_i \\ N_h \neq first_i}} (\Delta_{N_h}) \qquad\qquad [7.13]$$

Term [7.12] represents the technological latencies of the $|\mathcal{P}_i| - 1$ switches traversed by v_i. In the example of Figure 7.14, v_1 traverses the two switches $c1$ and $c2$. It therefore incurs two technological latencies that are materialized by the two black rectangles in the figure.

All the other terms are related to the delays in the queues and the transmission links.

Term [7.10] is related to the delay created by all the VLs v_j that share at least one output port with v_i. In the worst-case scenario of Figure 7.14, a frame of each of these competing VLs $(v_2, v_3, v_4, v_5, v_6, v_7)$ delays the frame of v_i generated at time t. There exist configurations in which several frames of a same VL delay the studied frame. This is the case in the example of Figure 7.15. This configuration includes 20 VLs $v_1, \ldots, v_{20}$ which all have the same maximum frame size of

$s_{max}(v_i) = 1500$ bytes. v_4 has a BAG of 2 ms. The other VLs have a BAG of 32 ms. Figure 7.16 shows a worst-case scenario for v_1. The output load of the switch $c2$ means that two consecutive frames of v_4, whose generation times are separated by 2 ms, arrive immediately after one another in the output port of $c3$. They both delay the frame of v_1.

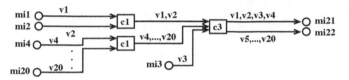

Figure 7.15. *An AFDX configuration*

mi1																					1	
c1																				2	1	
c2	20	19	18	17	16	15	14	13	12	11	10	9	8	7	6	5	4	4'				
c3																		2	4	3	4'	1

Figure 7.16. *Worst-case scenario for v_1*

Term [7.10] bounds the number of frames of every competing VL able to delay the frame of the studied VL.

Term [7.9] is related to the delay created by the transmissions of the studied frame and possibly of the frames of the same VL v_i that precede it. This phenomenon can be produced by the reasons illustrated in section 7.5.1.

In the example in Figure 7.14, terms [7.10], [7.9] and [7.12] lead to a delay of 372 μs, which is smaller than the delay observed in Figure 7.14 (442 μs). To understand this difference, we focus on $mi1$ and $c1$. The frame of v_1 is created at time 0 and it is fully transmitted at time 266 μs. This delay is composed of the technological latency of $c1$ (16 μs), one transmission time of the frames of v_1, v_3, v_4 and two times the transmission time of v_2. More generally, for every pair of nodes on the path of the studied frame, the transmission time of a common frame has to be counted twice. Determining which frame has to be counted twice would require an exhaustive exploration of every possible case. The trajectory approach therefore considers an upper bound on this additional delay by counting the transmission time of the largest common frame (term [7.11]).

Term [7.13] takes into account the fact that the frames coming from a same link do not arrive at the same time in an output port. It may then happen that some frames do not delay the studied frame. This phenomenon is illustrated in Figure 7.17, which takes the scenario of Figure 7.14 and considers that $mi3$ creates an additional VL (v_8). The frame of v_8 does not delay the frame of v_1. However, it will be counted in term [7.10]. Term [7.13] therefore allows to remove it. This term is pessimistic in some cases [LI 11].

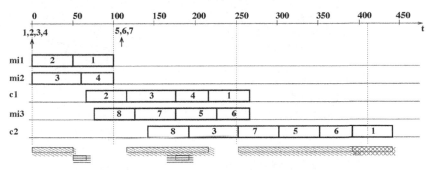

Figure 7.17. *A worst-case scenario with v_8 added*

7.6. Results on an embedded avionic configuration

Figure 7.18 shows the general structure of the industrial configuration analyzed in this section. It is composed of 120 to 130 end systems interconnected by two redundant AFDX networks, each including nine switches (the dashed rectangles in Figure 7.18). Around 1,000 VLs are transmitted by the various end systems on each of these two networks for a total of $6,400$ paths, given the multicast feature of the VLs. Table 7.2 shows the distribution of the VLs of this application in terms of BAG and of frame length. The BAGS used are powers of 2 between 2 and $128\ ms$ and the longest BAGs are the most used. The frame lengths are mostly smaller than or equal to 600 bytes.

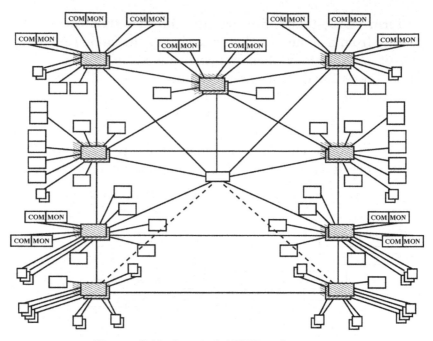

Figure 7.18. *A typical AFDX configuration*

Table 7.3 shows the distribution of the paths by length. In a typical industrial application, a path of a VL traverses at most four switches.

Figure 7.19 gives an overview of the load on each of the links of the network. The load of a link is defined here as its occupancy rate. It is obtained by summing the occupancy rates of all the VLs transmitted on this link. The occupancy rate of a link by a VL is the ratio between the transmission delay of a maximum length frame of the VL and the BAG. Figure 7.19 gives the number of links for the various possible loads. It appears that the links of an industrial application are lightly loaded. The load never exceeds 21%.

BAG (ms)	Number of VLs		Frame length (bytes)	Number of VLs
2	20		0-150	561
4	40		151-300	202
8	78		301-600	114
16	142		601-900	57
32	229		901-1,200	12
64	220		1,201-1,500	35
128	255		> 1,500	3

Table 7.2. *BAGs and frame lengths of an industrial application*

Number of switches traversed	Number of paths
1	1,797
2	2,787
3	1,537
4	291

Table 7.3. *VL path lengths*

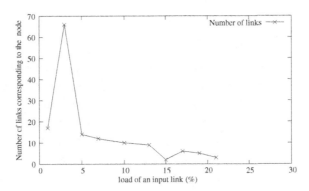

Figure 7.19. *Network link load*

The worst-case analysis is performed for each of the 6,400 paths of the configuration.

The exhaustive exploration presented in section 7.4 allows us to obtain the worst-case delay for $4,100$ paths (64% of all). For the other paths, the number of scenarios to consider remains too high. To give an order of magnitude, this number exceeds 10^{100} for 70 paths of the configuration.

This exhaustive exploration approach therefore remains insufficient for analyzing the entirety of a realistic configuration, but it can process a significant part of such a configuration.

The network calculus and trajectory approaches allow us to analyze the whole configuration. For every path analyzable by exhaustive exploration, the pessimism introduced by network calculus and trajectory is the difference between the worst-case delay obtained by the exhaustive approach and the bound calculated by network calculus and trajectory. This pessimism is on average equal to 6% for trajectory calculus and equal to 13% for network calculus. These results show that:

– trajectory calculus introduce less pessimism that network calculus;

– the pessimism is on average very limited.

7.7. Conclusion

Today, AFDX has become a standard for civil avionic networks. This has been made possible by the temporal analysis methods that allow us to bound the transmission delay of a frame of an avionic flow, insofar as the throughput of each flow is bounded. The calculated bounds are slightly pessimistic. Indeed, an exhaustive search of the worst-case scenario is not feasible today on a complete configuration, since the search space is too vast. However, the characterization of a candidate worst-case scenario has allowed to considerably limit this search space and a finer characterization would presumably allow this exhaustive search.

The analysis methods presented in this chapter do not make any assumptions on the generation times of the frames of the various VLs by the end systems. We have shown that it is possible to integrate into the analysis constraints between the VLs created by a same end system [LI 10]. These constraints are expressed in the form of minimum durations between the generation instants of the frames of the various VLs. They allow us to significantly reduce the calculated bounds on the delays of the flows. Now we have to study more accurately the functioning of the end systems effectively deployed in aircrafts in order to determine the gain brought about by taking these constraints into account in the case of an existing avionic configuration.

The differentiation of the flows transmitted in the AFDX network is nowadays envisioned with two main objectives. The first objective is to assign priorities to the avionic flows in order to obtain more homogeneous worst-case delays between the flows or take into account stronger constraints of certain flows. The second objective is to share the AFDX network between the avionic and the less critical flows. Preliminary work has been conducted in this context. A worst-case analysis method integrating priorities was proposed in the framework of AFDX [BAU 12]. The possibility to use Audsley's algorithm [AUD 01] to assign priorities to the flows transmitted on an AFDX network was evaluated [HAM 13]. The results are promising. Their use required the implementation of an AFDX switch with quality of service.

The bounds calculated on the delays are safe: there is no scenario that leads to exceeding the bounds. However, the scenarios leading to the worst case are very rare events. The network is therefore designed to support cases having a very low probability to occur. It is therefore very lightly loaded. The avionic functions being designed to support losses (in a very limited number) of frames, one solution to increase the load of the network consists of offering a probabilistic guarantee to respect the bounds. A primary solution was proposed in [SCH 09]. The obtained gain is small, since the network is aggregated in a node to respect the constraint of independence of the flows. It is therefore necessary to find alternative solutions.

7.8. Bibliography

[ADN 11] ADNAN M., SCHARBARG J.-L., FRABOUL C., "Minimizing the search space for computing exact worst-case delays of AFDX periodic flows", *Proceedings of SIES*, Västeras, June 2011.

[ARI 91] ARINC 651, specification 651, Design Guidance for Integrated Modular Avionics., Report, Aeronotical Radio Inc., 1991.

[ARI 97] ARINC 653, ARINC specification 653, Avionics application Software Standard Interface, Report, Aeronotical Radio Inc., 1997.

[ARI 99] ARINC 629, ARINC specification 629, Multi-transmitter data Bus Part 1-Technical Description, Report, Aeronotical Radio Inc., 1999.

[ARI 01] ARINC 429, ARINC specification 429, Digital Information Transfer System (DITS) parts 1,2,3, Report, Aeronotical Radio Inc., 2001.

[ARI 05] ARINC Specification 664: Aircraft Data Network, Parts 1,2,7, Report, Aeronotical Radio Inc., 2002–2005.

[AUD 01] AUDSLEY N., "On priority assignment in fixed priority scheduling", *Information Processing Letters*, vol. 79, pp. 39–44, 2001.

[BAU 10] BAUER H., SCHARBARG J.-L., FRABOUL C., "Improving the worst-case delay analysis of an AFDX network using an optimized trajectory approach", *IEEE Transactions on Industrial Informatics*, vol. 6, no. 4, pp. 521–533, November 2010.

[BAU 12] BAUER H., SCHARBARG J.-L., FRABOUL C., "Applying trajectory approach with static priority queuing for improving the use of available AFDX resources", *Real-Time Systems Journal*, vol. 48, no. 1, pp. 101–131, January 2012.

[HAM 13] HAMZA T., SCHARBARG J.-L., FRABOUL C., "Qos-aware afdx: benefits of an efficient priority assignment for avionics flows", *Proceedings of RTSS (WiP session)*, Vancouver, December 2013.

[LEB 01] LE BOUDEC J.-Y., THIRAN P., *Network Calculus: A Theory of Deterministic Queuing Systems for the Internet*, vol. 2050 of Lecture Notes in Computer Science, Springer-Verlag, 2001.

[LI 10] LI X., SCHARBARG J.-L., FRABOUL C., "Improving end-to-end delay upper bounds on an AFDX network by integrating offsets in worst-case analysis", *Proceedings of the 14th International Conference on Emerging Technologies and Factory Automation*, Bilbao, September 2010.

[LI 11] LI X., SCHARBARG J.-L., FRABOUL C., "Analysis of the pessimism of the trajectory approach for upper bounding end-to-end delay of sporadic flows sharing a switched Ethernet network", *Proceedings of RTNS*, Nantes, September 2011.

[MAR 06] MARTIN S., MINET P., "Schedulability analysis of flows scheduled with FIFO: application to the expedited forwarding class", *Proceedings of the 20th International parallel and distributed processing symposium*, Rhodes Island, Greece, April 2006.

[SCH 09] SCHARBARG J.-L., RIDOUARD F., FRABOUL C., "A probabilistic analysis of end-to-end delays on an AFDX network", *IEEE Transactions on Industrial Informatics*, vol. 5, no. 1, February 2009.

List of Authors

Malika BOURENANE
Department of Computer
Science
University of Oran
Algeria

Maryline CHETTO
IRCCyN Laboratory
University of Nantes
France

Liliana CUCU-GROSJEAN
INRIA
Rocquencourt
France

Christian FRABOUL
IRIT Laboratory
INPT/ENSEEIHT
Toulouse
France

Adriana GOGONEL
INRIA
Rocquencourt
France

Dorin MAXIM
LORIA Laboratory
Nancy
France

Abdelhamid MELLOUK
LISSI Laboratory
University of Paris-Est
Créteil
France

Dumitru POTOP-BUTUCARU
INRIA
Rocquencourt
France

Olivier SENAME
GIPSA Laboratory
INP
Grenoble
France

Jean-Luc SCHARBARG
IRIT Laboratory
INPT/ENSEEIHT
Toulouse
France

Daniel SIMON
Research Center of Sophia
Antipolis-Méditerrannée
Montpellier
France

Yves SOREL
INRIA
Rocquencourt
France

Ye-Qiong SONG
LORIA Laboratory
University of Lorraine
Nancy
France

Index

Summary of Volume 1

Contents

Other titles from

in

Networks and Telecommunications

2014

CAMPISTA Miguel Elias Mitre, RUBINSTEIN Marcelo Gonçalves
Advanced Routing Protocols for Wireless Networks

EXPOSITO Ernesto, DIOP Codé
Smart SOA Platforms in Cloud Computing Architectures

MELLOUK Abdelhamid, CUADRA-SANCHEZ Antonio
Quality of Experience Engineering for Customer Added Value Services

OTEAFY Sharief M.A., HASSANEIN Hossam S.
Dynamic Wireless Sensor Networks

TANWIR Savera, PERROS Harry
VBR Video Traffic Models

VAN METER Rodney
Quantum Networking

XIONG Kaiqi
Resource Optimization and Security for Cloud Services

2013

ASSING Dominique, CALÉ Stéphane
Mobile Access Safety: Beyond BYOD

BEN MAHMOUD Mohamed Slim, LARRIEU Nicolas, PIROVANO Alain
Risk Propagation Assessment for Network Security: Application to Airport Communication Network Design

BEYLOT André-Luc, LABIOD Houda
Vehicular Networks: Models and Algorithms

BRITO Gabriel M., VELLOSO Pedro Braconnot, MORAES Igor M.
Information-Centric Networks: A New Paradigm for the Internet

BERTIN Emmanuel, CRESPI Noël
Architecture and Governance for Communication Services

DEUFF Dominique, COSQUER Mathilde
User-Centered Agile Method

DUARTE Otto Carlos, PUJOLLE Guy
Virtual Networks: Pluralistic Approach for the Next Generation of Internet

FOWLER Scott A., MELLOUK Abdelhamid, YAMADA Naomi
LTE-Advanced DRX Mechanism for Power Saving

JOBERT Sébastien *et al.*
Synchronous Ethernet and IEEE 1588 in Telecoms: Next Generation Synchronization Networks

MELLOUK Abdelhamid, HOCEINI Said, TRAN Hai Anh
Quality-of-Experience for Multimedia: Application to Content Delivery Network Architecture

NAIT-SIDI-MOH Ahmed, BAKHOUYA Mohamed, GABER Jaafar, WACK Maxime
Geopositioning and Mobility

PEREZ André
Voice over LTE: EPS and IMS Networks

2012

AL AGHA Khaldoun
Network Coding

BOUCHET Olivier
Wireless Optical Communications

DECREUSEFOND Laurent, MOYAL Pascal
Stochastic Modeling and Analysis of Telecoms Networks

DUFOUR Jean-Yves
Intelligent Video Surveillance Systems

EXPOSITO Ernesto
Advanced Transport Protocols: Designing the Next Generation

JUMIRA Oswald, ZEADALLY Sherali
Energy Efficiency in Wireless Networks

KRIEF Francine
Green Networking

PEREZ André
Mobile Networks Architecture

2011

BONALD Thomas, FEUILLET Mathieu
Network Performance Analysis

CARBOU Romain, DIAZ Michel, EXPOSITO Ernesto, ROMAN Rodrigo
Digital Home Networking

CHABANNE Hervé, URIEN Pascal, SUSINI Jean-Ferdinand
RFID and the Internet of Things

GARDUNO David, DIAZ Michel
Communicating Systems with UML 2: Modeling and Analysis of Network Protocols

LAHEURTE Jean-Marc
Compact Antennas for Wireless Communications and Terminals: Theory and Design

RÉMY Jean-Gabriel, LETAMENDIA Charlotte
Home Area Networks and IPTV

PALICOT Jacques
Radio Engineering: From Software Radio to Cognitive Radio

PEREZ André
IP, Ethernet and MPLS Networks: Resource and Fault Management

TOUTAIN Laurent, MINABURO Ana
Local Networks and the Internet: From Protocols to Interconnection

2010

CHAOUCHI Hakima
The Internet of Things

FRIKHA Mounir
Ad Hoc Networks: Routing, QoS and Optimization

KRIEF Francine
Communicating Embedded Systems / Network Applications

2009

CHAOUCHI Hakima, MAKNAVICIUS Maryline
Wireless and Mobile Network Security

VIVIER Emmanuelle
Radio Resources Management in WiMAX

2008

CHADUC Jean-Marc, POGOREL Gérard
The Radio Spectrum

GAÏTI Dominique
Autonomic Networks

LABIOD Houda
Wireless Ad Hoc and Sensor Networks

LECOY Pierre
Fiber-optic Communications

MELLOUK Abdelhamid
End-to-End Quality of Service Engineering in Next Generation Heterogeneous Networks

PAGANI Pascal *et al.*
Ultra-wideband Radio Propagation Channel

2007

BENSLIMANE Abderrahim
Multimedia Multicast on the Internet

PUJOLLE Guy
Management, Control and Evolution of IP Networks

SANCHEZ Javier, THIOUNE Mamadou
UMTS

VIVIER Guillaume
Reconfigurable Mobile Radio Systems

CPSIA information can be obtained at www.ICGtesting.com
Printed in the USA
BVOW08*1123241014

372147BV00001B/1/P